High-Impact Consulting

High-Impact Consulting

Consulting

How Clients and Consultants Can Work Together to Achieve Extraordinary Results

Completely Revised and Updated

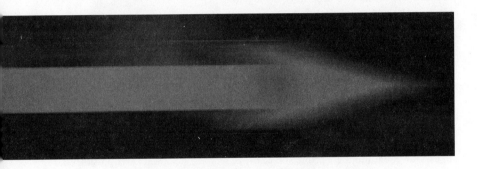

Robert H. Schaffer

JOSSEY-BASS
A Wiley Company
San Francisco

Published by

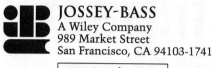

JOSSEY-BASS
A Wiley Company
989 Market Street
San Francisco, CA 94103-1741

www.josseybass.com

Jossey-Bass books and products are available through most bookstores. To contact Jossey-Bass directly, call (888) 378-2537, fax to (800) 605-2665, or visit our Web site at www.josseybass.com.

Substantial discounts on bulk quantities of Jossey-Bass books are available to corporations, professional associations, and other organizations. For details and discount information, contact the special sales department at Jossey-Bass.

We at Jossey-Bass strive to use the most environmentally sensitive paper stocks available to us. Our publications are printed on acid-free recycled stock whenever possible, and our paper always meets or exceeds minimum GPO and EPA requirements.

Library of Congress Cataloging-in-Publication Data

Schaffer, Robert H.
    High-impact consulting : How clients and consultants can work together to achieve extraordinary results / by Robert Schaffer.—2nd ed.
        p. cm.—(The Jossey-Bass business & management series)
    Includes bibliographical references and index.
    ISBN 0-7879-6049-7 (alk. paper)
    1. Business consultants. 2. Management. I. Title. II. Series.
HD69.C6 S27 2002
001'.068—dc21   2001005909

HB Printing   10 9 8 7 6 5 4 3 2 1   SECOND EDITION

The Jossey-Bass
Business & Management Series

To my wife, Natalie

CONTENTS

PREFACE

Most consultants and most clients have never heard of the phenomenon I call the "implementation gap," and yet it undermines, to a greater or lesser extent, most of the consulting projects ever carried out. The gap is the difference between (a) all the things that a client organization would have to do in order to benefit from a consultant's contribution and (b) what the client organization is, in fact, capable of doing. No matter how wise and creative the consultant's analyses and recommendations, they pay off only to the extent that the client does what is necessary to benefit from them. But the way consulting is practiced, the steps that might ensure the closest match between consultant's recommendations and client's reactions are not built into the process. The result is that many consulting projects fail to contribute nearly as much as they might because of the implementation gap, and a great many produce virtually no lasting benefit.

These mismatches are analogous to a recent experience of my own: I purchased a telephone system for use in my home that had some unique features that I needed. It arrived with an eighty-page book of instructions, the telephone supplier's version of the "consultant's recommendations." It was thorough in every respect and flawless. The trouble was, many of the instructions were beyond my capacity to follow, and the time required to work through the instructions was more than I was willing to spend. I got the system working to some extent, but was—and still am—far from deriving as much benefit as the product's designers imagined I might. So here was a superb system that the "client" couldn't benefit from because of the "implementation gap"—the gulf between what I would have had to do for successful implementation and what I was actually able to do.

A great many consulting projects suffer from the same kind of discrepancy.

This book, addressed to senior managers and the consultants they hire or employ, describes why and how this implementation gap sabotages so many consulting projects. And it describes a powerful, alternative model, *high-impact consulting,* which is designed explicitly to close the gap. Over a number of decades, many consultants have demonstrated it to be highly effective in hundreds of applications. It has been employed in some of the world's most successful organizations, including General Electric, Motorola, General Reinsurance, Bell Canada, Consolidated Edison, Johnson & Johnson, Rio Tinto, the World Bank, SmithKline Beecham, the states of Connecticut and Washington, Dun & Bradstreet, and dozens of others.

Development of the High-Impact Paradigm

Many years ago, the head of industrial engineering at a large chemical company described this dilemma to me: All of his people possessed a toolbox full of methodologies that could help the company make significant improvements. Yet it was often difficult to get their client managers to do what they had to do to benefit from the industrial engineering. The implementation gap!

I worked with this group and shortly thereafter I published an American Management Association monograph called *Maximizing the Impact of Industrial Engineering.*[1] That monograph marked the beginning of many years of work on how consultants and clients can ensure that client organizations fully benefit from consulting inputs. My associates and I have applied the lessons learned along the way in our own consulting practice and in educating other consultants. With this book I hope to share this experience with an increasingly wider audience of managers and consultants.

The Implementation Gap: Achilles' Heel of Consulting

Since those chemical company days, the world has become much more complex. Change has become more rapid and pervasive. The management consulting profession has proliferated beyond anyone's wildest expectations. Yet despite all this change, the dilemma faced by those industrial engineers—the implementation gap—remains the most significant barrier limiting the value of consulting. Although the consulting profession has grown at an intoxicating pace, it has largely failed to overcome this widespread problem—the gap between the changes a client organization is actually capable of carrying out and what they would need to do to benefit from their consultant's help.

It is important to note that when I use the word *consulting* I refer to expertise that has the explicit goal of helping organizations actually effect positive changes and improvements. One respected consultant told me of submitting a report to a client who appreciated it but took absolutely no action. The consultant maintained that the report, chock full of insight about the client company, was nevertheless very valuable. But to me this "value" was not consulting, but rather *technical outsourcing*—the provision of insights, tools, techniques, and systems to clients without a sense of responsibility for ultimate outcomes. Thus, while the project in question might represent high-quality outsourced technology, it fails as a consulting project. The term *consulting,* as used throughout this book, includes responsibility for results. Consulting projects that do not yield demonstrably improved client performance are, as far as I'm concerned, on a par with books on weight reduction that do not lead to any weight loss.

My criticism of the consulting paradigm grows from its frequent failure to produce demonstrable client results. And by "results" I mean actual client benefits, not just the delivery of a consultant product. This contrast is illustrated by the consultants who had just installed a new inventory control system in a client organization and told me they had achieved "wonderful results"—meaning the system was operative. No way. As my colleagues and I use the word, *results* can be counted only when the new system actually reduces inventory levels or increases inventory turns. The frequent failure to achieve such ultimate results is not generally the fault of consultant incompetence or client resistance to change. The failure occurs because in the conventional consulting paradigm, there is usually little or no effort devoted, in starting a project, to ensure a match between the changes that might be required of the client and what the client will be capable of doing. Thus consultants can expend substantial effort producing technically excellent reports that have little positive impact and installing superb systems that yield no benefit for the client.

If consulting falls short so often, why does its business continue to grow so rapidly? There are many reasons.

First, there is the matter of need. Many managers face enormous pressures to deal with a torrent of change that is accelerating exponentially. They want help, and consulting offers it to them.

Second, clients as well as consultants accept the notion that once the consultant has delivered the agreed-upon product, the project has been successful. Thus many projects that never demonstrate ultimate client benefits are nevertheless deemed successes by both clients and consultants.

Third, consulting projects have increasingly become so big, so complex, and so long that it is virtually impossible to trace outcomes back to consultant inputs. Huge systems are created over many months, major restructuring is carried out, new processes are implemented, but it is frequently impossible to tie client outcomes to these inputs.

Fourth, there are very few established facts to go on. There is no concerted effort on the part of consulting firms or academia to carry out research or publish information on consulting success. Most clients who are dissatisfied with consulting services are loath to say so out loud. There is little literature on the impact of consulting other than self-serving hype or various exposés. Thus, whatever is known comes through informal contacts, conversations, and the collection of anecdotes shared by client participants in projects.

Finally, consultants do help to produce a certain number of genuine successes in which real and measurable improvements in client performance are realized. Every large consulting firm's Web site features a few of these successes.

For all these reasons, a great many senior managers who need to improve their organization's performance call upon management consultants simply because they have won broad acceptability, no matter how unknown or poor the actual record of results. Hiring a consultant often seems to be better than doing nothing.

Who Should Read This Book and Why

Clients of consulting firms and of internal staff consulting groups should read this book. They will see that they may be deluding themselves if they select their expert helpers on the basis of subject matter expertise and assume that success will automatically follow. The book describes the price such managers and their organizations pay for remaining victimized by the traditional consulting paradigm. And it describes what managers must do differently (and require their consultants to do differently) to ensure significantly better outcomes from their consulting investments.

Of course, this book is also addressed to all consultants, whether or not "consultant" is in their job title. To me, you are a consultant if you provide unique knowledge, skills, insights, methods, or technology that is aimed at helping managers get better results, but you don't have any direct authority to require those managers to follow your advice. I want to be clear to all these consultant readers that virtually every one of you that I have met in my many years of practice wants to do well by your clients. My criticism is with the conventional modes of practice that prevent you from being as helpful to your clients as you'd like to be.

The book will be of particular interest to those professionals who want to become more effective change agents—those who feel that they are functioning too much as management technologists or high-level contract labor. The book's goal is to have management consultants measure their worth not by the excellence of their solutions and recommendations but by how much continuing benefit their clients derive from their input.

Finally, the book speaks to internal consultants and to corporate staff groups charged with improving performance, including finance, human resources, organization development, information technology, operations, logistics, and strategic planning professionals. Many books on consulting exclude these groups and focus exclusively on consulting firms. But, in fact, there are many more internal consultants than members of consulting firms. If you fit the definition given here, then you are a consultant, and this book is for you.

Throughout this book, I cite examples of companies' actual experiences with consultants. Where successful episodes are described, and the parties have given permission, they are identified. Since it is not my purpose to embarrass specific individuals, all failures are presented without identifying the participants except in the case of material that has already been published.

To write on this subject it is necessary to make broad generalizations, and I have certainly done so in criticizing the conventional consulting model. I do recognize, however, that a number of consulting firms and individual consultants have attempted to deal with the issues I raise in this book. While I name only a few of them here, there are others who have enjoyed varying degrees of success. The best way to deal with the generalizations in this book is to use an "if the shoe fits" approach.

Clients and consultants should assess their own experiences and decide what, if anything, they want to do to make their client-consultant relationships more effective. If you do that to your own satisfaction, I will have accomplished my purpose.

Stamford, Connecticut   Robert H. Schaffer
January 2002

ACKNOWLEDGMENTS

In this book I emphasize that it is just as important for consultants to learn from their clients as it is for clients to learn from their consultants. As one who has put this concept into practice during my professional career, I wish to acknowledge the wealth of learning I have garnered from the people in client organizations with whom I have worked. To them I offer my profound thanks and appreciation.

Many of the concepts presented in this book have been the subject of case conferences and informal discussions with my colleagues at Robert H. Schaffer & Associates, and I am most appreciative to them for stimulating my thinking. They have also provided abundant case material and counsel on the book as it developed. They include Ron Ashkenas, Regan Backer, Katie Beavan, Suzanne Francis, Claude Guay, Rick Heinick, Elaine Mandrish, Keith Michaelson, Matthew McCreight, Nadim Matta, Patrice Murphy, Robert Neiman, Catherine Paul-Chowdhury, Rudi Siddik, Wes Siegal, and Harvey Thomson.

I also benefited from case material and generously shared personal recollections from Tom Barron, Mike Berkin, Charles Baum, Rodney Blanckenberg, David Francis, Bob Gunn, Tom Kivlehan, Bob Moore, and Doug Smith.

Harvey Thomson researched the data available on large-firm consulting success and helped to prepare some material for the second edition.

Geoffrey Love of Rice University provided extensive help in editing the first edition manuscript. He and Catherine Paul-Chowdhury also gathered case material from both clients and consultants and carried out other research tasks.

Emilieanne Koehnlein did yeoman work on the intricacies of graphics and manuscript preparation for both editions. Joanne Young provided administrative support that helped me keep my consulting and managerial jobs going when I first wrote the book.

THE AUTHOR

Robert H. Schaffer founded Robert H. Schaffer & Associates, a highly innovative consulting firm. He was its head for many years and continues as a principal of the firm. Schaffer is the originator of the firm's unique results-driven approach, described in his 1988 book *The Breakthrough Strategy: Using Short-Term Successes to Build the High Performance Organization* (New York: HarperBusiness, 1988). The firm employs this strategy to help organizations achieve major performance improvement and accelerate the pace of change.

The firm has worked with such clients as AlliedSignal, Chase Manhattan Bank, Fidelity Investments, General Electric, General Reinsurance, IBM, Morgan Guaranty Trust, Motorola, Siemens AG, the World Bank, and many other companies. It has also worked with social agencies and governments, including the states of Connecticut and Washington.

Schaffer holds a bachelor's degree in engineering and a doctorate in counseling and management psychology, both from Columbia University. He has played a leadership role in the consulting profession as a founding director of the Institute of Management Consultants and as chairman of its Professional Development Committee for four years. He helped launch the *Journal of Management Consulting* and has served as an editor for many years. He inaugurated and continues to manage "High-Impact Consulting," the longest-running workshop for management consultants.

One of Schaffer's articles, "Demand Better Results—And Get Them," first published in 1974, was republished as a *Harvard Business Review* Classic in 1991. It then became one of the ten most requested HBR articles of the 1990s. He is also the author of five other *Harvard Business Review* articles, as well as about fifty additional articles on productivity, change management, and management consulting.

Robert Schaffer may be reached at

Robert H. Schaffer & Associates
30 Oak Street
Stamford, CT 06905-5302
(203) 322-1604
e-mail address: rhschaffer@rhsa.com

High-Impact Consulting

Part One

From High-Stakes Gambling to Certain Success

Chapter 1

Low-Yield, Conventional Consulting Versus High-Yield, High-Impact Consulting

Almost all the managers who engage consultants, and almost all the consultants they hire, subscribe to a model of consulting that severely limits the benefits of their collaboration. It is typically expected that the consultants are accountable for creating the best possible solutions and tools, while the clients are accountable for using those solutions and tools to produce the improved results. Success obviously depends on the client organization being able to do what must be done to benefit from the consulting input and being motivated to do it. If there is a gap between what is necessary for success and what the client is able and willing to do, then the anticipated benefits will not occur. I believe that such mismatching occurs very frequently and at enormous cost to clients and consultants alike.

The following story will convey the essence of the point. I always use it in the seminars I give for consultants because it captures one of the most profound issues in management consulting.

A family who had been unhappy for many years about the messy state of various storage spaces in their house heard about a firm of "closet consultants." After a hasty phone call from the family, the consultants arrived on the scene to provide a free preliminary survey. Shortly after that visit a proposal arrived by mail, outlining what the consultants would do with the master bedroom closet. The family initialed the agreement, and within two weeks a miracle was wrought. New equipment was installed, and everything in the closet was tastefully, even artistically, arranged. It was a pleasure for the family to witness the transformation, and they willingly paid the consultants' fees. It was a happy ending, except. . . .

Within three or four weeks, the closet was just about as messy as it had been before the consulting project. Except for the fixtures that had been screwed into the wall, there was little by which to remember the project.

The closet consultants exercised their professional skills and delivered a superb solution. Yet, although it exactly met the client's stated requirements, the "solution" failed to yield sustained value for the client. Was the consulting project successful? The answer to this question is important, because a great many management consulting projects have the same sort of outcome. Consultants labor long and diligently to produce technically excellent solutions that fail to produce the results desired by their client.

Success in Consulting

Many consultants rationalize that such projects are technically successful since the consultants have provided the "right answers," but for some reason— usually various client shortcomings—the clients were unable to benefit from the projects. I reject this explanation. "Right answers" that do not help clients achieve what they are trying to achieve are, in fact, wrong answers.

I believe that for a management consulting project to be called a success, three outcomes must be achieved:

- First, the consultant must provide a solution or a method new to the client.
- Second, the client must achieve measurable improvement in its results by adopting the consultant's solution.
- Third, the client must be able to sustain the improvement over time.

In other words, management consultants must be more than experts in their field. They must serve as effective change agents and share accountability with their clients for the ultimate outcome of their consulting projects.

4

Most consultants talk about the benefits of their services but are willing to be held accountable for the first success criterion only, not the second or third. While they always *hope* that their clients will achieve sustainable bottom-line benefits from their work, few consultants accept responsibility for ensuring those outcomes because they are so focused on developing the "right" answer.

Take this very simple, focused consulting project:

Updyke Supply, an automotive parts supplier with one center of operations near New York City and another near Cleveland, was suffering from an increasing number of logistical problems. Many orders had to be shipped in several installments for lack of needed parts in inventory. Yet at the same time the overall levels of inventory were well beyond budget, resulting in increased warehouse costs and excessive cash tied up. Updyke's chief operations manager invited a consulting firm to help.

After some initial exploration, the consultant proposed a study of the company's sales forecasting and inventory management procedures. It was a modest project, completed in about three months. The consultant developed a set of recommendations for an improved sales forecasting system and a modified inventory and purchasing system to impose a more orderly process of replenishing inventory.

Compared to many consulting projects, this one was rather sharply focused. Nevertheless, to carry out the recommendations, Updyke Supply would have to make many changes in many parts of its business. The way reordering decisions were made would have to change. The responsibilities of the people involved in these decisions would change. And as those decision-making processes changed, many other individual job responsibilities would also have to change.

New methods for tracking inventory and reporting on inventory status would have to be developed and implemented. The working relationships among individuals, and the relationships among units, would have to be modified as the new work methods were introduced. Exhibit 1.1 lists a number of the changes that this "simple" project would require.[1]

Exhibit 1.1. Changes Facing Updyke Supply.

- Work flows
- Design of individual jobs (skills, routines)
- Information gathering and processing
- Decision points
- Decision criteria
- Accountabilities
- How new work procedures created; how introduced
- Communication patterns (formal, informal)
- How to solve problems and diagnose and overcome weaknesses
- Record keeping
- Performance measures and criteria

If you set out to identify where all these changes would have to take place, you would discover that sales and marketing would be responsible for the new sales forecasting process. But they would have to coordinate these changes with manufacturing, finance, information systems, and various other groups. Changes would have to be made in production scheduling and order processing. Purchasing systems would be modified significantly. Human resources would have to revise job evaluations, compensation, and various related metrics. It would soon become evident that in addition to the many *kinds* of changes listed in Exhibit 1.1, the changes would have to take place in many different *functions* (as listed in Exhibit 1.2).[2]

Thus, to implement even this very focused, modest project, dozens and dozens of interrelated changes have to be carried out in decision-making processes, in the relationships among jobs and functions, in work flows and measurements—and they all would have to be made in some kind of coordinated way. While the consulting team might help install some of the new systems, it is doubtful that they would even be able to identify, never mind get involved in, all of the ramifications. The rest would have to be figured out and carried out by the Updyke people themselves.

Exhibit 1.2. Where Updyke Supply Would Have to Change.

- In sales department
- In order processing
- In plant production and scheduling
- In inventory control and logistics
- In purchasing
- In final assembly
- In shipping
- In accounting and control functions
- In human resources
- In product design
- In customer service

This case demonstrates that to successfully implement even a simple, focused consulting assignment requires that dozens of interrelated changes be carried out, a process calling for skills and capabilities and motivation that may be missing. Thus even a modest and sharply focused project can run the risk of failure—not because the consultants' recommendations or the methods they introduce are not sound, but because some or most of the associated changes may not be carried out properly. If that is true, consider what can happen when the complexity is multiplied many times over.

Just as in the closet consultants case, the Updyke project was carried out in the conventional consulting mode, which is based on the belief that consultants' value comes from their expertise, from their ability to make flawless recommendations or to install powerful new processes or systems. In the spirit of this philosophy consultants concentrate on making sure that their recommendations are "professionally correct." They pay much less attention to the great many changes their clients have to carry out in order to actually *benefit* from the consultant's recommendations.

Here is where both clients and consultants fail to recognize the fundamental flaw of the conventional approach: like Sunday sermons, parental advice, diet books, and doctors' admonitions about smoking and obesity, conventional consulting is based on the assumption that the key to progress is knowledge. In other words, once the client knows what to do, then the client will achieve greater success.

But real-world experience suggests that this is a false assumption. Mountains of data indicate that not knowing what to do is only rarely the main obstacle to organizational success. Much more often it is not being able to do it. Who would say that in the 1940s and 1950s Packard Motors, Studebaker, and Willys-Overland did not have the same market information and did not try to pursue the same strategies that enabled General Motors, Ford, and Chrysler to succeed? And who would say that in the 1960s and 1970s General Motors, Ford, and Chrysler were not privy to all the information they needed to prevail over their Japanese competitors? They simply lacked the capacity to translate their insights into effective action.

Or take this case, which occurred within a huge global corporation:

A consulting firm was retained by the corporate headquarters to study the marketing approach of a particularly powerful competitor and to develop an effective counterstrategy. Five divisions of the client company were to be involved.

The consultants began by interviewing a number of senior executives in the client company. They learned about the unique operations, goals, and strategies of each of the five divisions included in the project. They then conducted extensive research in many different marketplaces to gather information on the competitor.

The consultants prepared a thorough analysis of the threats posed by the competitor and offered a fairly detailed menu of possible counterstrategies for dealing with them. Although they had performed a first-rate analysis and produced some excellent solutions, when they tried to convene a strategy summit of the general managers of the affected divisions to discuss an action plan, they could not make it happen. No real action was ever taken on the report. Despite this fact, the corporate officers who had hired the consultants were very impressed with the high quality of their professional work and judged the project a success.

A success? I disagree. The elegant and creative recommendations prepared for the managers of the global corporation failed to advance the company's competitive position one iota, just as the closet consultant's efforts failed to improve the client family's lifestyle. Any solution—no matter how creative—that provides no direct, measurable benefits for the client is, in my view, a failure. Unfortunately, such "solutions" pervade the world of consulting.

Despite the occasional strategic victories that come from knowing which horse to bet on, more often the key to business success is the ability to translate strategic visions into needed change. The ultimate value of consulting inputs always depends on the ability of the client organization to absorb and use them to achieve better results. As people have known for thousands of years, even the best advice often fails to produce any noticeable progress. I would go so far as to say that providing clients with answers or recommendations or systems without ensuring their potential for successful implementation is really just plain technical outsourcing, even though most consultants and clients call it consulting.

Flawed Assumptions, Flawed Designs

Of course consultants understand the importance of successful implementation. Of course they want benefits to accrue to the client from their work. Most individual consultants and most consulting firm officers want to do good for their clients. The trouble is that most of them don't make client implementation a central focus of their consulting practices. Most are almost completely dedicated to providing managers with insights and ideas *about* change; they pay virtually no attention to helping the client *effect* change. In fact, client limitations in this area are generally not viewed as an appropriate focus for the consultant's attention. Rather, they are viewed as hazards to the practice of consulting, like sand traps on a golf course. Over and over again, I hear consultants complain about organizational barriers that prevent their clients from achieving good results from their recommendations—almost as if it were unfair to have to deal with these obstacles. No wonder that so many projects are undermined by the implementation gap—that gulf between all the changes that a client would need to carry out to benefit from the consultant input and the changes that the client is actually ready, willing, and able to carry out.

For example, a consultant-developed sales forecasting system fails because the sales force does not provide the required data and support. A corporation implements a consultant's recommendations for organizational restructuring but places the wrong people in some key roles. A client rejects a carefully developed marketing plan because it contradicts the CEO's beliefs. A company sets aside a major strategy study because it calls for directional shifts too radical for senior management to risk. Such occurrences are quite common, and when they occur, the disappointed consultants usually blame the results on limitations of the client organization. They never see that the very design of their consulting project contained the seeds of its failure.

Most consultants will thoroughly research almost every dimension of a client's problems but pay little or no attention to assessing the client's willingness and ability to implement the suggestions that the consultants might be making after they do their research. Consultants rarely discover what their clients are able to do with their recommendations until after the project is over and the reports have already been submitted. By then it is often too late.

Another self-defeating aspect of conventional consulting is the assumption that the best way to attack any subject—whether cash flow, marketing strategy, or inventory turns—is to examine it in its totality and, even better, in its relationship to everything else. Most consultants, particularly the larger firms with thousands of consultants to keep busy, want to produce a "big-picture" solution. Anything less is considered piecemeal or suboptimizing. But such large-scale, comprehensive studies usually take very long, are very costly, and result in change processes that are much too complex for most organizations to carry out successfully—even with the vast amount of consulting help the firms are happy to provide. Moreover, with everything being dealt with at once and dozens of consultants busy intervening all over the place, there is no way of ever being clear about what the consultants' contribution really accomplished.

Further, the serious research and deliberation that are at the heart of consulting projects are usually considered to be mainly within the province of the consultant. Although clients may be "involved," the consultants usually do their work and then hand over their products to their clients. The clients, with little opportunity to do this thinking and develop their own insights and skills—and busy with all the other aspects of their jobs—are nevertheless expected to fully accept and then implement the consultants' recommendations.

It is no wonder that a significant number of projects, directed by highly knowledgeable and motivated consultants, produce great ideas, great reports, powerful new systems and methods—but are undermined by the implementation gap. At the end of too many consulting projects, the consultants can honestly say, "We did a thoroughly competent job and showed them how to solve the problem." And the clients can honestly say, "We really wanted to deal with that, but implementing the consultant's recommendations would have required some changes we were not prepared to make." In other words, everyone did the "right" thing but the results were dismal.

This should not be permitted to happen. In fact, a number of consultants, sharing this feeling, have experimented with new techniques and have paid greater attention to implementation issues. But neither consultants nor their clients have questioned the fundamental paradigm of conventional management consulting. And that is where the solution lies—not in fixes and adjustments but in some basic shifts in the way consulting is practiced.

The High-Impact Paradigm

High-impact consulting is based on the premise that although the consultant's expert solutions are vital to the success of a consulting project, it is just as vital for consultants to make certain that clients absorb, use, and benefit from those solutions. Merely dishing up the consulting products with the assumption that the client can take it from there makes each project a gamble—and a poor one at that. Client success must be carefully designed into the process. And client success must include both client implementation and client learning.

To ensure success, each project must produce an action plan that the client is apt to be ready, willing, and able to implement. If a high-jumper has been able to jump sixty inches but no more, no coach would set the bar at sixty-six inches and say, "Try it." That's loaded for failure. But consultants do the equivalent to their clients every day of the week. Both client and consultant should take responsibility for making certain that a project not require client staff to do things they're not equipped to do. Instead of tackling a huge project all at once, the client and consultant can carve off subprojects, each focused on a near-term goal that both parties are reasonably certain can be achieved. These first subprojects can provide the reinforcement of success. They can provide experience that proves helpful in subsequent projects, laying a foundation for continuing, expanding cycles of success.

High-impact consultants devote as much energy to helping their clients tap into their own wisdom and develop new skills and confidence as they do to their technical studies. As clients experience success in the early phases of the process, they develop new skills and confidence and thus the ability to attack increasingly ambitious undertakings.

These fundamental shifts, the essence of the high-impact paradigm, take much of the gamble out of consulting. Because the strategy is designed to mobilize and exploit the client's own capabilities and to overcome the organizational barriers that often sabotage improvement, it can significantly increase clients' return on their investments in consulting.

P.S. An Action Note to Client Managers and Consultants

It will not be very difficult for managers or for consultants to make the shifts described in this book. Anyone ready to try it will be surprised by the results they get and the ease with which they get them. The difficult part is wrenching yourself psychologically from the conventional model, an approach that has for so long provided a cozy security blanket for so many managers and consultants. The essence of this shift to high-impact consulting is that neither consultants nor their clients will continue to regard the attainment of measurable bottom-line results and the sustaining of those results by the client merely as the desirable outcomes of consulting projects. They will be essential goals of consulting projects. Client managers: no matter how smart your consultants may be nor how busy you are, you have to play a key role in designing projects for success.

To get a feel for the difference, think of a recent project where you were either client or consultant. Select a project where good technical work was done, but the bottom-line benefits were disappointing. Was that disappointment identified at the time and confronted? Or was it overlooked to avoid difficult discussions and self-examination? In retrospect would you, the client manager, tend to blame the consultant for the lack of results? Would you, the consultant, feel that you had done a great job and believe that your client was remiss for not properly implementing the recommendations?

This tendency to blame the other party instead of blaming the essential flaws of the methodology will have to change if you are going to enjoy greater success. For the rest of your read through this book, try focusing not on what's wrong with any of the players, but on what it is about the method that needs to be changed.

Chapter 2

The Five Fatal Flaws of Conventional Consulting

I t is not at all unusual for consultants to deliver thoughtful and creative solutions that provide little or no ultimate benefit for the client organization.

Quotom Supply (a real company but disguised name) was the dominant office equipment and supply distributor in a large region of the United States. It ran a number of retail stores and a mail order operation and served large companies through a well-organized sales force. And it was making money in all of these businesses. It was doing so well that the company's managers decided that it would be worthwhile trying to figure out how to make their extremely successful enterprise even more successful. They engaged a well-known consulting firm to do an "opportunity identification study." The consultants did the study and developed more than a dozen possibilities for Quotom to expand into new business areas. They were highly creative ideas, and any of them, if actually implemented, might well have been successful.

None of the suggestions was followed, however. It was not that the managers were dissatisfied with the recommendations. The managers said that the consulting job had been done well, but they were simply not ready or willing to implement any of the suggested solutions.

Within a few short years the situation had changed. A large national distributor had begun to move into Quotom Supply's region. This competitor was undercutting Quotom prices because of its greater bargaining power with manufacturers. Quotom Supply's market share dropped significantly, and they felt they were in serious trouble. The same consulting firm that did the earlier opportunity identification study was invited back to help the company's management regain its market position. As a senior associate of the firm described it:

"We did a classic consulting strategy study. It encompassed understanding the economics, understanding the marketplace, including the supply chain, including customers and the key competitor, and understanding the role of the distribution channels.

"We discovered, for example, that there were significant differences in what various categories of customers felt were the most important value factors for them. We discovered that many of the services Quotom Supply felt it had to provide to all its customers were useless to certain groups of them. We discovered that Quotom was in a position to provide certain unique customer-by-customer services that the large national competitor couldn't possibly provide.

"We developed a set of recommendations for carefully segmenting the market, then reorganizing the operations of each of the units to reflect the unique needs of the segments it was serving.

"When we finally came up with our full array of recommendations, the heads of Quotom accepted them, and they put them into effect quickly and efficiently. As a result, the downward market share trend reversed. Within three years, in fact, the company was able to increase its market share by about 35 percent even though the national competitor continued to expand in Quotom's region."

Success a Gamble?

This second project netted tens of millions of dollars for the client. Yet just a few years previously, a team from the same consulting firm completed a project for this client that produced virtually nothing. In the latter, successful, case, the client was driven by a sense of urgency. Management had to get moving quickly. The consultant team's recommendations were clear and easy for the client to carry out.

In the earlier project, there was no similar sense of urgency. To implement the recommendations would have required the client's managers, without any strong motivation to do so, to venture into risky new territory where they had little experience or confidence.

Effective action ensued only when the consultants' recommendations were aligned with the client's motivation and skills. In the earlier project, where the client's motivations were not in alignment with the consultant's recommendations, there was no successful action.

Most consultants regard the risk of such misalignment as an unavoidable aspect of management consulting, a risk for which they cannot be held responsible. When the consultants were asked to do the first study, they devoted their energy to making sure that they conducted the necessary research and provided the correct solutions and insights. They would explain that the reason the client got nothing from that earlier study was due to lack of motivation. What most consultants refuse to accept is that if the level of client motivation had been taken into account *before* the first project was launched, the consultants could have anticipated failure using the design they had in mind. They might even have tried to design the project differently so that they produced some real progress. This might have even enabled them to help Quotom to anticipate and take some useful steps to avoid the near-disaster it later encountered. But by approaching both assignments in virtually the same way, they left the outcome to chance: Success when the project happened to align with the client's motivations; failure when it did not.

Unfortunately, clients' capabilities and motivations frequently do not happen to be well aligned with their consultants' recommendations. Thus consulting is too often a gamble. Clients can win big, as in the successful Quotom case, but often they fail to win at all as in the first one.

Some Evidence of the Problem

The available evidence suggests that the results in the earlier Quotom case are more typical than those in the later, successful project. Consider some of the most common change programs of the last ten or fifteen years. In the early 1990s, one of the most popular consulting products was Total Quality Management (TQM), in all its variations. Many consulting firms made TQM a mainstay of their practices. The results? The American Electronics Association conducted a survey in 1991 of TQM efforts at high-technology companies. Most of the more than three hundred companies that responded had an active TQM program under way. But of those, two-thirds reported that they had been able to reduce defects by only 10 percent or less.[1]

Similarly, an article in the *Economist* reported on a survey by Arthur D. Little of five hundred manufacturing and service companies.[2] Of these, only a third felt that their total quality programs were having a "significant impact." The article also quoted a study by A. T. Kearney of over a hundred British firms. Only a fifth of those companies believed that their quality programs had achieved tangible improvements. A number of other studies reported similar findings.

Later in the 1990s, reengineering replaced TQM as the most popular consulting product. As with TQM, the published evidence of results is bleak. Gene Hall, Jim Rosenthal, and Judy Wade reported in the *Harvard Business Review* on reengineering programs in over a hundred corporations.[3] They noted that in most of the companies the efforts produced some process improvements but little, if any, improvement in overall business results. And even James Champy, one of the movement's founders, reports that "even substantial reengineering payoffs appear to have fallen well short of potential."[4]

In 1994 *Consultants News* reported that "Business Process Re-engineering, the current darling of American management, is having a good run, with consultants, academic devotees and the business press all pushing it. Realistically, it's no different than dozens of other fads that have preceded it, and it's following the same life cycle." This was accompanied by a chart of over fifty fads, under the heading "Management's Field of Dreams, Headstones in Management's Graveyard: 50+ Fads and Panaceas in 50+ Years."[5]

In the late 1990s consulting firms moved aggressively into supporting client ventures into various manifestations of e-business. When large numbers of these dot-coms and e-businesses nosedived at the turn of the century, there is no evidence that consulting interventions made any difference

High-Impact Consulting

at all in the success or failure of the new ventures. The saddest but most dramatic evidence of this assertion is the fact that one George Shaheen left a "$5-million-a-year job running Andersen Consulting" to manage Webvan, a hot new dot-com company. That company quietly went out of business a few years later despite the best of what conventional consulting could provide.[6]

The short life cycle of various management fads that support consulting "products" further demonstrates the probable low success rate of conventional consulting. Nitin Nohria and J. D. Berkley reached this conclusion in 1994: "In the majority of cases, research shows, the management fads of the last 15 years rarely produced the promised results."[7] Most of these fads have been mainstays of consulting practice.

My own personal experience confirms these conclusions. For over thirty years my colleagues and I have had extensive opportunity to observe consulting at work. We have worked with dozens of the world's leading companies where other consulting firms were working or had worked; we have also served as consultants to management consulting firms and to internal staff consulting groups. We have attended consulting conferences, conducted consulting seminars, and talked with hundreds of managers who have been clients of both consulting firms and internal consulting groups. I helped launch the Institute of Management Consultants, served on its board, and served as an editor of *C2M (Consulting to Management)*. These experiences have all provided insights into how consulting is practiced and the results it produces or fails to produce.

Incidentally, the reason one is forced to rely on personal experiences and "reading between the lines" in the published literature is because there is virtually no published research information on the success rate in consulting.

Key Obstacles to Client Implementation Capability

Unquestionably, most management consultants are motivated by a strong desire to make a useful contribution to their client organizations. Their goal is to introduce changes that will help their clients achieve their goals more effectively. Yet, every consultant faces the dilemma faced by our closet consultants in Chapter One. The habits and lifestyle of the family that hired the consultants simply did not support the wonderful new closet arrangement that the consultants introduced. It was this mismatch between what the clients were willing and able to do and what the consultants' solution required of them—the implementation gap—that ultimately resulted in failure. In planning the closet project, the consultants did not consider the family's habits nor its willingness to change them. Yet these factors were critical to the outcome of the assignment.

Management consultants must deal with similar dynamics every day, as in the Quotom case at the beginning of this chapter. They deliver ideas for improved operations, new systems, better information, new strategies, and new processes for achieving results. But if those ideas are to be successful, members of the client organization must change their work patterns enough to be able to adopt and support the innovations.

The operational patterns of an organization, however, are just as intractable as the lifestyle and personal habits of a family, and they are much more complex to understand and influence.

Any number of obstacles may need to be overcome in order to change an organization effectively. There may be impermeable barriers between organizational levels or between the organization and its suppliers and customers. Organizational departments and functions may be worlds unto themselves. The organization's managers may have weak performance expectations, accepting minimal effort from employees. Or they might allow employees all sorts of escape hatches when challenging goals are not being met. There may be meager rewards for outstanding performance and no adverse consequences for poor performance. Goals may be vague or unmeasurable. Accountability may be ambiguous. Change may induce a crisis mode rather than being a routine part of organizational life. Anxiety avoidance may result in unproductive behavior. This is just a sampling of the patterns that can undermine a consulting project. These and other obstacles are outlined in Exhibit 2.1.

Most conventional consultants, highly sophisticated in their areas of expertise (such as business strategy, manufacturing methodology, information technology, finance, and so on), are woefully naive about dealing with

Exhibit 2.1. Organizational Obstacles That Derail Consulting Projects.

1. Psychological Myopia
   - Feeling we are "doing the best we can"
   - Denying or distorting reality
   - Assuming time will solve the problems
   - Avoiding risk and commitment

2. Wasteful Work Patterns
   - Following old, familiar routines
   - Being "too busy" to be thoughtful
   - Impulsively trying one thing, then another
   - Overlooking the views of others

3. Weak Performance Expectations
   - Having overly modest goals
   - Leaving escape hatches for those who miss goals
   - Valuing explanations as highly as results
   - Providing no real consequences for performance levels

4. Defective Work Management
   - Having too many goals
   - Having vague or unmeasurable goals
   - Lacking clear accountability
   - Having weak or nonexistent work plans
   - Conducting infrequent or ineffectual progress reviews

5. Cultural Barriers
   - Allowing confused decision-making processes
   - Letting change become a crisis, not a routine
   - Having low expectations
   - Letting each unit go its own way

the psychological, cultural, and other organizational issues outlined in Exhibit 2.1. The basic consulting methods of almost all conventional firms, including those that feature "change management" practices, fail dismally to address these issues, even though over 90 percent of consulting failures and disappointments stem from them. In fact, as noted earlier, the very design of the conventional consulting paradigm ignores these issues and thus dooms many consulting projects to failure.

The Five Fatal Flaws of Conventional Consulting

Whoever the client is, whatever the consultant's area of expertise, and regardless of whether an outside or staff consultant does the work, the conventional consulting process proceeds more or less in the same time-honored fashion:

- First, a client manager describes the need to the consultant.
- Responsibility shifts to the consultant, who prepares a proposal outlining the work the consulting team will perform and the products they will produce.
- Once the client gives the go-ahead, the consultants carry out their work: researching the problem, conducting interviews, analyzing the organization, designing new systems, and developing new processes or recommendations for change.
- When the consultants have delivered their recommendations or completed the new systems specified in their proposal, they are considered to have fulfilled their commitment. Now it is the client's responsibility to exploit the consultant's products and (with or without additional consulting support) to achieve the improvements that were the reason for hiring the consultant.

This nearly universal pattern has five intrinsic characteristics that I refer to as the "five fatal flaws." Each of these flaws contributes to failure rather than success.

Flaw #1: Project Defined in Terms of Consultant's Deliverables

Consulting projects are defined in terms of the work the consultant will do and the "products" the consultant will deliver, but not in terms of specific client results to be achieved. No matter what goals a client may have in mind when engaging a consultant, it is unlikely that the consulting project will be defined in terms of achieving those goals. Rather, the project will be defined in terms of the tasks the consultant will carry out and the systems, recommendations, or reports the consultant will deliver. The assumption, of course, is always is that the consultant's deliverables will eventually be translated into the client's desired results. But that is only an assumption; it is rarely part of the contract.

These two examples will show how this happens:

- A rapidly growing electronics manufacturer, its inventories and accounts receivable growing much too fast, is strapped for cash. Senior management identifies one urgent goal: *reduce inventory levels by significant amounts*. A consultant is hired to help. The consultant's project is defined as follows: *To help reduce inventory levels, we will design and install an improved inventory control system*. While the phrase "help reduce inventory levels" is in the proposal, the consultant makes no actual commitment to help reduce specific categories of inventory by a specific percentage by a specific date.
- A chain of retail stores is enjoying healthy growth, but major changes in the marketplace are producing some significant competitive pressures. Senior officers decide that store managers need to *increase sales volume per employee*. A consultant is called in to help, and the project is defined as follows: *train store managers to enable them to better provide the leadership required to boost store sales volumes and profitability*. Even though the phrase "boost store sales volumes and profitability" is included in the project definition, a careful reading makes it clear that the goal to which the consultant is committed is the training of store managers, not the real client goal of boosting sales volumes and profitability.

By accepting projects defined in this way, clients allow consultants to escape sharing the accountability for measurable performance results. The consultant is responsible only for delivering a product—a report, a system, a package of business intelligence or strategic recommendations, or some other output that the consultant knows can be delivered, risk-free. This narrow view of the consultant's accountability was illustrated for me in an article coauthored by the head of the change management practice of one of the world's largest consulting firms. In the article he describes a consulting project that used a copyrighted methodology practiced by his firm. After describing a complex analysis the firm carried out, undoubtedly for substantial fees, the case is concluded: "Putting all that information together resulted in a number that was guaranteed to turn any executive's head: Over a three-and-a-half-year period, the benefits would be $2.5 million."[8] Read it again. The *"benefits would be."* That a senior partner of a firm with tens of thousands of consultants illustrates success, apparently with pride, by the size of *identified potential savings* on a project, rather than by actual savings, illustrates the conventional consulting mindset. Once the consultants' product has been installed, they can say, "See how successful we were?" without any evidence of actual client results.

Flaw #2: Project Scope Ignores Client Readiness

Project scope is determined mainly by the subject to be studied or the problem to be solved, with little regard for the client's readiness for change. When consultants are asked to recommend improvements in some aspect of a client's organization, they begin by analyzing the system or process they have been asked to deal with: How is it working now? What is working well? What is not working well? How do the elements fit together? What might a changed or improved system look like? Such questions result in projects in which the consultants study certain systems, business processes, or strategies and then recommend how to strengthen them.

Rarely do consultants, in designing a project, consider questions like these: What kind of recommendations might we make at the completion of this study? What kinds of changes would the client have to carry out to make it work? How likely is it that our client will want to carry out those changes—and will have the ability to do so? Only at the end of a project, when the consultants are making their recommendations, do the client's motivations and capabilities come into focus as a matter of concern. At that point, dozens of factors influencing implementation suddenly become apparent and can overwhelm even the most competently designed solution.

Here is an illustration of what often happens:

A large national financial services company had always sold its products and services through a network of regional offices with an employee sales force.

Several senior officers thought that if the company could sell directly to the consumer and eliminate a full-time sales force, there was great potential for enhanced growth and earnings. To make this decision, they needed to better understand their customers' motivations: How did they feel about the company's products and services? How did they view the competition? And how would they respond to alternative sales methods?

They invited a consulting firm, well known for its strategy work, to provide the information needed to decide for or against the radical redesign of their overall market strategy. Because of the complexity of the assignment and the rather large stakes, the consultant invested several months in designing a project proposal that would encompass all the relevant factors. And then many more months were spent carrying out the study and developing recommendations, for a total of more than a year and a half to complete the study. As many as a dozen consultants at a time worked on the project, and it cost the client around $5 million.

At the end of the project, several volumes of consultants' findings and recommendations were prepared. At a formal presentation to senior management the major findings were summarized, and a rather creative way to launch the new strategy was proposed. At this presentation, management suddenly understood the enormous size of the effort required to make the changes they were considering and also the risks that would be involved in doing so. At that moment the potential gains suddenly paled by comparison. After a few more sessions to explore the strategy in greater detail, the consultants were paid and the project terminated.

The consultants conducted a thorough study and devised a creative plan to accomplish what the clients said they wanted to do. But the consultants, focusing on the question the client posed, did not pause at the beginning of the project to explore what the client might actually be willing and able to implement. Thus they spent many months and millions of dollars generating imaginative recommendations that never had a chance of being implemented. This happens all the time because the consultants focus too much on the business issues they are supposed to study and not enough on client readiness for change.

Flaw #3: Grandiose Solutions

Projects aim for one big solution rather than incremental successes. The managers of the financial services company just cited might well have been willing to take some modest, low-risk steps to test some of the ideas and assumptions behind the consultants' ultimate recommendations. But they were never given that choice. Such steps were never considered because this consulting firm was geared to studying the issue in its totality and offering a complete remedy. The aim was to go as far as possible toward having the problem completely diagnosed and solved. This stems from the fairly common view of the consultant as the heavy hitter who provides answers and solutions but is not responsible for execution and results. This tendency is most true of the very large firms.

A few years ago, the *Wall Street Journal's* lead article lambasted one of the top employee benefits consulting firms because "The vast majority of the advice given to seven clients was identical." The advice concerned the companies' diversity programs and was packaged in reports consisting of 100 to 120 pages. The *Journal* went on to say that for the seven clients studied, the consulting firm's recommended "Strategic Action Plans were identical" and, moreover, they replicated "nearly all" of the firm's fifty-four basic strategies and tactics.[9] While the article naturally focused on the fact that similar reports were given to different clients, what should arouse indignation is what the article conveys about conventional consulting. Hundred-page reports with fifty-four strategic concepts to be pursued! And clients are expected to make use of that all-wrapped-into-one final solution with apparently zero attention to the different levels of readiness among them?

In the same spirit, the senior partner of the very large firm cited previously under Flaw #1 puts it this way: "No consulting intervention can be successful unless it addresses all aspects of a company—its strategy, processes, technology, and people. . . . It must focus on the complex cause-and-effect relationships throughout the system."[10] The Updyke Automotive parts case cited in Chapter One showed how many different changes were needed in many different functions on even a simple project. The blockbuster projects require untold thousands of simultaneous, interrelated changes, often by client organizations with only modest change capability. Moreover, they allow the consultant to recommend changing everything that can be improved without having to identify the most critical few changes that will make the greatest difference.

Another negative result of the blockbuster consulting design is that many projects end up taking many months or even years from the time they begin until the consultant delivers the recommendations or installs the system. While the behemoth consulting project inches forward, month after month, life moves on. The external world continues to change. Management priorities shift. Management personnel may change. All these shifts influence client implementation motivation and capability. Yet, like a glacier moving down the mountain, the project grinds on toward its ultimate destiny, the presentation to the client of huge, complex change requirements.

Flaw #4: Hand-Offs Back and Forth

Projects entail a sharp division of responsibility between client and consultant; there is little sense of partnership between them. In the financial services example, once the client described its need and accepted the consulting firm's proposal, the consultants took over and went to work. The consultants conducted hundreds of interviews and discussed them informally with one another, developing some important insights into the buying patterns of their client company's customers. They clarified the nature of the relationships between various kinds of customers and the company's salespeople. They uncovered a number of insights into the dynamics of the client's business. They devised a number of possible solutions and explored each of them thoroughly. Eventually, they narrowed their solutions down to a few possibilities that seemed very exciting to them. But the client company's people were not involved in this creative process. Of course, the consultants did present occasional progress reports—but listening to progress reports is not the same as talking to customers and brainstorming options. By the end of the project the consultant team had coalesced around a set of well-conceived concepts, in which they had real confidence. But to the client the recommendations were all very new, very strange, and very risky.

This illustrates the fourth fatal flaw, the sharp division of responsibilities between clients and consultants. In a conventional consulting relationship, project responsibilities are handed off, back and forth, between consultant and client. The financial services company case shows how client managers go blithely on with their daily routines while the consultants are exposed to a wealth of data that the client never sees. As a consequence, the consultant may develop a strikingly different point of view on the project.

There are other risks in the back-and-forth hand-off mode. Client managers with strong views on the subject under study or with unique insights into the issues may not be sufficiently involved in helping shape recommended solutions. Individuals who will have to play a key role in implementing the consultant's recommendations may be similarly ignored until the recommendations are presented.

These are all time bombs waiting to go off at the conclusion of the project. The more work the consultant carries out without close client involvement, and the longer the cycle time from start to finish, the greater the likelihood of missed connections, of recommendations that call for actions that are too complex for the client to comprehend or carry out.

This hand-off choreography of consulting projects is similar to the way new products used to be developed. First, a company's marketing or sales department would identify a consumer need. Then, with a project authorization in hand, engineering or R&D would begin developing the new product. They would then go back to marketing and present their tentative designs. Marketing would react, and then the technical people would go do their part again. Finally, after marketing and R&D agreed on the product design, it would be taken to manufacturing. Manufacturing would study the drawings and announce what elements of the design could or could not be manufactured. In response, the plans would be modified. Perhaps the plans would have to go back to marketing for approval of the design changes. Then manufacturing would estimate the cost of the product. And so it would go, until a few years later when the product would arrive in the marketplace.

Most companies have learned that new products can be developed in a fraction of the time and at a fraction of the cost if they are developed by teams representing all of the key functions, working together throughout the process. But too few consultants have experimented with replacing the hand-off mode of consulting with a more effective, collaborative mode.

Flaw #5: Labor-Intensive Use of Consultants

Projects make labor-intensive use of consultants, instead of leveraged use. In the case of the financial services company, a team of twelve consultants worked for over eighteen months to develop a comprehensive but indigestible set of recommendations. Such labor-intensive use of consultants illustrates the fifth flaw of conventional consulting.

This flaw is the virtually inevitable consequence of the other four flaws. When the consultant is oriented toward a comprehensive solution, and the client and consultants agree that this will require extensive study, and it is understood that the consultants will do the bulk of the work, then it is not surprising if the project involves a large number of consultants. No one will be surprised to discover that the large-firm senior partner cited earlier for advocating the all-or-nothing view of project scope, advocates that clients be supplied with an abundance of consultants. Since the project must focus on everything all at once, he recommends, "Expertise must be found to assist with the interventions at each level. It's not enough to bring in just a strategy expert, or a technology expert, or a human resources expert. Expertise provided by multiple teams must be coordinated and managed, much as a general contractor manages the experts required to construct a building or house."

With all of this expertise required, it is no wonder that projects are consultant labor intensive. When consultants fail to get client personnel to play major roles on projects and fail to transfer knowledge to client personnel, that is the essence of labor-intensive consulting. It really is very similar, as the senior partner previously quoted explains, to the way "a general contractor manages the experts required to construct a building." They do all the work and turn the finished product over to the client. It ignores the gains that are possible if the consulting effort is leveraged by having client people learn from the consultants and take over increasing amounts of the work of the project.

Some cynics point to consultants' economic incentive in heavily staffing a project. While that is certainly part of it, the entire structure of conventional consulting leads inevitably to a labor-intensive mode.

Many consulting firms and internal consultants recognize that this is not a good way to work. They may even make some attempts to get their clients involved in project work. The great majority of consultants, however, seem to be unwilling or unable to depart from the conventional, labor-intensive consulting model. And, as I'll discuss later, clients not only accept this state of affairs but have a real psychological stake in the game being played this way.

So much resource, so much creativity, so much motivation, yet so much lost along the way.

The Cost of the Flaws

Not all five flaws afflict every consulting project. In most conventional firms, however, enough projects are affected by enough of the flaws that many clients receive much less benefit than they paid for. Moreover, the longer a project, the more organizational units it affects, and the more different changes it introduces, the more likely it is to fail. Take the case of this fairly large project in a specialty insurance company, carried out by a well-known, respected consulting firm:

> The company had a serious problem with falling profits. It needed to significantly reduce its expenses and improve the effectiveness of its operations. Even though the company's senior managers were not clear on the strategic direction the company should take, they did agree that expenses had to be cut by about 20 percent. The head of the consulting firm promised the company's president that a comprehensive reengineering project could accomplish that goal.
>
> The consultants provided a team of about twenty-five consultants (mainly newly minted MBAs) and augmented them with a group of about forty company employees. This group was divided into process redesign

teams to study six primary processes, with many subteams organized around related subprocesses.

The assessment and redesign activities of these various teams went on for about a year. Although senior managers were given periodic progress reports, they were not really encouraged to become active in the project. They were expected to listen and approve. Similarly, company personnel serving on the teams quickly discovered that the consultants incorporated only those ideas that they viewed as acceptable to themselves.

At the end of the redesign phase, the consultants presented the company's senior managers with voluminous documents containing masses of data. The consultants' plan called for all sorts of radical work-process and related changes to be carried out more or less simultaneously at headquarters and in the field. Various offices were to be consolidated, moved, or redesigned. The company's products and services were to undergo fundamental shifts. The company was to reduce its staff. And all of this was supposed to be carried out by a management team that had little experience in managing change. The company tried to implement the consultants' recommendations, but the effort soon bogged down. The net effect was that the business was worse off than it had been before.

Talk about the five fatal flaws! The client wanted to reduce its expenses, and after a year it received a complicated *plan* to do so, but no actual reductions. After a year of work and untold millions of dollars of cost, the consultants had not done a single pilot test of any redesign recommendation to see if their plan would actually work for their client. Moreover, the consultants' plan gave no consideration to the client's ability to implement change, so there was a huge implementation gap. Nor was this gap closed during the year-long study by steps to develop the client's change management capability. The project followed the characteristic labor-intensive, one-big-solution model. All five fatal flaws (summarized in Exhibit 2.2) were honed to a fine edge by this large, well-respected consulting firm, which, as you read these words, has hundreds of consultants out repeating this flawed pattern with other clients.

Exhibit 2.2. The Five Fatal Flaws of Conventional Consulting.

1. Project defined in terms of consultant's products (not in terms of client results to be achieved).
2. Project scope based on subject matter logic (not on client readiness for change).
3. One big solution (rather than incremental successes).
4. Hand-offs back and forth (instead of client-consultant partnerships).
5. Labor-intensive use of consultants (instead of leveraged use).

Most books and articles on consulting take for granted the conventional big-picture, one-time-around, lengthy and labor-intensive consulting model. When such an effort works, it can produce wonderful results. When the moon and stars and planets are all in alignment and the consultant's recommendations mobilize effective client action, there can be some powerful outcomes that the client could never have achieved on its own.

The evidence suggests, however, that such successes are more the exception than the rule. Dozens of things can go wrong, and these things are not typically controlled within the framework of the conventional consulting model. It is much more common for the moon, stars, and planets not to align. High-impact consulting offers an alternative for clients who want more assurance of success and for the consultants who want to provide it.

Chapter 3

The Bottom-Line Results of High-Impact Consulting

D uring the 1930s, one of President Franklin Roosevelt's top priorities was to revive the country's ailing agricultural sector. Thousands of "county agents" were deployed by the Department of Agriculture to provide education and consultation to farmers. One such agent in western Nebraska encountered a farmer who had not made use of this assistance. After some small talk, the agent said, "Say, Calvin, how about if I come by next week to see if I can be of some help?" "Thanks very much," Calvin responded, "but you needn't bother to visit. I ain't farmin' half as good as I already know how to farm."

Calvin's situation matches that of many senior managers. Most already know what their organizations should be doing differently; they simply are not capable of making it happen. For every manager I have encountered who was in the dark about what strategic direction to pursue, I have met twenty or thirty who knew what they wanted to do but were frustrated by not being able to do it fast enough or well enough.

The ability to make things happen, to effect change, is thus the most critical dimension of organizational success. A new management tool or a strategic vision can be created in a relatively short time by a few bright people. To significantly enhance an organization's capacity for improvement, however, requires very hard work by many people over time. As professor Arthur Turner of the Harvard Business School put it, in a more sophisticated expression of Calvin's insightful remark, "It is often easier, but less useful, to transmit to a client a valid diagnosis of what is wrong and what should be done about it, than to interact with members of the client organization in such a way that the things which 'should' happen actually come to pass."[1]

As noted earlier, the conventional consulting paradigm is not designed to mobilize organizational change. High-impact consulting, by contrast, focuses on implementing solutions as much as on discovering them. It is explicitly designed to produce all three elements of consulting success: expert recommendations, bottom-line results, and client capacity to sustain improvements. Indeed, high-impact consulting aims to expand the skills, confidence, and enthusiasm of the client to go even further. It is designed to help the Calvins of the world to farm as well as they know how to farm, and then to learn even more.

Here's an example of high-impact consulting in action:

The United Aluminum Corporation, a rolling and processing mill in Connecticut, invested large sums over a five-year period in technical consulting to install the rolling-mill control equipment the consultant recommended. The resulting productivity gains were only a few percentage points a year, however.

A colleague of mine, Keith Michaelson, collaborated with an internal consultant at the company to address the need for greater productivity. A small group of mill operators and supervisors were invited to help the company capture greater benefits from its investment by further increasing the rolling mill's throughput.

In a series of brainstorming sessions, the consultants tuned in to the participants' resistance to improvement as well as to the participants' ideas for achieving it. The consultants encouraged senior management to respond to a number of "hidden agenda" items that surfaced.

Once management had met with the team of mill personnel and dealt with their questions, the group agreed to shoot for a 15 percent gain in six weeks. The team ran the project. It was made very clear—by word and deed—that the consultants were there to provide methodological help but were not the ones in charge of the project. All members of the team were encouraged to contribute their ideas. By the end of the six weeks, productivity had actually increased by 17 percent—five or six times the amount gained over the preceding several years. And this level was not only sustained in subsequent years but actually increased to higher levels, again without further capital investment.

The Next Step

At around this same time, company management decided to take action to improve their on-time shipment record, which was down around 80 percent. They were about to engage a consultant to recommend and install an order-tracking system, at a cost of about $2 million.

The company's experience in the rolling-mill productivity project suggested that a purely technical solution might not solve the late shipments problem. So the company postponed the systems study and asked Michaelson to help them shoot for some rapid results on the on-time shipments problem.

In collaboration with several internal consultants, Michaelson proposed and then helped carry out the following pilot project, without making any changes in the information system. The mill managers agreed to try, with some consulting assistance, to ship 100 percent of orders on time during a one-week experiment by "doing everything right." One month of preparation was scheduled before the trial week. The managers were not asked to commit to maintaining that level of service after the one-week experiment. Employees in every department were asked to help prepare for the experiment, and everyone's ideas were welcomed.

During the one-week pilot (and the following week, too) every single order was shipped on time. Thereafter, delivery performance never fell below 95 percent. Some modest information-system improvements were needed to sustain the performance, but nothing like a $2 million system.

Reversing the Five Fatal Flaws

These two projects illustrate a consulting process that eliminates most of the risks of conventional consulting and adds dimensions that can multiply the benefits of consulting many times. The approach sharply contrasts with conventional consulting because it reverses the five frequently fatal flaws of the conventional model, transmuting them into techniques that reduce risks and enhance returns:

1. Instead of defining projects in terms of the consultant's expertise or the consultant's deliverables (solutions, reports, systems, and so on), high-impact consulting defines projects in terms of specific client performance goals that will be attained.

2. Instead of determining a project's scope in terms of the subject to be studied, high-impact consulting determines project scope based on an assessment of what the client is likely to be willing and able to implement.

3. Instead of aiming for one big solution that will require a long cycle time and huge up-front investment, high-impact consulting divides projects into increments with rapid cycle times for quicker results.

4. Instead of passing responsibility back and forth between clients and consultants, high-impact consulting encourages both parties to work and learn together, in full partnership mode, through every stage of the project.

5. Instead of making labor-intensive use of hordes of consultants, high-impact consulting makes leveraged use of small consulting teams.

By reversing each of the five frequently fatal flaws of conventional consulting, high-impact consulting creates a low-risk, rapid-return developmental process. Each project is designed not only to produce some tangible result but also to expand the capability of both client and consultant to tackle increasingly ambitious projects with increasing competence.

Tapping the Client's Latent Potential

High-impact consulting is based on the belief that fostering an organization's ability to implement change is the key to strengthening its fundamental capability. As that Nebraskan farmer knew perfectly well, there's no sense in giving more advice to someone who is already not doing half as much as he knows he should be doing.

How can consultants strengthen their clients' implementation capability? One important clue can be found in the fact that when a crisis or must-do situation suddenly arises, virtually every organization can spontaneously mobilize a response. Let the possibility of landing a new important account arise, or let a fire or flood occur, and suddenly there is a surge of effectiveness—as much as double or triple the normal level. The world of business is replete with events like these:

- Some years ago, an Exxon refinery with 2,800 employees (a number the plant's managers had complained was inadequate) was hit with a sudden wildcat strike. Unable to plan for a safe, orderly shutdown, the managers kept the refinery going, assuming the stoppage would be over quickly. Instead, it continued for months, while about 450 managers and engineers kept the refinery going at full capacity.
- In 1993, northern Georgia had a record snowfall of about nineteen inches. The roof over part of a Mohawk Carpet mill, unable to support the load, collapsed, destroying one of two production lines in a fully loaded factory. Within days, thanks to the inventiveness and dedication of the people in the mill, the remaining line was producing what both lines had been producing before the storm.
- A group of health insurance claims examiners whose productivity was low and whose work was fraught with errors was, as part of an experiment, offered time off if they reached some new levels of output. Within hours they increased their output by about 50 percent, and the error rate dropped.
- After the Chicago poisonings temporarily put the company out of business in the early 1980s, Tylenol developed a triple safety packaging system and restarted production within three months, instead of the more normal twelve to eighteen months to develop such a system.

Every manager can cite similar miracles of response to fires, floods, or earthquakes, or to sudden sales opportunities or client-imposed deadlines. It is obvious that none of these organizations' capability was created at the moment their crisis occurred. Consider that to achieve such dramatic improvements, an organization's people must modify their personal work patterns, shift their priorities, and reorganize their work processes, eliminating those of little value. That they can do it so fast and so well, and without any consulting help, means that they must already have possessed the know-how and capability.

To capture this potential every day, it is necessary to know what releases it in must-do situations. My associates and I have asked thousands of managers and consultants what they think is the answer to this question. They all responded quickly, and every group enumerated virtually the same list of causes—I call them the "zest factors"—listed in Exhibit 3.1.[2] The more an undertaking is characterized by these zest factors, the more a group will mobilize its energies, overturn barriers, and set aside low-value-added activities. If you test most consulting projects against the zest list, you will find that there was probably plenty of zest for the consultants but little or no zest for the clients. Projects are rarely focused on a few critical results. Clients rarely feel they are working toward goals that are "clear, measurable, and short-term." Nor do most consulting projects have a sense of urgency about them. It is no wonder, therefore, that most conventional consulting projects fail to mobilize the client's hidden potential.

Carving off and achieving a rapid-cycle results goal, however, does provide a sense of zest. There is a clear-cut focus. Clients feel a sense of responsibility; they are invited to be creative in devising and implementing solutions. From the first moment, both client and consultant are focused on identifying and implementing actions that will liberate zest and yield results quickly.

Exhibit 3.1. The Zest Factors.

- The focus is on a few critical results.
- The goals are clear, measurable, and short-term.
- The project carries a real sense of urgency. It must be done.
- People see that success depends on them—and they assume the responsibility.
- People realize they must experiment to achieve their goals.

Achieving Success: The High-Impact Paradigm

Simply put, using high-impact consulting is like loading the dice for success. Each project is designed to exploit the untapped capabilities of the client, with the help of the consultants. Focusing on real results that have some urgency mobilizes people's energy. Designing rapid-cycle subprojects means people have a chance to see the results of their efforts quickly. Having clients work in partnership with the consultants encourages people to share their creative ideas and to experiment to see what works.

Following sections show how each of the five shifts from the conventional model to high-impact consulting contributes to liberating the client's untapped capability. I'll describe these shifts briefly here, and then cover them in more detail in Chapters Four through Eight.

Success Factor #1: Every Project Defined in Terms of Client Results

High-impact projects are defined in terms of measurable client results that client and consultant agree to achieve together. This is in contrast to defining them in terms of the work the consultants will perform and the products they will deliver, which is how virtually all consulting projects are defined. For example, suppose a company wants consulting help to speed the pace of new product development. A high-impact consultant would define the project in terms of achieving actual reductions in the time to develop new products. If the client wants to enter a new market, the high-impact consultant's goal would be to help the client enter that market. If a company is experiencing errors and delays in processing orders, a high-impact consulting project would have the goal of reducing errors and delays by some specified amount within some specified period.

In each of those assignments, the consultants would of course contribute technical know-how and introduce new systems and work methods. But the project would not be defined in terms of those tools. It would be defined by the measurable results that must be achieved for the project to be considered successful.

Many consultants, on reading this last paragraph, would leap to their feet and assert that of course they focus on client results. Helping clients achieve their goals is their only raison d'être, they would assert. But, as mentioned in Chapter Two, a quick scan of any of their typical proposals would suggest otherwise. A proposal for an order-entry project, for example, might define the consultant's task as something like this: "Study the company's present order-processing system, identify needed improvements, and recommend and install new processes designed to reduce errors and eliminate delays in order processing." Although the project definition uses the phrase "reduce errors and eliminate delays," the consultants in fact have committed only to recommending and installing new processes. Of course those processes are intended to reduce errors—sometime in the future. But the consultants are not accountable for those ultimate results.

Many consultants (and clients) confuse the issue by using the word *results* to describe almost any product of a consulting study. A truly results-focused definition of a consulting project, however, needs to be very specific about achieving measurable client results. In a semiconductor plant, for example, a high-impact quality project might be defined as follows: "In a joint undertaking, increase second-pass yields from the current 60 percent level to 80 percent or more within ten weeks." With such a project definition in hand, client and consultant will both be focused on the same goals, and both will assess their success by the same criteria.

Of course, the consultants will provide some expert input to help improve the targeted process or system, but success in providing that input won't be considered success on the project. Rather, those inputs will be but one contribution to the project. The consultants, no matter how elegant their solutions, will not consider themselves successful unless tangible, measurable results are achieved—that is, rejects are reduced or yields are improved.

Focusing on a real bottom-line result important to the client adds zest to any consulting project. Rather than being a distraction from the client's efforts to achieve a desired goal, the project becomes the effort. Such a focus generates more commitment than a consulting project that promises great results sometime in the distant future.

Certain types of projects may be more difficult to define in terms of concrete results. Strategic planning projects and major systems projects are examples. I will show in Chapter Four, however, how virtually every kind of consulting project can be translated into results-oriented terms.

Success Factor #2: Projects Designed to Match Client Motivation and Capability

To ensure success, it is essential that the client and consultant, at the earliest possible moment, assess what kinds of changes the client organization is likely to be ready, willing, and able to carry out. Then the project can be designed so that the amount of change it eventually calls for will not extend far beyond that estimate. That's designing for a win.

A client exploring a new project with a consultant should insist on discussing the possible actions the consultant might recommend. Both parties need to consider which of the possible changes might actually be feasible.

Often when consultants are asked at the beginning of a project to speculate about its possible outcomes, they will hedge: "We can't predict what the recommendations might be until we do the study and get the results." In fact, though, any experienced consultant, even after only brief exposure to a new situation, should be able to provide a range of possible recommendations and outcomes. It should always be possible to make some educated guesses. And clients should insist on hearing some of those guesses. Only when you, the client, have a sense of what your organization might have to do in order to benefit from a consultant's work can you reliably assess whether the project is a certain winner or not. And you can't do that unless the consultant shares with you, while the project is being designed, some of the possible outcomes. Without such a discussion the project is a real Las Vegas crap shoot.

As both client and consultant sharpen their sense of the client's readiness to act, they can carefully design (or redesign) the project so that their expectations for change will align with the organization's estimated capabilities. This process shifts the essential nature of a consulting project from a gamble to more of a sure bet.

Success Factor #3: Divide Large Projects into Rapid-Cycle Subprojects

The faster a project gets finished, the more likely it is to deliver the desired results. When the project drags on for six or eight or twelve months, the client's needs (or how it views them) are apt to change while the work is under way. Some of the key players in the organization may change jobs or priorities. Market and competitive conditions may shift. Time and again I have heard about large information-systems projects that cost tens of millions of dollars and extended over several years but had to be abandoned along the way because they had not been modified to meet the client's changing needs. The worst risk is that as projects get larger and larger, the more likely is it that they will conclude with large, complex, and elaborate changes that will overwhelm the client organization.

The most reliable and powerful way to minimize these risks is to carve off from the overall project a series of subprojects, each of which will yield some results and some success in a short time—five or six weeks, if possible, or fourteen or fifteen at the high end. For example, the first project at United Aluminum, described at the beginning of this chapter, began producing major gains in six weeks. Here is another example:

> An office machine distribution company engaged a consulting firm that practices in the high-impact mode to help increase the productivity of its national sales force. Client and consultant both agreed on the general approach that would be used, but instead of trying to launch a change effort in all twelve of the company's branch offices, they decided to try it first in one branch. The branch selected for the trial was one whose manager had expressed some interest in receiving help to increase sales. Several interviews with personnel at that branch revealed that the most urgent need was to increase sales in the major account categories. After some further dialogue, a project was designed with the goal of increasing major account sales by $100,000 a month over a period of ten to twelve weeks.
>
> By focusing intently on one goal, they succeeded. Equally important, both client and consultant learned something about what would work and what would not. They were able to sharpen the design of the project as

they moved forward within the first branch and then expanded the effort to the other branches.

Carving off rapid-cycle subprojects may be the single most important contributor to stimulating the zest factors in an organization. When there is a clear, short-term end result in sight, people can get enthused about making it happen. Since the goal is more contained, there is less risk, so people feel freer to experiment. And as people enjoy some successes, their willingness to shoot for tougher goals expands.

Carving off shorter-term projects from large-scale, long-term undertakings is often mistaken for being tactical instead of being strategic. Those who are wed to the conventional consulting paradigm often retort that the use of rapid-cycle projects that deliver quick results is nothing more than "picking the low-hanging fruit." But these short-term projects are not carried out at the expense of pursuing a more strategic vision. In selecting rapid-cycle goals, managers are asked to make certain that those goals align with the company's longer-term strategies. In fact, as each rapid-cycle project is carried out, one of its aims should be to gather and test more information about those longer-term strategies. Many large-scale change projects, such as the GE Work-Out process in the 1990s and the Motorola Organization Effectiveness Process in the 1980s, were built on a foundation of specific incremental achievements.

Success Factor #4: Develop a Working Partnership Between Client and Consultant

Once a consulting project aims at achieving some targeted, measurable improvements in a relatively short period of time, the conventional consulting project's back-and-forth hand-offs of responsibility disappear because they simply won't work. Clients and consultants must work together as partners, agreeing on what must be done, allocating tasks, and working together to achieve the desired results.

Suppose, for example, that a client wants to find out whether a new product is likely to succeed. The client and consultant might decide that instead of undertaking a massive study of the possible markets, they will collaborate on a real-time test of the product in one or two major markets. They discuss between themselves how the test might be carried out. Perhaps they obtain the views of other people in the organization. Then, together, they create a work plan for carrying out the project. Now they share a common, results-focused, rapid-cycle goal, a conviction that the goal is achievable, and a common view of how they will carry out the project.

One indication of the shift from conventional to high-impact consulting is that the project design statement is no longer prepared by the consultant and conveyed to the client. Since a high-impact consulting project is a collaborative process, it can only be described in a document that is prepared jointly.

The partnership relationship also makes each project a learning experience for both the client and the consultant. During each rapid-cycle subproject, the client's people learn how to identify a goal and achieve it. They learn how to use the consultant's expert inputs, adapt them, and put them to work. They also learn how to implement changes—and how to get various groups to collaborate in carrying them out. Thus every project carried out in the high-impact mode yields management-development and organizational-development benefits for the client, as well as tangible bottom-line results.

The consultants learn too. In conventional consulting, the consultants are assumed to be the font of all knowledge and wisdom. Many consultants cultivate this aura of omniscience to prop up their professional image and self-confidence. But consultant learning is a key developmental building block of high-impact consulting. At the very least, the initial projects in an organization teach the consultants what it takes to make things happen in that organization.

One of the most important things that both client and consultant learn from collaborating on a rapid-cycle project is how to proceed together to attack the next-step goals. That is, as client and consultant work together on their initial projects, they gain insight into how they can best move forward with their collaboration. They share the task of identifying goals for the next steps and the best way to move forward to achieve them. This is in contrast to the heavy dumps of material and recommendations at the end of a conventional consulting project, which often make clients plead with their consultants, saying things like, "Please go away and give us a chance to absorb what you've already given us."

Thus the partnership mode kindles a sense of shared responsibility on the part of client staff. They are not just standing around answering the consultant's questions and waiting for the consultant to drop the final blueprint on them.

Success Factor #5: Leverage Consulting Inputs

Consulting projects aimed at rapid-cycle, measurable results with the active participation of the client require far fewer consulting hours than the typical labor-intensive conventional project. A principal objective of high-impact consulting is to help clients make better use of their own talents and skills. With this perspective, and with more emphasis on achieving results and less on producing voluminous studies, consultants need do much less, because the client accomplishes so much more with what the consultant provides. That is why high-impact consulting is also high-leverage consulting.

A drastic reduction in costs is only one of the benefits of high-leverage consulting. At least as important is the implied message to everyone in the client organization: "This is our project, and we are the ones who will have to make it succeed, with the help of the consultants." The zest aroused by this sense of personal responsibility contrasts markedly with the malaise and cynicism that follow when twenty or thirty or fifty consultants are scampering around, poring over files, sitting in client meetings to take notes and share their views, calling their own meetings, and sometimes acting, perhaps unconsciously, as though they were running the show.

As consultants and clients plan projects in ways that leverage the costly consulting inputs for maximum effectiveness, they will discover that small amounts of consultant input can go a long way when the client is prepared to absorb and use it.

So, as summarized in Exhibit 3.2, high-impact consulting takes the five frequently fatal flaws of conventional consulting and reverses every one of them. The result is an entirely different way of looking at the consulting process.

Exhibit 3.2. Conventional Consulting Versus High-Impact Consulting.

Conventional Consulting	High-Impact Consulting
1. *Defining the project* Project goals are defined in terms of the solutions, systems, recommendations, or techniques to be provided by the consultant.	Projects are defined in terms of measurable improvements in clients' bottom-line results.
2. *Determining the project's scope* The project's scope is determined by the systems or technical issues to be studied.	The project's scope is determined by assessing what the client will be willing and able to absorb and implement.
3. *Designing the project* Projects are large-scale, with long cycle times and the speed and maneuverability of a glacier.	Projects are divided into steps to produce rapid results and to gain the experience that enables further progress.
4. *Working on the project* First the client passes the problem to the consultant; then the consultant does the job and passes the results back to the client.	The client and consultant work together as partners at every stage of the project.
5. *Deploying consultants* Large consulting teams do the work, with little client involvement.	Consultants provide focused support to client teams, who take major responsibility for the project.
Consequences Big up-front investments and long cycle times before value can be assessed; high risk and frequently low returns; may be little or no client learning.	Low risk, high returns; consultant time highly leveraged; short cycle time, so there is little investment before seeing a payoff; client capabilities expand with each cycle.

Blending Content Consulting with Process Consulting

Many writers on the subject divide the consulting world into two sectors. Most consultants are "content consultants," functioning as experts on substantive issues such as information technology, logistics, manufacturing processes, strategy, finance, and so on. "Process consultants" offer help in determining how things should happen in an organization, but they don't devote much energy to content issues (or to achieving results).

It seems obvious that effective consulting as I have defined it requires a blend of content consulting with process consulting, with a strong added emphasis on achieving results. Arthur Turner advocated this shift in a 1983 paper titled "Expert or Facilitator?" In it he describes the consulting process as a "collaboration between consultant and client in discovering and mobilizing readiness for action to improve performance, [with the] desired outcome [of] more effective task accomplishment and relevant learning within the client organization."[3] In the paper, Turner quotes Carl Sloane, former head of Temple, Barker & Sloane and then professor at Harvard Business School, who wrote, "I have never seen an issue of any significance that is entirely substance or entirely process."[4] High-impact consulting offers a results-oriented framework for blending substance and process.

P.S. An Action Note to Client Managers: Change Is Long Overdue

Hundreds of success stories reveal that you can significantly reduce or eliminate the usual risks of management consulting and multiply its payoffs. It is amazing that clients have permitted consultants to stick with the dismal conventional paradigm so tenaciously.

Why must mountains of information, data, insights, ideas, and innovations be amassed during a project, assembled in final reports, and then dumped onto the desks of client managers in doses beyond their capacity to absorb and use? Why should consultants be pushing projects in your organization that take time, effort, and money without any direct bottom-line results? There is no reason. Projects can be designed to yield recommendations that you, the client, can respond to. Further, why should you, the client, manager, have to assume full accountability for translating the consultant's inputs into bottom-line results? There is no reason. The achievement of some meaningful results, as you, the client, define results, can be made the central focus of every consulting project. Highly leveraged consulting is not only a more valuable way to work, it is a more pleasant way to work. You and your consultants will have much more fun working together to produce real results in a short period of time.

One way to ensure that consultants adopt more of a high-impact strategy is for you to be unrelenting in your demand that consultants demonstrate their worth by producing measurable results very early in the relationship—and then on every step of the way.

P.S. An Action Note to Consultants: You'll Win Too

In this book I advocate that conventional consultants experiment with high-impact modes. I don't advocate that you attempt a sudden shift to the high-impact model on all five factors. Rather, experiment with adopting the high-impact consulting ideas that seem most compatible with your own individual modes of practicing. As noted in Chapter Two, many consultants have already adopted some elements of higher-leverage, high-impact strategies. And I urge them to keep moving. Even the giant firms that seem financially and psychologically attuned to the labor-intensive, high-cost traditional consulting patterns can find ways to practice high-impact consulting. They can even do so and still retain their large-scale projects, but they'll have to think of them as outsourced technology, not as consulting.

In the chapters that follow, I show how both clients and consultants can move toward results-focused high-impact consulting. You might want to think of a specific consulting project that you are working on or plan to begin in the near future. Keep that project or potential project in mind as you read so you will have a tangible, real-world situation against which to test the ideas in this book.

Part Two

The Results-Driven Architecture of High-Impact Consulting

Chapter 4

Define Goals in Terms of
Client Results Instead
of Consultant Products

Even when the need for improvement is painfully clear, it's easy for a company to allow conventional consulting to spiral off track:

I was once invited to explore the possibility of assisting a rapidly growing food service company with an urgent problem. The preceding year its creditors had imposed some very tough restrictions because of the company's serious cash problems. Those restrictions had recently been eased because the company had forecast breaking even in the current year. After the first five months, however, sales were running well behind the company's projections.

Initial discussions with senior managers quickly revealed one major step that could generate some immediate progress and possibly ensure the company's viability. That step was to focus major attention on increasing sales in the one major division that was the company's worst performer. There were many ideas among senior managers about how the laggard division could step up its performance. But none of these ideas were being acted on. Why? Because an internal consulting group, with the CEO's approval, was engaging the senior management team in a number of developmental and planning activities.

Here are some of the activities that were being carried forward by the consultants in the earnest belief that they were building a necessary foundation for future success:

A Plethora of Planning and Preparations

- They created a "timeless vision" for the company, developing a set of corporate goals with carefully honed wording—for example: "Profitability: To maximize the long-term value of the company" and a number of similar statements.
- They created a set of corporate values—such as "Sustain our energy and commitment to the company mission while maintaining a healthy balance between personal and work life" and similar statements.
- They developed a company strategy that included selling the company's product "not only through our own retail stores but through any channel (wholesale, retail, or mail order) that facilitates customer access to products."
- They discussed and wrote out an expansion strategy.
- They laid out a list of items under the heading "Strategic Focus" that began with "Our organizational excellence will become more and more important in the increasing competitive environment" and continued with a number of similar platitudes.
- They created a one-year plan that began with "To *focus* our efforts on improving our business processes with a major focus on investing in people and with the goal of being profitable in the fiscal year" and continued with a number of similar statements.
- They created a six-year vision, which began with "To be one of the top three companies" in their business in their part of the country "with the best business processes to support this," and continued with a number of similar statements.
- They created a company planning process and a calendar of the key planning events for the coming year.
- They launched a number of "process and planning" activities, each under the aegis of the CEO or another senior manager: developing a model for expansion; developing a prospecting telemarketing system; developing an on-line inventory system; developing a production forecasting sys-

High-Impact Consulting

tem; developing a production planning and scheduling system; developing a plant process and equipment control system; and perhaps twenty or thirty more.

Here was a business in difficulty, with some very urgent performance improvement requirements, but its management group was investing endless time in implementing the internal consultant's vision of the right answer. The consultants felt no compulsion to produce results; just the opposite. They felt that the key to attaining better results was to strengthen the organization's structures, systems, and processes. Then results would follow—some day.

The orientation of this consulting group illustrates the fallacy that guides most conventional consulting. According to the conventional paradigm, if you want to produce better results, the first step is always to build in all the *presumed contributors* to better results. After you lay that groundwork, and only after you do so, results will naturally follow in due course,

When we explored with this company's management the possibility of focusing directly and immediately on achieving some performance improvements in the poorly performing division, a few of the senior managers favored the idea. But the concept created consternation among the consultants. The idea of aiming directly at achieving some better results at once—the heart of the high-impact consulting paradigm—sounds as odd to most conventional consultants and their clients as the roundness of the earth sounded to many of the contemporaries of Christopher Columbus. The conventional paradigm encourages consultants, with the support of their clients, to focus on studies, preparations, reformations, training, new systems, and anything except trying to get an immediate bottom-line result. That is somehow considered to be cheating.

Consider, for example, an automotive-parts plant whose customers were turning away from it because of quality and delivery problems:

A group of consultants determined that it was crucial for employees in the plant to become involved in quality improvement. To stimulate this involvement, they helped management launch weekly employee-involvement team meetings focused on quality. After six months these teams had generated hundreds of suggestions and abundant goodwill among plant employees but no significant improvement in quality or delivery. It was a typical preparations-first consulting process. First the consultants would concentrate on getting employees involved (the presumed contributor to better results). Once that was accomplished, results would follow. But as in many conventional projects, the up-front work was done, but the results never came.

When the division general manager became impatient with the process, he introduced the plant's management to a high-impact, begin-with-results consultant. They agreed to try the approach on one production line. The manager of that line began by setting a specific improvement target with his people: they would try to reduce by 30 percent the frequency of their most prevalent defect, and do so within two months. They concentrated all their efforts on this one sharply focused goal, and it was achieved. The success created a model for an expanded, plantwide improvement process that quickly spread the method across the entire operation.

Mistaking Means for Ends, Activities for Results

The conventional consulting paradigm encourages preparations-first strategies. The focus is on introducing new management tools, techniques, systems, or directions. One reason for the rapid growth of consulting is that many managers believe that if they can only discover and carry out the right improvement *preparations,* lay the right *foundations,* it will inevitably lead to actual *improvements.* That is certainly what the food service CEO and consultants whose adventures open this chapter believed. This perspective confuses ends with means and processes with outcomes. Consultants encourage this view by telling managers that they need not—in fact, *should not*—focus on improving results directly, because that approach is bound to be tactical and shortsighted. Only after the consultant has ensured that the fundamentals are in place, managers are told, will results unfold in ways that are sound and healthy.

But, in fact, preparations-first conventional consulting often has little or no impact on the client's bottom line. One reason for that is that the consultants running such projects accept no accountability beyond creating and handing over their deliverable in a form their client will accept. They do not, in contracting for the project, place their reputation on the line and agree that they will collaborate with the client to help deliver specific and measurable improvements. And since the consulting product itself is what they are evaluated on, consultants operate on the idea that the more thoroughly their product is developed, the better. This adds to the problem because it encourages long cycle times as the consultant focuses on doing a thorough and correct job of research and analysis and avoids trying to help the client take direct aim at some results rapidly.

Beginning with Results

In the high-impact consulting paradigm, clients and consultants take aim from the first moment at achieving some tangible results. Not programs. Not systems. Not reports. Not recommendations. Not studies with better answers. Not strategy formulations. None of these, unless they inherently include the delivery of some measurable bottom-line results in short order. This means that if the client's goal is lower manufacturing costs, for example, then the *project's* goal will be to produce measurable cost savings in manufacturing. Whatever tools or methods the consultants might introduce, the aim of the project will be to actually lower the client's costs.

This idea of focusing directly on the attainment of results as step #1 in consulting is the most critical difference between the conventional consulting paradigm and high-impact consulting.

Here's how this concept played out in the Department of Mental Health in Connecticut.

Like every other state, Connecticut has been plagued by rising workers' compensation costs from on-the-job employee injuries. In the Department of Mental Health, the most serious safety hazards for employees were the patients themselves. Lifting and transferring patients caused one category of problems. In addition, a small minority of violent patients caused many injuries. Employees were hurt. Morale suffered. Work was disrupted. And providing workers' compensation indemnity and medical care was increasingly costly to the state.

Consultants knowledgeable in safety issues had encouraged a number of "preparations" steps. These included safety training, researching accident causes, publicity to educate employees about the costs of accidents, safety rules. And so on. Some of these programs were developed by state-employed staff consultants and some by outside consultants. The results were the same: the injury rate continued to increase, hurting employees, disrupting ward equanimity, and undermining patient care. The cost of disability compensation continued to accelerate.

Fairfield Hills: A High-Impact, Results-Focused Effort

As part of the state's Executive Management Program, a consultant from my firm was working with a group of managers that included the head nurse of the wards at Fairfield Hills, one of the state's mental health institutions. She thought that more training and additional staff might help solve the worker injury problem. Since there was no evidence that past training had had much impact and there was no budget for more people, my colleague suggested that perhaps they might try setting a specific goal for the reduction of worker injuries and then try to achieve it. While the suggestion seemed odd, since the head nurse felt that the goal had to be zero injuries, they agreed to try to reduce the incidence of patient violence by 10 percent. This very modest goal reflected their lack of confidence that they could really reduce worker injuries. They focused on two wards only, to make sure the approach would work before involving other wards. After some further discussion, a team was assembled under the leadership of a nursing supervisor and given the task of achieving the goal within three months on wards A and B.

Now for the first time there was some accountability for results, shared by client and consultant. There was a measurable goal. With some consulting assistance, the team began to create a work plan, based not on ideas about what would be good to include in a safety program, but on what they believed they had to do to reduce the frequency of the incidents that were causing injury on those two specific wards. In the first week or two, they created new charts for tracking the nature and time of patient incidents. They tested new ways to anticipate and avoid incidents. Nursing staff, aides, administrators, and psychiatrists worked together on this effort as they had never done before.

During the three months of the experimental period, the number of staff injuries dropped to two, compared to eight during the same three months the previous year, and lost work days were 11, compared to 144 the previous year.

By realizing these dramatic results, the hospital's management and the participants in the experiment moved from being victims of a problem to being problem solvers. They began to develop some confidence that they might be able to manage an effective safety improvement process.

The head nurse at Fairfield Hills extended the process to all six wards, and the injury rate from patient incidents actually dropped by 85 percent and stayed there, year after year. Beyond achieving these dramatic results at Fairfield Hills, the experiment proved to be the spark that ignited a statewide effort.

They demonstrated the power of going for immediate results.

Norwich Hospital: Building on Success

In response to the urging of the state's workers' compensation manager, Bob Finder, Garrell Mullaney (the superintendent of Norwich Hospital) decided to test the results-focused approach to controlling the skyrocketing cost of workers' compensation. Norwich was a much larger facility than Fairfield Hills, and at the time it had one of the highest worker injury rates in the state. The work was sponsored by the Connecticut Quality of Work Life Committee, a state-sponsored union-management collaboration. Rather than tackle the problem all at once in the hospital's more than twenty wards, Mullaney and consultants Suzanne Francis and Matthew McCreight agreed to focus at first on just two high-incidence wards. He asked a team from each of these high-incidence wards to make significant measurable reductions in the number of staff injuries, and he made it clear that the role of the consultants was to help the teams do that. The hospital union, Local 1199, supported and collaborated in the project.

The consultants helped the team members visualize how a results-focused experiment might work. Each team established some specific, ambitious goals. Both teams enjoyed considerable success in meeting those goals. The initial projects at Norwich reduced incidents of patient violence more than 60 percent from the previous year. That project, in 1988, was the beginning of a three-year program during which Mullaney expanded the program to all of Norwich, mobilizing more than twenty teams in the effort. Eight internal facilitators were trained to support the teams' work; the external consultants supported the internal facilitators and helped hospital management provide overall leadership and direction.

Meanwhile, other facilities began to participate. These used an even more leveraged approach, training their own internal facilitators right from the start. The first four pilot wards at Connecticut Valley Hospital reduced safety-related incidents by 30 percent and lost work days by 70 percent compared to the previous year.

In 1990, the third year of the program, Norwich continued to expand its effort. Connecticut Valley added eight additional wards and support departments to its program. The outside consultants' main role by that time was to train internal facilitators to support the work of an expanded number of teams. And Cedarcrest, another hospital, began its participation with three projects.

In 1993, the Quality of Work Life State Steering Committee asked my firm to extend the safety improvement process statewide, not only in the Department of Mental Health but also in other departments. Consultants Suzanne Francis, Matthew McCreight, and Keith Michaelson worked with steering committee staff members Jane Fleishman and Chris Lassen, together with Paul Ashton of the Department of Mental Retardation, to implement the program throughout that department as well as in the Mental Health and the Public Health and Addiction Services Departments.

The head of each institution and the union representative chose two people to be trained as facilitators. These individuals in turn helped launch the teams at their own institutions, with backup from the Quality of Work Life staff and the external consultants. The work was increasingly supported by internal staff members trained by the consultants to advance the process. In addition to building a large group of internal facilitators in the facilities of the three participating agencies, a few state-level people were developing the ability to spearhead an expanding statewide effort with very little outside consulting help.

In 1994, the Department of Mental Retardation's safety ombudsman, Paul Ashton, with help from Quality of Work Life staff, worked across the entire state in a number of the department's facilities and succeeded in reducing workers' compensation costs by $5 million a year, a 23 percent reduction. Ashton and the Quality of Work Life staff produced an additional $3 million a year in savings in workers' compensation the following year.

Thus, step by step, the project expanded through different state agencies, producing huge cumulative savings for the state. It was able to do so because each step along the way consisted of a results-focused project that produced measurable improvement.

Making measurable results the primary, immediate goal of a consulting project, as my colleagues did in Connecticut, is the first and most radical shift traditional consultants and their clients must make in adopting a high-impact, results-focused strategy. It is also the most critical, for the following reasons:

- Concentrating on a clear, short-term goal stimulates the performance-enhancing zest factors described earlier, because the client organization's own people are clearly accountable, with the consultant's help, for obtaining results.

- Client and consultant share the common goal of producing real results, so they are motivated to work together. A partnership mode is encouraged, in contrast to the conventional approach of having the consultant do the studies and the client then attempt to produce the results.

- With a sharp focus on results and clearly measurable outcomes, both client and consultant can ascertain what works and what does not.

- Finally, achieving a measurable success together is a joyous and reinforcing experience for both client and consultant. This is quite different from the typical conventional project, in which the consultant labors long and hard and then dumps a massive implementation task in the client's lap.

Translating Client Requirements into Results-Focused Projects

Making the shift to focusing on results is not difficult, but it is a major psychological wrench for most consultants (and many clients). Consultants frequently assert that results-focused projects are possible in only a very limited number of situations. By contrast, my associates and I have found that it is possible to carve out results-oriented projects in response to virtually any client requirement.

Michael Hammer and James Champy, in their book *Reengineering the Corporation* and in numerous articles, have pointed out that many business processes evolved over time without being studied in a disciplined way.[1] Consequently, many are wasteful and inefficient. Reengineering and process redesign projects are aimed at remedying this situation. These techniques are focused on improving processes, however, rather than on achieving measurable results. Results can be designed into reengineering projects, however, as these examples show:

Process Mapping and Process Redesign

The order processing system at MVE, Inc., a company that manufactures cryogenic containers, was not working well. There were many problems and complaints. Instead of aiming at the broad goal of improving the entire order processing system, an initial project was undertaken, focusing on reducing the error frequency in one category of orders through process improvement. Success on that project produced the confidence to move rapidly to a more ambitious attack on the problem.

Manulife Insurance in Toronto was trying to reduce its turnaround time for issuing a certain category of new policies. Many activities had been launched to help achieve this goal, but they were not working. Seven different functions were involved in meeting the goal. One of the worst delays was caused by employees' placing problem applications in a "pending file." With the help of a consultant, they selected a first project: to "improve the processing of applications so that in six weeks we reduce the average number of applications in the pending file from 1,200 to under 1,000."[2] This project broke the logjam, and the turnaround time was significantly reduced in a short time.

Cost Reduction

General Electric Lighting was dissatisfied with the costs being incurred by breakage of fragile lamps. Traditionally the manufacturing function, the warehouse, and customer service had each worked on reducing breakage within its own bailiwick. As part of GE's "Work-Out" process (described in Chapter Eight), however, an interfunctional team was given the job of reducing breakage. With the help of a consultant, they decided that instead of doing an exhaustive study of breakage for hundreds of products and a dozen or more handling points, they would select one product and try to achieve some measurable reduction within sixty days.

They selected six-foot fluorescent tubes, a high-volume and relatively high-breakage product. Over several days a small subgroup traced the product from manufacturing to delivery and reported back to the full team. The team suggested using better (though slightly more costly) pallets and some space fillers in the trucks used to ship the product. Well before the sixty days had passed, the savings achieved were worth several million dollars a year. The expenses incurred were minor. Less than six consulting days were needed, and the dividends were already rolling in as the other product lines were attacked.

Rodney Blanckenberg, a South African consultant, helped managers at Hunt, Leuchars & Hepburn conduct a "hundred-day action project" to increase the number of eucalyptus logs the company could load onto a single railcar. Costs had to be reduced because the logs were for use as supports in gold mines, which were then suffering some economic hardship. Step one was a two-day workshop on the subject with all the company's managers involved in the process. With a total of about four or five consulting days from Blanckenberg plus some internal facilitation by a human resources officer, John Murray, the average load per car was raised from thirty-two tons to thirty-seven tons. This was followed by a similar project that achieved major savings in the costs of the labor and wire used in loading the cars. These projects launched thirteen years of continuing improvement at the company.

New Product Development

A division of Motorola wanted to reduce its fourteen- or fifteen-month cycle time for developing new products. Projects to improve long cycle times are almost always abstract and process-oriented. At the time, however, there were two specific (and important) new products that the division had promised to release many months before but had not yet managed to complete. A consultant helped them design a results-focused project to bring those two products successfully to market within ninety days, the currently promised date. To achieve this result, the consultant helped the client team test some new approaches, including parallel instead of sequential development steps and more disciplined management of all the elements of the project. When the team was able to achieve the targeted results, the methods were then tried on several other products and gradually institutionalized as part of the division's new product development process.

This project not only illustrates the power of beginning with results but illustrates how rapid-cycle projects, even of limited scope, can provide the impetus for major strategic shifts.

Improved Customer Relationships

An office products company was having difficulty shifting the orientation of its salespeople away from small stationery and office supply outlets and toward the new superstores that were beginning to dominate the marketplace. It had many activities under way to facilitate the shift but little to show for the effort. With the help of a consultant, management selected one important superstore chain and set the goal of moving from an "acceptable supplier" rating to a "preferred supplier" rating and getting at least one sale as a result of this shift within four months. With this sharp focus, the goal was easily met.

The Integration of Acquisitions

Grupo Industrial Saltillo is a large, multibusiness Mexican corporation. To expand market share, it purchased a company called Cal-O-Rex, the Mexican water heater business of American Standard. As the due diligence was being completed, Paco Rodriguez was named integration manager, and a team representing the key functions in both companies was formed.

A huge number of details need to be dealt with even in a simple acquisition. Such teams typically work very long hours trying to amalgamate the sales forces, deciding on which products to continue and which to abandon, deciding on the new organization structure and reporting relationships, deciding who owns common customers, deciding on the integration or separation of advertising and marketing programs, deciding which information systems will be used in the new setup, deciding on HR policies, deciding on travel policies. And these are just some of the integration steps that have to be carried out. No wonder some integrations don't start showing results until the second or third year.

Rodolfo Fernandez and Cesar Cardenas, the GIS senior managers, did not want to wait that long. Despite the extra challenge in their case of the cultural differences between the two companies, they insisted that the targeted ROI be achieved in the first year. They asked my colleagues Rick Heinick and Rudi Siddik to help them get started. In response, even before the acquisition was consummated, Paco Rodriguez and his team began to identify immediate cost reduction and revenue enhancing steps. Once the deal was signed, the team got to work on all the integration issues enumerated earlier, but also devoted a major portion of their energy to achieving bottom-line results. They designed hundred-day projects to reduce costs through rationalized purchasing, through changing the components used on certain water heaters, and through manufacturing efficiencies. They hired a new sales team to penetrate markets that had been of no interest to Cal-O-Rex. They launched enough of these projects during the first few months that, among other results, the first year's cost reduction goals were reached in three months and the first year's EBIT shortly thereafter. The profits achieved in the first year outstripped the due diligence target figures. But more than that—as groups achieved success after success, the typical cultural barriers that impede such integrations evaporated, and the new unit generated great momentum toward its ambitious goals.

Backlog Reduction

At SmithKline Beecham, accelerated product development was placing a tremendous strain on the company's clinical data management unit. Each year the unit processes thousands of case report forms (CRFs) containing data from clinical trials at sites around the world. Though some of their work had been contracted out, the group was faced with a backlog of eighty thousand CRFs, plus an accelerating flow of new ones. The group's management set a goal of reducing the backlog to ten thousand CRFs within four months. A consultant worked with fifty of the group's people to collect their ideas on how to achieve what looked like an almost impossible goal. They devised five major new ways to process the CRFs; each was advanced by a "champion" and some team members. Each team agreed on specific short-term deadlines. At the end of slightly more than three months, the number of CRFs had been reduced to fewer than ten thousand.

Management Development and Training

Matthias Bellmann, managing director of Siemens Management Learning at the time, decided to collaborate with my firm in reversing the usual development and training paradigm. Typically, management development (like management consulting) is based on the preparations-first principle.

The idea is that *first* managers are trained and developed, and, when sufficient training and development has taken place, *then* better results should be expected to follow. Our notion: If managers could figure out how to accomplish some performance breakthroughs and deliver some tangible results, they would learn a lot about managing that they could never learn in an academic setting. So we designed the Siemens program so that managers attending their learning program formed themselves into teams, and each team had to select a specific performance results goal that they would achieve in the four months between their development seminars.

Several thousand managers have participated in the program around the globe, and the teams have produced tens of millions of dollars of benefits. The learning that has come through the experience of achieving results has put these managers in position to execute performance breakthroughs back on the job. Academic courses, like consultant recommendations, provide intellectual insight into what's needed. But the achievement of a tangible, measurable, bottom-line result provides a visceral learning experience that can not be duplicated any other way.

Systems Installations

As part of the drive to expand its business around the world, the Global Business Group of CNA Insurance decided to update its information systems. One of the major objectives was to create a common system for its five international businesses. This would reduce the extra costs of maintaining a number of different systems and would permit different CNA units to serve the same customers more easily.

To get started, the systems consultants interviewed the key managers and staff of each business. How could the new system best serve their needs? What did they want to automate and how? They then took this list of requirements, created the specifications for the system, and began to design the software. Their cost estimates began to escalate. The president of the group called for a program review to assess more fully the expected costs related to the expected benefits and then to devise ways to move forward under better control.

In preparation for this review, the systems development teams assembled specific data about the system, including its estimated cost. Each business unit was also asked to prepare its ideas for utilization of the system—with particular focus on the business payoffs to be achieved—cost and profit gains. The president was astonished to discover that what he had assumed would be an $8 or $9 million project was growing to possibly over $40 million. He was impressed with the business projections for potential gains, but saw that they could be achieved with a more modest system than was being designed.

Given the collective "facts of life" revealed by these analyses, he called for an immediate change in direction. The aim was to get the system plans and investment much more closely keyed to the business values to be gained. A number of specific-results goals were identified. For example, they agreed that with certain systems improvements they could reduce the cost of claims administration as well as the actual cost of claims.

As a result of this shift of orientation, the overall size and cost of the project were scaled back drastically. And the program shifted from pure systems development to a dual-track effort—performance improvement along with systems development. Not only were the necessary systems delivered at a fraction of the cost, but many operational improvements, such as claims cost reductions, were achieved at the same time.

Strategic Planning

Some years ago, Frank Green, then head of PPG Industries' Fiber Glass Products division, realized that a drastic shift in the nature of the fiberglass business was beginning to occur. After twenty-five years of growth as essentially a commodity business, the industry would in the future have to provide tailor-made products possessing a high degree of technical sophistication. This meant that the competitive advantage would no longer be with those companies that could manufacture an acceptable product at lowest cost but rather with those that could engineer products to meet each customer's unique requirements. Green eschewed the idea of cranking up a large-scale culture-change program. Instead, working with a re-sults-focused consultant, he and his key associates selected one new product family for which they wanted more sales. They set this goal: they would develop three new "chopped-strand" products and be selling at least eight hundred thousand pounds per month of those products to six or more new customers within three years. This rather long-term results goal was broken down into a series of subgoals. Thus, with this specific result targeted, the business had taken its first step into the new era.

These examples, summarized in Exhibit 4.1, show how a focus on results can be introduced into almost any type of consulting project if there is determination to do it. Targeting a concrete result does not obviate the need for research, conceptual and strategic thinking, and many of the other traditional consulting activities. Nor does it shift attention from long-term strategic issues to narrow tactical issues. It just keeps everyone focused on some measurable end product as a first step toward large-scale change. It permits more rapid testing of what works and what doesn't work—before millions of dollars and many months have been expended. Thus it makes go/no-go decisions feasible in short order—increasingly important as the pace of change accelerates and as organizations need to change directions rapidly in response to changing conditions.

Obstacles to a Focus on Results

Although the results-focused consulting project has many powerful advantages and is not all that difficult to implement, both consultants and client managers are often resistant to trying it. And for some important reasons. Even though designing projects that aim at results has many advantages over the begin-with-studies-and-preparations mode of conventional consulting, it also has some risks that keep client managers and consultants trapped in the old mode. Both clients and consultants need to understand these psychological traps if you want to move past the barriers.

Exhibit 4.1. Examples of Projects Defined in Terms of Client Results Instead of Consultant Products.

Situation	Consultant Product	Client Results
1. *Process Mapping and Process Redesign*		
MVE, Inc. (manufacturer of cryogenic containers): Many complaints about errors in the ordering process.	Redesign the end-to-end ordering process.	Reduce the frequency of the highest-volume error through process improvement in twelve weeks.
Manulife (insurance company): New policy applications being sidetracked into "pending" file, causing backlog.	Redesign the end-to-end new policy issue process.	Reduce the average number of applications in the pending file by 15 percent in six weeks.
2. *Cost Reduction*		
GE Lighting (manufacturer): Significant breakage of fragile lamps.	Undertake a study to determine the primary causes of breakage across the spectrum of products and create process to reduce breakage.	Reduce the breakage of high-volume and expensive six-foot fluorescent tubes in sixty days.
Hunt, Leuchars & Hepburn (timber): Excessive transportation costs.	Study the transportation issues and develop recommendations for reducing costs.	Increase by 15 percent the tonnage per railcar in transporting eucalyptus logs (used in mine shafts).

Situation	Consultant Product	Client Results
3. *New Product Development* Motorola: Foreign competition introducing new products into the market much faster.	Put a dedicated team to work on redesigning the new product development and commercialization process.	Get two new products facing stiff competition out as promised in ninety days.
4. *Improved Customer Service* Office products company: Difficulty in shifting sales force to concentrate on large superstores.	Train sales force and develop an enhanced electronic commerce system.	With one large, national chain of superstores, move from an "acceptable supplier" to a "preferred supplier" rating in two months and make a new sale.
5. *The Integration of Acquisitions* Grupo Industrial Saltillo: Acquires a business from American Standard.	Study the acquiring company and the acquired business and create a plan for integrating the two and a business strategy to implement once the two units are integrated.	Create hundred-day projects to achieve a number of immediate cost reduction and revenue enhancement results.
6. *Backlog Reduction* SmithKline Beecham: Faced with a large, and increased backlog of data files from clinical research studies.	Study data file work flow and work station layout and make recommendations for improvement.	Reduce the data file backlog by 80 percent in four months.

(Continued)

Exhibit 4.1. Continued.

Situation	Consultant Product	Client Results
7. *Management Development and Training* American Greetings (greeting card manufacturer): Rapid growth led to the need for accelerating the development of senior managers.	Send high-potential managers to leadership programs; develop an in-company leadership development curriculum.	Assign specific challenging improvement goals to high-potential managers, requiring them to learn new skills as a by-product of achieving the results.
8. *Systems Installations* Global Business Group (CNA Insurance): New information system needed to reduce costs, support expansion, and serve common customers.	Design a huge, comprehensive system based on expressed needs of managers in all the units.	Have each business specify the gains the new system should help them achieve, then modify systems to match these potential gains.
9. *Strategic Planning* PPG Industries (industrial materials manufacturer): Increased product customization required by the market.	Develop a strategic plan, including steps to shift the culture from cost-focused mass production to customer-responsive customization.	Develop and sell eight hundred thousand pounds per month of three new customized products.

A Note to Consultants: Why You May Resist Focusing on Results

Even though achieving rapid, tangible results for the client will provide all sorts of rewards, consultants have an emotional block against trying it. Here are the main reasons:

Fear of Losing Control. When consultants define a project in terms of the tasks they will perform and the products they will deliver, they are confident they know how to fulfill their promises. The steps are clear, and nothing stands between the consultant and certain success. As soon as a bottom-line result is promised, your success depends on the client's behavior as well as your own. This can be very uncomfortable for consultants since you no longer control all the success factors. "We can't make the client do something they're not prepared to do, can we?"

Information Addiction. Consultants are often convinced that they cannot set any specific results goals, even short-range get-started ones, until they do all their research and diagnosis. "How do you know what is really possible until you do the study?" you might ask. Or you might think, "Even worse, if we set a goal at the beginning and it is not the right one, we might take the client down the wrong path."

Need for an Escape Hatch. The conventional split, with the consultant responsible for delivering the deliverables and the client responsible for achieving results with those deliverables, provides a real escape hatch. If for some reason a job doesn't work out, you can explain that the project was great, but the client failed to implement it properly. For example, some years ago, professor Chris Argyris of Harvard demonstrated in crystal-clear terms how this is done. Here is his explanation of a client's termination of a project that he was conducting with the senior management of a major newspaper (disguised as the *Daily Planet* in Argyris's book): "The fact that the client did not choose to continue beyond these learning experiences is a sign of their own failure, not failure of the intervention process. What we are left with is strong evidence that when forty top members of the *Daily Planet* had an opportunity to make their organization one that learns and examines itself, they retreated from the challenge."[3] Consultants' use of the escape hatch has not changed much in the twenty years since the Argyris quotation. Here is James Champy explaining shortfalls in reengineering efforts: "The obstacle is management."[4] Many consultants feel this way every time a project goes sour, a rationalization that would evaporate if you shared accountability for results with clients.

A Note to Clients: Why You May Resist Focusing on Results

Even though getting the consultants to share accountability with client managers reduces many of the risks of failure in consulting, there are some reasons why you as a client may not always feel particularly enthusiastic about the approach.

Risk Avoidance. When you hire a consultant to do a typical activities-focused consulting project, you take a very modest risk. If the project works out, you can claim credit for it. If there are no results, you can blame the consultant's work. Once there is an explicit commitment to a result that you and the consultant contract for, you are now exposed to the risk of failure if that result is not achieved.

Comfort with Competent Consultants at Work. There is something reassuring to impatient managers about having seemingly competent, confident consultants bustling about their organization. As these consultants go about their work, they cite previous successes, they spotlight weaknesses the managers have been concerned about, and they set about installing tools and methods that appear to be big improvements. All of these can provide some psychological comfort when you have reached the limit of what you are capable of doing, but the results are still not good enough. There is a sense of purpose, of directed action, of high-level professionalism. And if the consultants doing the work come from a well-known firm, so much the better.

Comfort with the Familiar Paradigm. Most senior managers who supervise internal consultants or engage consulting firms are used to the conventional consulting paradigm and derive a certain comfort from it. They don't expect consultants to commit to more than doing the consulting work and carrying out their programs. They have never seen consultants work as partners with clients in a results-oriented mode, and thus have no mental model of how it ought to work. They expect that their people will be able to keep doing their jobs during a consulting engagement, not take their valuable time to work on the project. And they may, in fact, be a bit uneasy that if they or their people work closely with the consultants, then they will reveal their lack of knowledge in certain areas.

P.S. An Action Note to Client Managers: Require Results!

Managers, it is time to liberate yourselves. Only when your consultants agree to help you produce some measurable results have they really cast their lot with you. That is the moment when they abandon the consultant's traditional safety net, the rationalization that "We gave them a good system, but they just weren't able to get the results."

Thomas Kivlehan, at the time vice president of reengineering for the publisher Simon & Schuster, reported that several large consulting firms agreed to bid on a project for him in which their fee would be keyed to the achievement of some measurable results. When asked whether there was any difference between their approach to that project and their more usual approach, Kivlehan responded: "There was a big difference. They were much more insistent about demanding participation by key individuals from our company. And all of a sudden they were spelling out requirements that we in management had to meet in conducting the project. They wanted assurance they could meet with the executive committee to resolve issues. They wanted a certain amount of executive committee involvement in the project and support for it. Consultants basically don't pay any attention to these issues when they are doing one of their regular jobs."

As Kivlehan's quote makes very clear, focusing a consulting project on specific, measurable results produces a healthy shift in the behavior of both the consultant and the client. When consultants actually share accountability for achieving measurable results, for lowering costs or improving quality, they will exert more effort to find ways to use the skills and talents within your organization. They will concentrate on finding the shortest path to results. They will work toward the outcomes that are easiest to produce. And when the consultant shares your results goal, they must join forces to produce it and will collaborate in ways that do not come so naturally in the split responsibilities of the conventional mode.

P.S. An Action Note to Consultants

This is a test for you: focusing your initial projects with clients on achieving specific bottom-line results may require a more modest project than you had in mind. It may not require as many consultants. It may make you a bit uncomfortable because you now have to pay a lot more attention to what the client will and will not be able to do. But all that struggle is worth it when you produce the first results together with your client. At the end of a project, you will share with your clients a sense of accomplishment that is vastly different from your satisfaction with having installed a new system or changed a method without knowing whether the client benefited from it.

Moreover, you and the client have both learned about what the other party can contribute to success and how to best pool your knowledge and skills. You will have created momentum that can open the way to more ambitious progress and a continuing collaboration. And you'll be able to keep your people just as busy, but the added value for the client will multiply manyfold.

Chapter 5

Match Project Scope to What the Client Is Ready to Do

I sometimes pose the following question to groups of consultants: "Assume you are going into a gambling casino, and you have this choice—you can walk directly to the roulette wheel and start betting your chips at once, or you can walk over to a reference manual that will tell you fairly reliably how the numbers will come up that evening. Which would you do?" This question is always rejected as too ridiculous for serious consideration.

Then I point out that most consultants choose the "ridiculous" first option over the second one practically every day. Most consultants will thoroughly explore the technical and operational issues related to a new assignment, but will fail to investigate the client's willingness and ability to actually implement the recommendations the project might produce. Thus they ignore information that will guide them toward success. Take this example:

> The publisher of a large metropolitan newspaper invited a large conventional consulting firm to do a study on how the paper could reduce costs. "With the cost of newsprint rising and competition for the advertiser's dollar getting tougher every day," the publisher told the consultants, "I need to cut costs significantly. And I don't mean nickels and dimes." The consultants proposed a study design, and the publisher accepted it. He encouraged the consultants to study anything they thought might be relevant.

The consulting team was able to identify major opportunities for cost reductions in nearly every part of the organization. It was a gold mine of opportunity for cost reduction. Non-value-added work was being performed in nearly every function. Work that flowed from department to department was poorly coordinated, and when errors occurred, the main preoccupation was with shifting blame rather than making corrections. The reporting and editing staff, who were responsible for many large expenses, felt that reducing costs and boosting efficiency were not subjects they should be concerned with.

The consultant team gathered it all in. Then they assembled a report outlining the major opportunities and suggesting a comprehensive plan to achieve significant improvements. They looked forward to the possibility of a great deal of exciting and productive work helping make it all happen. The publisher met with them alone to hear their report. "I want to get a sense of it first before I drop it on my people," he told them. He spent several hours with the consultants and listened to their report thoughtfully. He asked many questions, but he did not make any commitments to take action. "This is pretty fundamental stuff," he said. "I need to think about it."

A few weeks later, when the consultants called, as agreed, to set a time to plan the next steps, the publisher put the meeting off for a while. And then he put it off for a few more weeks. And he did it again. And again. Finally the consultants realized there would be no big assignment for them. Nor any big cost reductions for the paper. An implementation gap of disastrous proportions!

To see this senior executive turn his back on so many millions of dollars in annual savings that were within such easy reach rankled them. They spoke disparagingly about the publisher's "lack of guts," and then they turned their attention to the next client.

Since the newspaper publisher seemed so interested in reducing costs, the consultants assumed that he would do whatever was necessary to implement their recommendations. So they examined staff size, reporter deployment, use of news services, information systems, accounting and

High-Impact Consulting

control systems, office operations, newsprint purchasing, and printing and distribution procedures.

The consultants did not, however, attempt to investigate the lengths to which the publisher might actually be willing and able to go to effect their recommended improvements. The consultants did not find out whether he had discussed the need for cost reduction with his associates and, if so, whether they understood and supported his view. They did not find out whether the publisher had ever managed to effect any significant changes within the organization. They did not find out how willing he might be to tangle with his associates if they insisted that the consultants' ideas were unsound. In short, the consulting team walked in and threw all their chips on the table for one big bet, without first digging into the "manual" that contained the clues about what might work and what would be unlikely to work in that situation.

As the newspaper example illustrates, such gambles often fail. Moreover, consultants rarely seek to discover *why* such a failure occurred. They're more apt to ascribe it to the client's lack of motivation, lack of real interest in obtaining better results, and so forth. As the consultants see it, they have provided the "right" answers or solutions, and if the client fails to capitalize on them, there must be something wrong with the client.

Sadly, clients are all too willing to accept the blame. Perhaps because consultants almost always deliver the products they promise to deliver, and because they usually deliver it in impressive formats, it is rare for clients to come right out and blame the consultants when a project's results are disappointing. In fact, it is not unusual to hear a client manager say about a consulting project that didn't accomplish much, "There were some very good ideas in that report. Too bad none of our people really wanted to do anything with it," or, "Too bad the marketing people didn't buy it." Or client managers reassure themselves, as the newspaper publisher may have done, that they have not really discarded the consultant's recommendations but have merely delayed implementing them.

Whether the client blames the consultant or the consultant blames the client or they both pretend a failure didn't occur, a consulting effort that doesn't yield results is a terrible waste. Whenever bright and able consultants join with managers who want to effect improvement, but no real progress is achieved, a tragedy has occurred.

It is my firm conviction that virtually every consulting assignment could be successful if consultants, with the help of their clients, would develop the equivalent of that hypothetical casino reference manual. The process of creating this manual is the process of "assessing client readiness." That means finding out while designing a project what the client is and is not likely to be willing or able to do when the time comes for decision and action. With this information in hand, the client and consultant can design the project to match what the client probably will be ready and able to do. It is a method for avoiding an implementation gap on every project.

The rest of this chapter describes how such a manual can be developed to enable clients and consultants to pursue a sure-win approach to consulting.

Assessing Readiness in the Closet Case

Back in Chapter One, I told the story of a magnificent consultant-installed closet system that went for naught when the family failed to maintain it. A good way to illustrate the concept of client readiness is to try to identify the readiness factors in that case. After discussing the case with a group of consultants, I challenge them to think of questions that the closet consultants should have asked before they got started if they wanted to be certain the project would be successful. Within six or seven minutes, a typical group of consultants generally think of forty or fifty questions that the closet consultants might have asked. See if you can think of eight or ten questions that you feel should have been asked before redesigning the closet. Then compare your questions with those suggested by other consultants (see Exhibit 5.1).

The exhibit contains only a small sampling of the kinds of questions that need to be asked to eliminate the possibility of an implementation gap, but that consultants rarely ask. If even some of the information suggested by the questions had been elicited, the closet consultants might have realized that the fully redesigned closet project would be a failure. Then they might have tried to conceive and suggest a more limited, "get-started" project.

Exhibit 5.1. Readiness Questions in the Closet Consultant Case.

Factual Issues
- What exactly do you keep in the closet?
- Who uses it?
- How many times do you go into your closet each day?
- Do you change the contents each season, or is it the same year round?
- When was the last time you sorted through the closet and tossed out any unused articles?
- Are there other closets in the house, and what do you use them for?
- What's your ideal sorting system?
- What kind of shelving, lighting, or floor covering would you like in the closet?
- How quickly do you need the job completed?
- What do you think about the closet we redesigned for your friend?

Psychological Issues
- Why do you want to redesign your closet?
- What do you think doesn't work about the closet? What does?
- Do each of the people using the closet agree on what needs to be done—and how to use it?
- Does everyone in the family feel equally strong about the goal of closet redesign?
- Have you ever attempted to make improvements like this before? What was the outcome?
- How willing do you think the people who use this closet will be to change their habits, especially if they're in a hurry, to maintain a new setup?
- What do you envision will be different in your life after you redesign your closet?
- What behavior do you think you'll need to change after the new closet is finished?

Defining the Project Goals
- What are you really hoping to accomplish from our work?
- Describe how things would be different were this project to be successful.
- Do you plan on using the closet for the same purposes after you redesign it?
- Do you want the new design of the closet to reflect utility, aesthetics, or both?
- How involved would you like to be in the project?
- What role or roles would you like to play?

When I ask consultants to suggest some possibilities for such get-started projects, inventive answers come rapidly. "Why not start by helping the family to get rid of stuff they don't use any more?" "How about seasonality? See if they can remove and store all the items not needed in the current season." "How about starting with just one category? Shoes, for example. Provide a way to store them. Then come back a few weeks later and see how that's working out."

Thus consultants who in their own practice may totally ignore readiness issues can devise many possible readiness questions for the closet consultant case. And even though they never do it in their own practices, they can also quickly devise a dozen get-started projects to match the client readiness they discover.

If the newspaper's consulting team had used this very same approach with the publisher, their project could easily have been a success instead of a failure. Some simple questions would have revealed that the company had never carried out any major improvement projects. The publisher was an intellectual leader with a brilliant grasp of good journalism and deep convictions in his editorial stance. But he had never had to deal with any major conflicts within the organization. He had never had the experience of cutting people's budgets or requiring them to achieve challenging new goals. It would have been clear to the consultants that a large-scale project was doomed to fail.

With this knowledge in mind, they might have suggested a few get-started projects designed to succeed without too much controversy. Reduce overtime in a few departments, for example. Eliminate newsprint waste caused by mishandling the rolls. Reduce the frequency of typographical errors that require rework. With a menu of such possible projects, they could have explored with the publisher which he thought he could make happen successfully.

But wait. How could the consultant suggest such modest projects when the publisher had clearly said he was not interested in just cutting "nickels and dimes"? Consultants need to remember that by the time managers call for consulting help, they may be frustrated and irritated. Their grandiose comments may reflect such feelings. No matter how dramatically managers declaim their wishes, however, consultants should not be panicked into taking self-defeating action. Even if the client hopes for the largest-scale changes imaginable, there is nothing inconsistent with suggesting some get-started projects to create momentum and test the waters. Doing so imposes no limits on how fast it can go from there.

How to Assess Readiness

Once a client and consultant have agreed on the general aims of a consulting project, the next step should be for them to agree to assess readiness and then to design their project to match that readiness. This precludes the possibility of the project foundering in a big implementation gap at the end. If the client has visions of gains that far outrun the organization's capacity to implement, the consultant needs to keep those visions in play, but emphasize the importance of getting started with some successes that are within the client's current capability—thus discovering what it will take to achieve the really big gains.

Exhibit 5.2 provides a systematic checklist of suggested readiness questions. It is written as though it is addressed solely to consultants, but clients also need to ask these questions of themselves. There may be some readiness issues in your own practice (if you are a consultant) or organization (if you are a manager) that are unique to your situation. Think about possible additional readiness factors not on the list that might be relevant in your situation. One way to create your own personal readiness checklist is to think back on consulting projects that were disappointing to you (either as a client or as a consultant) and ask, "What kinds of information did we discover only after the project was under way or completed that we should have found out about before we began?" Those need to be added to the categories in Exhibit 5.2.

Getting Comfortable with Assessing Readiness

One obstacle to good readiness assessment is the fact that in the initial, exploratory stages of a project, both the client managers interviewing the consultants and the consultants they are interviewing want to look good to the

Exhibit 5.2. Readiness Assessment Checklist.

1. Overall Motivation and Drive
   - What is the client's motivation for this project? Is the client enthusiastic? Passive? Resistant? Does motivation seem to be different in different groups within the client organization?
   - What is the client's view of possible project gains?
   - Who wants change to take place? Who doesn't care? Who is against change?
   - To what extent does the project respond to a goal everyone says is important but on which they seem reluctant to work?
   - Are there other motivation issues?

2. Resource Allocation and Commitment Level
   - What is the client's view of the time, energy, and support that will be required to carry out the project?
   - Does the client expect to participate in the work? Is the client ready to pull a full share of the load?
   - If other groups' or people's commitment is required, has it been (or is it being) secured?
   - Is it clear what the budget will be? Does the client's view of an appropriate budget match the consultant's?
   - Are there other resource issues?

3. Climate for Change
   - What kinds of pressures for change exist in the client organization? Where do they come from?
   - Where does the particular issue the consultant is focusing on fit into the client's hierarchy of concerns? Is it a top-priority issue or just something they feel they need to deal with?
   - Will the organization's climate support the kinds of changes the project might require?
   - Are there other climate issues?

4. Client's Technical Capacity and Change Management Skills
   - What is the client's capacity to implement innovations and change? What do recent experiences suggest about whether the client will be able to carry out the changes and adaptations that the project might require?
   - What is the client's demonstrated capacity to absorb new ideas and exploit them usefully?
   - What is the client's experience with and knowledge about the particular issue the project is focusing on?
   - Are there other knowledge and skill issues?

5. Client's View of the Consultant
   - Has the client had some recent experience with this consulting group or with a similar group? How did that work out?
   - How does the client feel about these experiences? What can be learned from previous experiences that will strengthen the design of this project?
   - What is the client's overall attitude toward the consultants who will be working on the upcoming project?
   - Are there other client-consultant relationship issues?

6. Client Understanding of the Project
   - Has the client already defined clear project outcomes? What will be the client's measure of success?
   - Does the client understand the implications of the project for the organization?
   - What is to be the specific output or product of the project? Who is going to use it, and how? Is this understood in the same way by all key players?
   - Are there other client understanding issues?

7. Scope and Pace of Project
   - What is the client's "project attention span"? How quickly must the client see some tangible results? What kind of results?
   - What is the client's view of the appropriate scope and pace of the project? How big a project seems right to the client? What sort of pace does the client wish to pursue?
   - Are there other pace and scope issues?

8. Other Success Factors
   - Are there certain solutions that will be taboo or unacceptable in the client organization?
   - Do the client and consultant mean essentially the same thing in their use of key words describing the project?
   - Are there other issues not yet addressed?

9. Historical Perspective
   - How did the current need evolve, and how long has the client been aware of the need?
   - How has the client attempted to deal with the issue until now? What has worked? What has failed to work?
   - How did the idea of using consulting assistance arise?

other party and to their own associates. The desire not to be seen as weak or unknowledgeable may lead some participants, often unconsciously, to keep their doubts and uncertainties covered up. This tendency is definitely an obstacle to accurate readiness assessment. Both parties have to work diligently to make certain they identify the realities of the situation and design a sure-winner project instead of trying to project desirable images to each other.

The list in Exhibit 5.2 is a suggested list of topics, but it does not suggest how the consultant can best open up these topics with the client. If you're a consultant accustomed to asking the "factual" questions but not readiness questions, it will take a bit of practice to discover how you want to do it.

A consultant who wants to develop sharper readiness assessment skills should begin by experimenting with a relatively few readiness questions that seem most useful. Until the process becomes second nature, consultants should prepare, in writing, a list of questions that might be relevant in advance of client meetings. Exhibit 5.3 provides a few for starters.

In asking readiness questions, it is very important to ask questions that call for elaboration and description rather than a simple yes-or-no answer. Consider these two ways of eliciting information about the motivation of client people to make the project succeed:

- Option 1: Do you think your people are going to be willing to support this project?
- Option 2: Tell me about how you think some of your key people feel about this project.

The "tell me about" form always draws out more information and initiates a more lively interchange.

The "What If?" Test

Another useful way to test client readiness is for client and consultant to speculate about a project's possible outcomes at the outset and then discuss them. Asking "What if—?" avoids the risk that the client will be surprised and, at the project's conclusion, say, "Oh, this isn't what we were expecting." The "What if?" scenario is one additional way to avoid nasty surprises.

Exhibit 5.3. Some Suggested Readiness Openers.

The questions below provide some illustrations of how the subjects listed in Exhibit 5.2 can be addressed with clients.

- What is your view of the main differences between how your department is operating now and how it will operate if this project is successful?
- Why have you decided to get this project started at this particular moment?
- This project seems to focus on a goal that is critical to your unit. What are some of the other major challenges you are facing in your job? How does this project relate to them?
- Who will have to participate in this project? To what extent do they share your views of the situation?
- Have your people worked with consultants before? How did it work out?
- Do you have any thoughts on how your people and the consulting team should work together?
- Are there any aspects of the project that make you a bit uneasy or that may contain some risks?
- Have you ever carried out any projects like this one? How did they work out?

One division of a corporation in the chemicals, plastics, and glass business was interested in the possibility of achieving forward integration through an acquisition. And the first step was to identify likely acquisition candidates. The division hired a large, well-known consulting firm that had done considerable work for it in the past and asked the firm to conduct a study to forecast future industry trends and predict the likely winners and losers.

The study's primary finding was that within each of the industry segments being considered, the top one or two firms had excellent prospects while the others had much less promising futures. The dilemma was that the price-to-earnings multiples for the top one or two firms in each segment were unacceptably high. So, although the consultants made some specific acquisition recommendations, no action was taken.

This wasteful project could have been avoided. The outcome was virtually inevitable from the outset. Almost any of the key players in the company

could have been able, with the information they already possessed, to identify the same acquisition candidates that the consultant identified. Moreover,
they would have known right away that the cost of acquiring those companies was far too high. The only way this project might have succeeded would
have been if the consultant had found a relatively unknown company that
could be purchased for a reasonable price. But there were very few companies in the segments studied, and all were already known to the client.

A "What if?" readiness assessment at the start could have saved this
business time, money, and embarrassment. In such a scenario the consultants sketch some possible outcomes of their study before they take the first
step. These are shared informally with a group of client people, and together
the clients and consultants examine what it would take to act on the imagined recommendations. Would the possible benefits be worth the costs?
What kind of resistance might be encountered? In the acquisition case, the
price of the desirable companies would have surfaced in the very first discussion. The study would never have been done as it was done. Perhaps
some more constructive directions might have been pursued.

Another way to conduct a "What if?" readiness assessment is for the
consultant to simulate, for discussion with the client, the products of the
project. If one of the outcomes is to be a work flow, for example, the consultant can mock up a hypothetical model of what the process might look
like after the project is complete and ask, "Would this help you get better
results? How might it be made more useful?" Or sometimes consultants
rough out a sketch of the kind of information the project would make available to the client, and both parties can see whether the new report provides
information that will be truly useful.

Hidden Verve

It would be a mistake to think of readiness testing solely as a method for
limiting the scope of a project. As described in Chapter Three, organizations often possess considerable unexploited capabilities, and readiness testing can sometimes reveal them and lead to a more ambitious project. Here
is an example of how readiness testing mobilized the client to undertake an
exciting project that had not been visualized previously:

In 1990 Motorola's Components Division was told it had to become a profitable business. This was a change from its previous role as a "strategic supplier" to other Motorola divisions. This shift required the division to make a 30 percent improvement in its bottom-line results. In working to achieve the goal, the division made many improvements in its cost structure, its product lines, its marketing and sales methods, and its manufacturing processes. Nevertheless, improvements in profits came very slowly. My firm was working with Motorola at the time, and Jerry Bruning, the division's general manager, invited us to help. He told us that the present plan called for arriving at break-even in twenty-four months. That seemed too far in the distant future. Worse, the rate of progress was not even sufficient for that modest goal. The process had to be accelerated. After several discussions, Bruning suggested we meet with his top team of about fourteen people to get their views.

At the meeting, after some preliminary introductions, my colleague Bob Neiman turned to the group and said, "We understand there is a two-year schedule for your division to become profitable. Further, we understand that there isn't even clear agreement on how that can be accomplished. I'd like to ask all of you to put yourself in the place of Jerry Bruning. If you were the general manager of this division, when would you insist that the division must break even? Write down the number of months you would allow, fold your paper, and pass it in. Do not sign your name."

A scale was drawn on the board, and as each paper was unfolded, Neiman marked the number. The lowest number was four months. The highest was eighteen months, a full half a year ahead of the budgeted time. The rest ranged in between.

This demonstration had a powerful effect on the group's motivation. Instead of the general manager or consultant having to convince them to move up the target date, their own estimates said it was possible to accelerate the schedule. And sure enough, an acceleration plan was devised within the framework they had provided, and break-even was reached in less than a year.

On hearing that story, cynics sometimes ask, "But what if they had estimated that it would take much longer than twenty-four months?" Well, that too would have been important to know. Jerry Bruning, the general manager, would be no worse off, and he would at least be aware that there was no basis for his confidence that the pace could be accelerated. The priority for the consulting project in that case would have been to experiment with some very short-range action steps that might create momentum and open the minds of the group to the possibility of acceleration.

In this case, a successful acceleration strategy needed to start from the base of what the key players thought was possible. To believe that a consultant can do a study and then somehow prove to the members of an organization that they can do better than they believe they can do is pure fantasy.

Bringing Readiness into Focus

Sometimes it is necessary not only to diagnose readiness but to take steps to influence the level of readiness of the people who will be working with the consultant. This is a task for senior management with the help of the consultant. Here is an example of how this played out in a specialty glass manufacturing facility (with names disguised), from the diary of the consultant who led the work.

> When we first started working with Vitrine Products, one of the first projects was to improve the efficiency of the 712 jet-air furnace, which provided the molten glass for the bulk of the company's products. The furnace had been performing at well below industry standards for five years, and a variety of managerial efforts had failed to raise its efficiency.
>
> Joel McCray, the vice president of manufacturing, and Ted Stevens, the plant manager, told us that every percentage point of improved efficiency on this one furnace would contribute significant sums directly to the company's bottom line, not to mention the added throughput such gains might create.
>
> When I met with Hank Granowski, the furnace superintendent, it quickly became clear that he was not ready to work with anyone to improve furnace efficiency, least of all a consultant who had no prior experience in the glass industry. He explained that he already had commissioned a technical team, headed by himself, to study the problem. They had been at

work for the last four months, and he felt they had the situation well in hand even though no results could be demonstrated yet. He also believed that unless major capital expenditures were made to improve the furnace, progress would be minimal. Just one of the new systems he was proposing would have cost well over a million dollars. He explained also that the scheduling of products to be run through the furnace was very poorly done and was a big contributor to furnace disruptions and inefficiencies.

Vice President McCray would not back away from the need to improve the furnace efficiencies and to do so without further capital investment. Plant manager Stevens drafted a fairly strong project assignment to Hank, stressing the importance of showing measurable results and doing so fairly soon. This was followed by a second strongly worded memorandum by vice president McCray.

After these memoranda, Hank agreed to meet with me again to develop a strategy. We decided that I would interview a number of the supervisors, process engineers, and hourly workers on the furnace to get their thoughts about possible improvement ideas. I talked to them and then summarized their suggestions in a work session with Hank and his furnace team. We also agreed, in order to avoid overlap with Hank's technical team, that this project would focus only on operational improvements, not mechanical fixes. We were also able to get Stevens to agree to freeze the "disruptive scheduling" during a one-week experimental period.

Hank was reluctant to set a goal more ambitious than raising efficiency by 2 percent. I pointed out that with a frozen schedule it should be possible to gain more. After further discussion, Hank agreed to set a goal of a 7 percent improvement. That was a very daring step since he had no experience to indicate that it could be done, but there were three factors that enabled Hank to venture: first, the agreement by the plant manager to freeze the schedule; second, the fact that we were going to provide some hands-on consulting help; and third, the fact that his commitment to the goal was only for the one experimental week and not beyond.

Once Hank had agreed, we met with his people and went over the project ideas with them. They agreed to shoot for the seven-point increase, but only after it was pointed out that they were committing themselves for just the one-week experiment. Next we secured their ideas for making the improvement, and decided to concentrate on those that had the highest potential payoff and were easiest to implement.

Six project teams were organized, each with one specific area of responsibility. We helped those teams get organized. By the time the experimental week came, just three weeks after the start of the project, furnace efficiency had already improved 8 percent, four times Hank's original target. A number of new procedures were tested during the experimental week. The ones that worked were continued, thus ensuring that the output would remain high after the experimental week. The paradox was that two weeks later, the scheduling went right back to the same old patterns (which, as Hank had correctly pointed out, was somewhat disruptive), but performance continued at the high levels reached during the experiment. It never dropped below that peak level until eighteen months later, when it was time to rebuild the furnace due to its age and deterioration.

Vitrine's vice president of manufacturing and plant manager both supported this consulting project, but when the consultant put his toes in the water he saw that there was no match between the project goal and the readiness of the working level client who would have to achieve that goal. Even if the consultant had been the world's greatest expert on furnaces, his failure would have been guaranteed had he not moved deliberately to have the vice president and the plant manager create more readiness on Hank's part. The importance of this kind of demand is discussed further in Chapter Ten.

Mapping: Casting Light into the Shadows

When the hero in a Hollywood thriller walks into a darkened room, everyone in the audience anticipates that some shadowy figure will leap out and attack him. So it is in consulting projects, too. Wherever there are dark corners, a threatening figure may emerge from the shadows to announce that there is no budget for the project or the consultant's recommendations are simply unworkable.

The idea behind readiness testing is to gather information that will permit clients and consultants to design projects that guarantee success. One element of information that helps achieve this goal is the identification of all the people whose approval or cooperation will be essential for success. To avoid nasty surprises, the client and consultant need to shed light into all the dark corners where these figures may be lurking and identify them and the roles they might play. The process for accomplishing this is known as *client system mapping.* Its aim is to develop a clear *Who's Who* that identifies all the key players and influencers.

Mapping can be done by the consultant team, by the client team, or, preferably, by both working together. Step one in client mapping is to identify the full cast of characters, not merely the managers who are talking with the consultant. Exhibit 5.4 offers a checklist to help identify both the obvious and the less obvious players.

Step two is drawing the map. Once the cast of characters is identified, it is useful to sketch a diagram that portrays the place of each of the key players and the relationships among them. This should be a dynamic portrayal that

Exhibit 5.4. A Project's "Cast of Characters."

1. The client—the one person (or a clearly designated small group) with the principal accountability for achieving the targeted results, with the support of the consultant.
2. People who are active participants in the planning and implementation of the project.
3. Contributors to the project who are not involved directly in the work.
4. People whose job or job environment will be affected by project results; obvious winners and possible losers.
5. Project user groups and their representatives—such as a steering committee, a project review panel, and so on.
6. Senior managers, whose general support and positive views can have subtle but crucial impact.
7. The ultimate decision makers and budgetary authorities.
8. (Add your own categories. . . .)

best conveys the client's and consultant's views of the interrelationships among these people—it should not be a conventional organization chart. It should make it possible for the client and consultant to discuss readiness and relationship issues with greater clarity.

Some teams use various symbols to help sharpen the map, drawing circles around names of people who are crucial to the project but have not been sufficiently involved in its planning, for example, or check marks next to names of people who may oppose elements of the project or its conclusions.

Then step three is to look at the map and to make certain that all the key players have been identified and that project plans involve all of them in appropriate ways. Exhibit 5.5 shows a few client maps sketched by various consultants. They need not be works of art—just portrayals of the interrelationships as best you can do them, quickly. They should provide a framework so that when several people are discussing the project, they will have the same picture in mind.

Loading the Dice for Success

The most expensive way to learn about a mismatch between a project's design and the client's readiness is to carry out the project and then, after the time, money, and effort have been invested, discover that a big implementation gap will prevent the possible benefits of the project from being realized.

Readiness testing, "What if?" scenarios, and client mapping can prevent this outcome. These steps take much of the gamble out of consulting work. Only after consultants and clients have carefully assessed all of the readiness issues that might be relevant to a project they are about to launch are they able to load their project for success. They do this by carefully designing the project so that its goals are clearly achievable by the people who have to achieve them. In other words, so that there will be no implementation gap.

Readiness exploration is an ongoing process, not a one-time event. After a project has begun, if any doubts arise about the match between the project design and the client's readiness to go forward, client and consultant

Exhibit 5.5. Sample Client Maps.

Project: **Nurse Management Development**

George
Martha

LMC
Union
Support

Sarah

Louise

RN Directors

sabotage

FD

LD / MS

Josephine
Y Director

? SC ?
LC
? CB ?
GS

Help
Agent

NURSE MANAGERS

info
control

MD

Leadership
Case Mgt
Pharm
ResP Bldgs

??
? PATIENTS
??

??
STAFF
??

"Pressing points"
PHYSICIANS ?
??

(Continued)

Exhibit 5.5. Continued.

Project: _Rebax 609 Cycle Time Reduction_

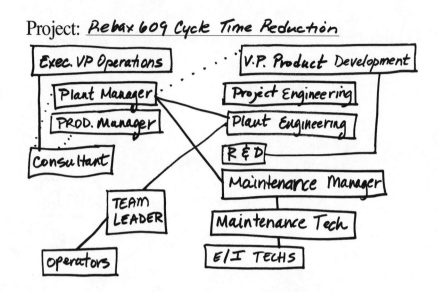

Project: <u>PLANNING /BUDGETING PROCESS IMPROVEMENT</u>

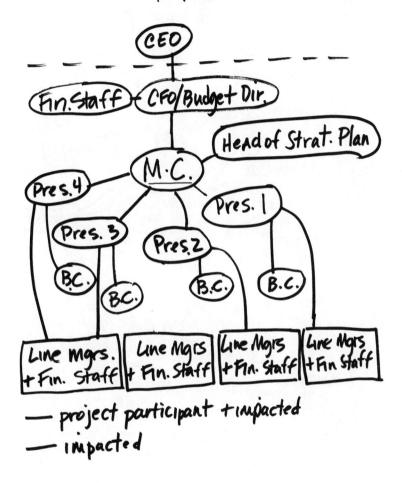

— project participant + impacted
— impacted

(Continued)

Exhibit 5.5. Continued.

Project: Reduce Workers Compensation Cost

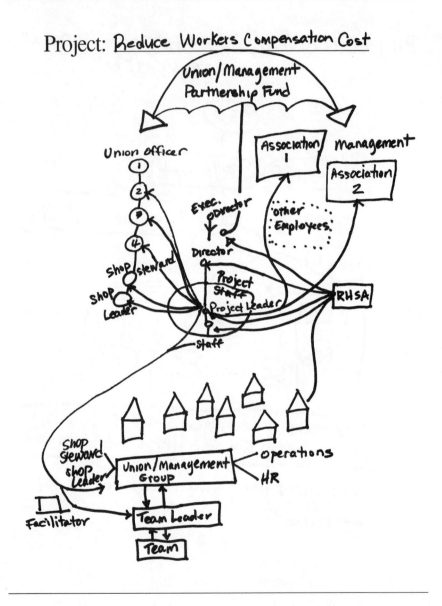

share responsibility for insisting that the issue be addressed and the project design modified if necessary.

P.S. An Action Note to Client Managers

If you are having a consulting firm or an inside consulting group undertake any project for you, you should insist, at the beginning, on some thoughtful speculation with them concerning possible project outcomes. What might be required of you and your people to make the project succeed? Then consider carefully whether you and the consultants are confident that you will want to carry out those changes and be capable of doing it. If you are uncertain about your answer, then you need to redesign the project until you can be more certain of the match between what will be required and what you will be able to do. This careful readiness testing and the design of projects to match readiness make it almost impossible for the project to be sabotaged by an implementation gap.

Consultants who are designing long-term, large-scale, complex projects—say, totally redesigning a company's operations or replacing a series of outdated information systems with one massive new system—point out that it is virtually impossible to assess readiness accurately in such cases. They assert that the project's completion is so far off that it is impossible to predict at the beginning of the project what the consultant's recommendations might be. But that view of an assignment can easily be the first step toward a massive failure. It asks you, the client, to bet all your chips on one gigantic spin of the wheel, without knowing whether you and your associates will be able to make the decisions and carry out the actions needed to make the consultant's input yield results for you. Rather than abandoning the idea of matching the project to the level of readiness, a more logical choice in such cases might be to change the design. From the massive overall project, carve off a first-step subproject that does look as though you'll be able to complete it quickly so that it can serve as a stepping-stone toward larger goals. The next chapter describes that strategy.

If the consultants say they can not provide any ideas about possible project outcomes until they have done their research, you have a decision to make. Either you can go along with the project as a big Las Vegas gamble. Or you can say that you don't want to squander the time and the money the project will require unless you are more certain of a successful outcome. They'll have to change the design or you'll change consultants.

P.S. An Action Note to Consultants

If you are a consultant, you need to experiment with including readiness testing in your exploratory discussions. This is not just a matter of proceeding through a long checklist (like the one in Exhibit 5.2) but of developing sensitivity to the issues. As with so many of the concepts in high-impact consulting, most experienced consultants already possess many of the skills needed to assess readiness. You just need to try it out on your next project, and the one after that. You will easily develop more skills as you practice.

Chapter 6

Aim for Rapid-Cycle Successes to Generate Momentum

S ometimes too much success can overwhelm a company.

Avionic Instruments designs and manufactures electronic control equipment for aircraft. For several years everybody in the company had been running faster and faster to keep up with the rapidly expanding demand for its products. Already breathless, senior management suddenly realized that demand was accelerating in 1996 at an even more radical pace. To respond would require major improvements in production planning, manufacturing processes, purchasing, inventory management, and quality control. At the same time, the company also needed to upgrade the skills of its entire workforce.

To help with this somewhat overwhelming situation, a traditional consultant would undoubtedly have begun with a comprehensive study of the company's operations (or perhaps several studies) and then the comprehensive report . . . but you already know the rest.

In fact, consultants Keith Michaelson and Rick Heinick, working in a high-impact mode, saw that it would be easy to overload this already stretched company. Michaelson asked the company's managers whether there was any one product that was more critical than the others. They easily named such a product, so he helped them organize a cross-functional team to expand its rate of production. The team set a goal: to double output of that product within two months.

The team worked on ensuring parts availability, coordinating the scheduling of subassembly production with final assembly, and identifying and overcoming production bottlenecks. Within two months, they were able to double production. They set a similar goal for the next two months, and sure enough, they doubled production again.

They had obviously achieved dramatic success with this sharply focused project. But what was even more important, they had developed considerable insight into how to manage expansion of the company's overall output. So, in a few short months, they had achieved some major progress and they had also enabled a number of managers to get the feel of what they'd have to do to expand capacity. The managers involved in the initial project were developing a greater sense of what the overall production expansion strategy needed to be. That is high-impact consulting.

The aim of conventional consulting is to formulate a comprehensive solution and to share that with the client. But this all-or-nothing approach on the part of the consultant almost inevitably leads to large-scale, long-term project designs that often outrun the client's capacity to act. In this case such an approach undoubtedly would have led to a major implementation gap.

A landmark study on major organization change done at Harvard confirms the fallacy of attempting large-scale corporate transformations. In some companies studied, "wave after wave of programs rolled across the landscape with little positive impact." By contrast, the more successful transformation efforts started "at the periphery . . . in a few plants and divisions." In those get-started steps, the successful companies "created ad hoc organizational arrangements to solve concrete business problems."[1] This is the essence of the high-impact consulting design. Rather than design an overall solution at once, the aim is to carve off a series of rapid-cycle attacks. One purpose of this is to create some measurable results for the client in the shortest possible time. The reinforcement of success, plus the knowledge gained by both client and consultant, creates the foundation for accelerated progress. The cumulative gains of a series of incremental improvements is actually as great as (or greater than) what large projects promise they will achieve "some day."

Many conventional consultants assert that shooting for rapid results should be avoided. Taking action before conducting the big study, they say, may cause clients to focus on tactics instead of strategy, or improve a system that should be eliminated, or head south when they should be heading north.

My associates and I have used rapid-payoff projects as steps in large-scale client change projects in many dozens of organizations for over thirty years, and I have never seen a single example of these tragic outcomes. Nor have any of the other consultants who work in parallel modes. Selecting the initial project is a thoughtful process, not simply plucking some "low-hanging fruit" out of thin air. Initial projects can usually be carried out rapidly and for relatively little cost. In half the time it takes for just a study and analysis of a big blockbuster project, an initial rapid-cycle project will likely be over and done with and have paid for itself several times over. Moreover, it provides real data for client and consultant on what works in the particular organization. Until the parties have shared some successful experience in a number of modest projects, any attempt to formulate and carry out a complex, long-term change is basically just a Las Vegas crap shoot. And the client often loses.

Rapid-Cycle Project Design

Choosing to pursue a rapid-cycle attack does not mean opting for the tactical instead of the strategic. To use a sports analogy: When I am on a steep snowy slope, I want my ski instructor to provide some tips that I can translate immediately into greater control. Also, I want to hear only as many instructions as I can absorb at once, there and then. Despite this focus on the immediate, however, neither of us, student or instructor, has lost the strategic view. We both know what an ideal skier looks like, and we both know that this is the goal that I, the instructor's client, am striving for. Why shouldn't an organization get from its consultants what I always get from my ski instructor—help that is immediately useful, achieving what must be accomplished at once while also moving the organization toward its more comprehensive goals.

On any consulting project there are almost always steps that can be taken to produce results and produce them quickly. Clients ought to insist that their consultants help them start this way. This chapter shows how even the largest-scale projects can be carved into meaningful, productive, rapid-cycle subprojects. It also demonstrates that such subprojects, rather than obfuscating large-scale change strategies, actually provide fresh insight and momentum for them. For example, each of the initial rapid-cycle projects for the State of Connecticut, United Aluminum, and Motorola described in Chapters Three and Four contributed to the formulation of comprehensive change strategies for those clients.

Selecting rapid-cycle subprojects is not actually difficult to do; what is difficult for clients and consultants is shifting from the conventional mode and embracing the new idea. The selection of the first subproject or two is particularly important, because they will serve as momentum builders. Client and consultant first need to define, as well as they can, the strategic goals of the overall project. Then they can carve out some shorter-term, stepping-stone subprojects. Sometimes a workshop can be organized to permit a larger number of key players to participate in considering and selecting the initial rapid-cycle projects. The GE Work-Out process is a well-developed method for involving large numbers of participants in identifying which projects should be worked on and how they should be attacked. Chapter Twelve describes the major turnaround from loss to profit at Zurich Financial UK, where the key to creating momentum was the use of the Work-Out process to define dozens of projects that collectively saved tens of millions of pounds.

Naturally, a rapid-cycle project must focus on the client's most urgent goals. In the Avionics case, increasing output was the most urgent goal, and that's where the project began, with the single most needed product. In addition to the importance of the goal, four other criteria will help with selection of the initial rapid-cycle projects. Basically, each must be

- *Focused on achieving measurable results.* As described in Chapter Four, the goal must be defined in bottom-line terms, and it must be something the client can measure.

- *Matched to client readiness.* While the goal should be a real stretch for the people who have to achieve it, they should feel both able and willing to achieve it.

- *Short-term.* It is good if the results can be achieved in five or six weeks, if possible, or at most within fourteen or fifteen weeks.

- *Strategic.* The goal should clearly be a logical step toward achieving the client's overall strategic aims. This makes certain that immediate progress will contribute to longer-term change and not simply win a momentary tactical gain.

The Vitrine Products furnace output project described in Chapter Five illustrates a project that met the rapid-cycle criteria: the aim was to achieve a measurable step up in furnace efficiency of over 7 percent (measurable results) within a few weeks (short-term goal). Considerable effort was made to be certain that even though the goal was a significant step beyond past performance, it would be achievable in the eyes of the furnace superintendent and his people (matched to client readiness). Finally, the project was a first step in implementing a multiyear performance improvement effort to be undertaken by the company that eventually returned many millions of dollars annually (strategic).

Laying a Foundation for Large-Scale Change

It is as logical to say that rapid-cycle projects are carried out at the expense of long-term strategies as it is to say that the use of individual I-beams is in conflict with conceiving and building a huge skyscraper. The rapid-cycle projects that are integrated into a logical framework serve as critical building blocks of strategic progress.

Here, for example, is how the Garrett Products Division of Group Dekko used rapid-cycle projects to launch a major turnaround.

Garrett was a profitable manufacturer of office lighting products. In 1995, however, the division began to experience difficulties. Its scrap rates rose and its on-time delivery declined. Profits suffered. Andy Barker, the division's general manager, launched several teams to study and correct the problems. They had some modest success, but not nearly as much as Barker wanted.

In thinking about what had happened, Barker realized that the difficulties resulted, in part, from Garrett's expansion into non-lighting products. That move introduced a number of new, and possibly distracting, challenges for his people. In addition, there was some ambiguity in Garrett's relationship with its largest customer, Custom Lights, which happened to be another division of Group Dekko. Barker was the general manager of Custom Lights as well as of Garrett. This dilemma was exacerbated by the fact that the newer non-lighting products were not nearly as profitable as the traditional lighting products.

Had Barker invited a conventional consultant to help resolve his problems and increase profitability, there is little doubt that the first step would have been a number of studies. First, operational studies would be needed to determine the cause and cure of the quality and delivery problems. Next, strategic and market analyses would have been needed to determine the wisdom of continuing as two separate businesses and to see whether it made sense to continue manufacturing the new non-lighting line. Many months would have elapsed before management even had a chance to see the diagnoses and recommendations, never mind getting on with a cure.

Instead of trying to understand and resolve all the issues at once, Barker, with the help of an associate of mine, formed three teams, each with members from both companies. He charged each team with producing some measurable improvement within a few months. One team worked on resolving the problem of overlapping roles and responsibilities between the two companies with the aim of reducing indirect expense. The second team was assigned to simplify the ordering, production planning, and scheduling processes with the goal of reducing work-in-process inventory.

The third team piloted ways to streamline selected steps within the over-all order-to-shipment process to reduce the time required and to eliminate duplicate inventories. Within ninety days of launching these team projects, the order cycle time shrank by more than 50 percent, from over six to under three days. Work-in-process inventory dropped by 25 percent. Overhead costs were decreased by about 15 percent. And quality defects declined by two-thirds.

These rapid-cycle projects enabled Garrett to return to its former level of profitability far sooner than it could have done with a long, detailed study to decide on the "correct" strategies and actions, followed by an equally long process to try to implement and benefit from them. Beyond the immediate results, the experience of working with the intercompany teams on these projects provided Barker with some fresh insights that enabled him to formulate a new strategic direction for the two companies, while continuing the rapid-cycle performance improvement process.

Infrastructure improvements—changing organizational structure, modifying the measurement system, revising incentive plans, conducting training, or improving processes—by themselves do not constitute rapid-cycle projects. They are only the support elements that can help achieve results. Unless tied to demonstrable outputs, such support activities rarely achieve the intended results. They tend to dissipate energy and resources and achieve little or nothing. By contrast, shortening production cycle time, reducing inventory, cutting costs, improving yields, and eliminating non-value-added work, and the like are the "measurable results" essential to rapid-cycle projects.

Carving Off Rapid-Cycle Projects from Large-Scale Goals

The first challenge in designing for rapid-cycle success is to visualize how to divide large-scale diffuse goals and programs into incremental steps. Exhibit 6.1 lists some of the ways to do it, and these are elaborated in subsequent paragraphs.

Exhibit 6.1. Carving Off Rapid-Cycle Projects.

1. Start small: If there are many dimensions that must be changed, start with only one or a few of them.
2. Pick your target: If there are many units to improve, start with only one or a few of them.
3. Bite off what you can chew: If major reengineering is the aim, start with one or a few subprocesses.
4. Make the most of what you have: Get the present system or technology to produce better results instead of waiting years to revolutionize or replace it.
5. Find a door instead of a wall: If groups in the client organization are not ready to proceed because of some delaying issue, use your ingenuity to find a piece to get moving on.
6. Make a low-risk test before taking the plunge: When the clients are focused on large-scale, long-term goals, carve off an achievable step toward those goals.
7. Try for an end run: If it seems absolutely impossible to carve off a first-step goal from the project itself, then design and conduct a rapid-cycle test project in an adjacent area or on a related subject.

Start Small

If there are many dimensions that must be changed, start with only one or a few of them.

The systems group in the Hartford Insurance Company's Commercial Lines Group was facing a twenty-six-person-year backlog. The group seemed to be trapped forever in maintenance catch-up and never had a chance to develop the new systems the division needed to automate its operations. They had carried out a great many activities-type improvement efforts with no impact on the backlog.

My colleague Robert Neiman helped them conduct the following project. The department's senior managers selected three work groups and charged each with achieving a 25 percent increase in productivity within the next three months. Each team leader was free to choose the approach they would use in the experiment and to use consulting support as needed.

The specific focus at last gave them something they could successfully attack; and their subsequent success shed light on how they could keep the effort moving.

Pick Your Target

If there are many units to improve, start with only one or a few of them.

Dun & Bradstreet's Information Services Division needed to revitalize the entire business. Douglas Smith, who was a McKinsey & Company partner at the time, describes the situation in his book *Taking Charge of Change*.[2] According to Smith, Dun & Bradstreet's Information Services Division (DBIS) provides its customers a plethora of information and analysis about millions of businesses. The company's credit report is so well known that many people even refer to competitors' products as "D&B's."

"When Ron Glover became president of DBIS in 1990, the warning signs of trouble were flashing. Financial performance had dipped after decades of predictable growth. Internally, the heads of various functions were so powerful that they literally considered their individual parts of DBIS as separate companies and rarely communicated with one another. A culture of isolation and relentless profit pressure had taken its toll."

To help accelerate a turnaround, Glover asked Mike Berkin to introduce total quality management to DBIS. Mike began with steps common to most TQM programs. More than two hundred managers participated in intensive training sessions, for example. At that point, Berkin wanted to get moving toward achieving results. He described it to me in this way a few years later:

> I wanted to produce some real results. Our people didn't have to be convinced that something needed to be done. And I established some design points for the effort. We wanted an approach that was easy to understand; that would not require more investment in training or anything else until we began to see some results; that would be fun, that people would enjoy doing; and that we could do quietly and have some success and let the word slip out gradually rather than make any big splashes. There were too many cynics ready to pounce.

This was a rare occurrence: the client, without using the term, was asking for high-leverage, rapid-cycle consulting. Douglas Smith invited Charles Baum to play an active role in helping Berkin get moving toward his goals. Berkin describes the experience this way:

> Doug and Charlie said we should do four or five or six projects to try it out. They did not want to have us gamble on doing just a few. Since the projects were all achievable in a short time and the approach was focused and hard-hitting, we did not mind doing that number. We chose eight projects in different functions where the rest of the business would be impressed if there was some success and where there would be some specific business gains to be made—not like working out the color combination for the dining room, which some quality programs I know about have done. And we picked leaders for those projects with the help of Charlie and Doug to make sure these initial projects were loaded for success.

So Berkin began with eight projects that he was certain could be carried out successfully and quickly. Having the confidence that you can do it is the key, not the exact number of projects to be launched.

Bite Off What You Can Chew

If major reengineering is the aim, start with one or a few subprocesses.

Large-scale reengineering projects typically manifest all of consulting's five frequently fatal flaws. Here is how consultant Elaine Mandrish helped a major electric utility company carve off a rapid-cycle subproject from a large-scale reengineering project:

> One of this company's generating plants had been having serious problems with its equipment maintenance. Besides having a huge backlog of work, when the maintenance staff finally got to the jobs, more than 25 percent of the time the repair plan was incorrect or the needed parts were not available.
>
> For two years the plant had been trying to reengineer its maintenance process to correct these problems, but they had not been able to dedicate

the key resources needed for months on end to complete the reengineered design. One day the new plant manager decided it would be futile to keep trying to reengineer the whole process at once. Instead he and his management team identified maintenance planning as the major bottleneck, and decided to try to improve it. They set an objective to redesign the planning process so that for 95 percent of all jobs the parts would be available when needed and the jobs completed on time.

A group of ten people representing all the relevant functions was brought together in a two-day workshop. They first mapped the current process on a white board, using self-sticking note sheets to describe each main step and colored markers to show the flow of work.

When team members saw how the process really worked, they were appalled. It was obviously too complex, with too many hand-offs, too much paper, and too many checkpoints. Too many people were involved in approving the plans and no one was clearly accountable for the process.

With the benefit of these insights, the team turned to a new white board and created a template for how the process ought to work. They eliminated most of the hand-offs and approvals and made a small cross-functional team responsible for planning each major job.

In addition, the process mapping had shown that while more than 60 percent of the maintenance jobs were very simple, the same complex planning process was followed for these as for the large-scale turnaround maintenance jobs. For these simple jobs they recommended substitution of a simple three-page document to guide the maintenance staff.

At the end of the workshop the team presented their recommended redesign to the senior plant management team and obtained approval to proceed. Within a few months the team carried out their plan.

The new process not only reduced the backlog significantly, but also saved the plant millions of dollars a year. In a subsequent external audit, the new process and the teamwork involved in it were cited as key strengths of the plant.[3]

Results-driven process redesign also differs from reengineering in its approach to infrastructure and organizational changes. With standard reengineering, such changes are done on a large scale. With results-driven process redesign, they are done incrementally, as needed.

Make the Most of What You Have

Get the present system or technology to produce better results instead of waiting years to revolutionize or replace it.

The 74th Street Station, part of the Consolidated Edison Company in New York City at the time of this story, had six "package boilers" that could produce steam within several hours of start-up. This permitted flexibility in responding to changing customer demand. The station's large boilers had to run all the time, and they required at least twenty-four hours to be turned off or on.

The package boilers were all quite old, however, and to achieve their purpose they had to be able to run reliably and in conformance with stringent environmental regulations. If they violated any environmental regulation, they had to be pulled off-line. To ensure reliability, the plant's managers decided that new electronic controls were needed on these boilers. Designing and installing such controls was going to require at least a year, and the present mode was intolerable to management. Consultant Keith Michaelson suggested trying to reduce the environmental operating problems right away. Since the plant had previously had some success on similar projects, the managers agreed to try. They had been experiencing two or three costly and inconvenient shutdowns a week; they set a goal of less than one per week.

They identified the most vulnerable points in their operating procedures and then worked on how to minimize those risks. For example, they saw that the greatest danger of opacity (dark smoke) occurred when starting up a package boiler. So a team of operating and maintenance people would meet at dawn each day to make certain that the start-up was done properly. They did all this planning and modifying of their operating methods during their first month of work.

They had only two incidents during the entire second month instead of the eight to twelve they had been experiencing. It was an improvement far beyond their goal. Now they had confidence that they would be able to operate reliably for the year or more it would take to install the new controls. They also discovered that some of their hopes about what the electronic controls would accomplish were illusions. A number of the potential pollution factors would have to be controlled through better operations. Instead of waiting a year to discover this, they were able to put the knowledge to work at once.

Find a Door Instead of a Wall

If groups in the client organization are not ready to proceed because of some delaying issue, use your ingenuity to find a piece to get moving on.

It is not uncommon for managers to be reluctant to venture into rapid-cycle breakthrough projects. One reason is that as soon as they select a specific goal and commit themselves to achieving it, they are exposed to the possibility of failing. It may be safer to study the situation and delay taking action. Of course, this pattern matches perfectly the conventional consultant's inclination to conduct all the preliminaries before getting on with the main event. So both parties conspire—unconsciously, of course—to extend the preliminaries so that the day of reckoning is delayed. To shake that pattern often requires considerable dedication and creativity:

> Some years ago, when working with an acquired Nortel subsidiary, my firm discovered that the unit's inventory levels were out of control. The unit's officers agreed that the situation was bad, but said they couldn't deal with it until they got their new inventory tracking and control system installed. Even though completion of the new system was still many months away, the managers insisted that there was no way to take effective action. "We don't even know how much inventory we have, nor where it is," they said, "so how can we do anything to reduce it?"
>
> Refusing to give up, a dauntless, results-focused consultant kept probing and eventually discovered that there were certain categories of inventory that management had more information about than others. In fact, there was one category for which management had a very good sense of both the amount and location. It was the "SNA inventory," that

is, inventory that has been "shipped but not accepted." The company manufactured complex electronic products. When customers believed the performance of a newly installed product was inadequate, they didn't pay the invoice. This equipment remained on the company's books as part of its inventory. This was a serious customer relations as well as inventory control problem.

The consultant suggested that they might want to focus on lowering SNA inventory by solving the quality problems and getting the customers to pay. It had never occurred to management that they could deal with a single category of inventory, but they were more than willing to try it. As is usual in such projects, they were able to make some significant progress in a matter of weeks. Not only were they able to reduce SNA inventory (and the associated customer complaints), but the experience provided some fresh insights on how to strengthen the inventory control system then being constructed.

Make a Low-Risk Test Before Taking the Plunge

When the clients are focused on large-scale, long-term goals, carve off an achievable step toward those goals.

The General Reinsurance Corporation (now GeneralCologne Re) provides a variety of risk-transfer mechanisms and other services to insurance companies. Traditionally, each General Re client company was contacted independently by professionals from each of General Re's different lines of business. In 1992, senior management decided that to provide the best possible service to their clients, teams representing all of General Re's specialties should be formed to provide integrated support for each client. It was planned that once the switch was thrown, hundreds of such teams would be formed—a monumental transition.

My firm was working with the company to support this process. We encouraged the company to select a few clients and test the idea before throwing the switch. Six clients and two potential clients were selected, and a team was assembled for each. Without too much concern for spelling out detailed ground rules in advance, team members were given some brief training and were asked to identify a few critical goals they could accomplish with their joint client (or potential client) in ten or twelve weeks. We carefully documented each team's work. Instead of devoting three months to studying what such teams might produce, we simply had a number of teams get to work. They each accomplished some important gains, both with active clients and with prospects. And they gained a wealth of practical experience, providing senior management with sufficient information and sufficient confidence to move forward with the project.

General Reinsurance's experience illustrates that no matter how complex or far-reaching a client's goal, it is always possible to carve off some rapid-cycle steps. For example, instead of undertaking a formal study of whether to design and market a new product, there might be a way to simulate the product, or buy it from another supplier, and try selling it in one test market. Or carve off one element of a broad strategic plan and make it work over the short term in one place.

A number of years ago, a number of engineers in the division of Motorola that manufactures portable radios (such as those carried by security people) got the idea that fast-food restaurants would provide a large market if the division could develop the right kind of radio. Together with their results-focused consultant, the engineers decided that the company's formal new-product-proposal pathway would take too long. Instead, they took a few samples of a current product, made some quick fixes to it in their shop, and took these informal prototypes out to a local fast-food restaurant to test their idea. This project clearly demonstrated that rapid cycle zest can be injected even into strategic projects that are long-term and large-scale.

Try for an End Run

If it seems absolutely impossible to carve off a first-step goal from the project itself, then design and conduct a rapid-cycle test project in an adjacent area or on a related subject.

Sometimes both the client and the consultant are absolutely convinced that there is no way to divide a huge project into increments. But I believe that even in these cases, clients and consultants who have never produced significant results together should avoid the gamble of tackling a big project in their first work together. Instead, the parties should invent a short-term project that is akin to, even if not exactly a part of, the proposed big project, to gain experience working together. In a few months, both parties will know how well they work together, and if they decide to move ahead to the large-scale job, they will be more clear about how to ensure success.

One example of such a project was suggested to me at a meeting of information-technology executives representing various units of a very large corporation. I was expounding the merits of rapid-cycle design to them when one of the participants interrupted me. "The concept is a good one, Robert, but you probably don't understand how systems projects work. There is no such thing as an incremental step. Projects require a minimum of six or nine months, or even much longer." Before I could say anything, another participant rose and responded as follows:

> Yes, that may be true. But let me tell you about a time when we were called into the x plant to work on their inventory management system. The problem was in raw materials inventory. They had too much inventory overall but at the same time suffered from frequent stock-outs. It seemed clear that we would have to revamp the entire system and that it would take many months. Before trying to lay out a design, we spent some time chatting with people in the plant, trying to get a sense of how the place worked. And we discovered one reason for their problems: they were having a hard time seeing what they actually had on hand.
>
> Following these interviews, we drafted a letter for the plant manager to send to all of the plant's vendors, telling them that if they wanted to remain on the approved vendor list, they should sign and return a copy of the letter, indicating they would conform with its requirements. The letter specified six vital pieces of information that were to be (a) listed in any paperwork accompanying (or electronic communications about) any order and (b) plainly printed on the outside of anything shipped to the plant.

114

That one step went a long way toward solving their immediate raw materials inventory crisis, and it provided some important perspective on the system we were going to develop.

Someone asked how long it took to do that. The answer was three days.

Big, Big, Systems: The Elephant in the Canoe

Information Technology people often agree with the specialist quoted earlier, who commented on the impossibility of dividing large systems projects into rapid-cycle increments. One reason is that these jobs are conducted as huge outsourced technical projects more than as consulting assignments. Another is that most of the client and consultant people working on them are systems experts, focused on the design and functionality of the system more than its actual use.

These large-scale systems are big and powerful tools, but to do their job, they need to be integrated with all the company's other activities. Thus for a new system to succeed, hundreds or thousands of related changes have to occur simultaneously. Often neither the technical people building a system nor the client managers who expect to use it deal adequately with all of these associated changes. As a result, many implementation gaps open along the new system route.

For example, a large insurance company decided that to grow and prosper would require major changes in how it did its business—new branch operation configuration, consolidation of products, new underwriting approaches, and comprehensive automation. Several new large integrated systems would serve as the central support mechanisms. As these systems were built, they grew so large and complex that even with very heavy investments in consultants, vendor support, and internal staff, delays were threatening the success of the entire transformation.

The key to getting back on track was to shift to a much more segmented approach. The managers of three branches were given the specific assignment to move into the new mode at once. They could use whatever elements of the new automated system were available, and use the old where the new was not ready. A multifunctional support team from the home office worked with the selected branches to carry out these steps. Soon it became clear that a great deal of progress could be made in implementing the new mode without waiting for many more months for all the automation. There were struggles to be sure. But they were also beginning to see bottom-line gains, and to break down the huge automation job into much more workable sub-elements that were fed into operations as rapidly as they proved workable.

The PNC Bank, headquartered in Pittsburgh, once faced a similar situation. It had expanded from a single bank to a regional powerhouse by the acquisition of seven other banks. Several new systems were needed if the bank was to function as a single entity and exploit the cost savings inherent in a large-scale operation. A team was assembled with delegates from all eight banks and asked to create a single retail sales system for the integrated bank, as the first step in creating new corporate systems. They went to work with the help of consultants and vendors, and designed a huge multifaceted system capable of all the functions in retail sales. Several years were spent agreeing on the specifications and details of the new system. Every decision required extensive debate as each of the formerly independent banks tried to advance its own views of how the systems should be configured.

At that point Richard L. Smoot, formerly head of operations for the Federal Reserve Bank of Philadelphia, joined PNC and took charge of operations and systems across the company. He was alarmed at the tons of paper in the complex plans and the growing potential cost of the retail sales system. He quickly decreed that the project had to be completed quickly and for much less expense than had been contemplated, and he engaged a consultant, my colleague Robert Neiman, to help in achieving that result.

The Bank's chairman, Tom O'Brien, issued a formal charge to both the retail organization and the systems organization to recast the whole project to speed up the installation while reducing its costs. In response, a core team got to work under the leadership of Tim Schack, head of systems, and managers representing the retail business. In a month they streamlined the system plan into seven components and assigned a small joint team to manage each one. Each team was asked to select one of the eight banks, and for that one pilot bank, design a prototype solution for their component and install it within three months. All of the teams met this focused goal, yielding seven workable components, each operating in its pilot bank. Next they began to roll out the new systems from their pilot bank sites as rapidly as the other banks became ready to use the systems. The whole system was installed in eighteen months versus the original three-year timetable. And the costs came in 25 percent lower—$19 million versus a planned $26 million.

Once this incremental pattern had proved successful, it was applied to the creation of other corporate-wide systems. For example, the new core deposit system was installed on the basis of short-term, rapid-cycle increments. Beginning in one bank, the installation was done in three months. Next it was installed in two additional banks, then in three. Even this basic system, which affected virtually every transaction in the business and was seen as nothing less than a total integrated system change, could still be broken down into workable components and installed incrementally.

Any business that takes all its chips and puts them on the table for a single, high-risk roll of the dice must have some sort of death wish. Client managers, no matter how strange it may seem to your systems consultants, insist on the low-risk rapid-cycle pattern even when launching the largest, most complex systems installations. Let me change that—*especially* when launching the largest, most complex systems installations.

A Rapid-Cycle Project Is Not Just a Phase

When I discuss the value of rapid-cycle breakthrough projects with consultant groups, many of them tell me that that is exactly the way they work. They break their large-scale projects into short-term phases: the preliminary study, the detailed proposal, the first-step study, the creation of prototypes, and so on. But these are merely steps in a long process, not separate sub-projects. Even though a conventional project may be divided into discrete stages, each one is merely a part of a lengthy process that does not give the client a chance to see results until it is all over and some sort of implementation has occurred. A rapid-cycle project goes from beginning to end in a few months and produces a result—a measurable, palpable result. It may attack only a narrow dimension of the subject but it is a complete project.

To illustrate the contrast: In an inventory reduction project, the conventional approach might have as an initial phase a study of the various categories of inventory and a determination of the turnover rates for those categories as well as the frequency of stock-outs. The study might also include an assessment of what steps might be required to increase inventory turns or to reduce stock-outs. At this point the client may have some ideas about what to do next, but has no tangible benefits from the work. By contrast, a rapid-cycle project might focus on one category of inventory (as in the Nortel case) and set a goal of reducing the level by x percent within a hundred days without allowing stock-outs to increase—or even while also reducing the frequency of stock-outs by some amount.

P.S. An Action Note to Client Managers

Even in cases where a consultant has convinced you that a large study with a very long cycle time and a very big budget is needed to accomplish your goals, if you are insistent you may find a way to carve off one or several small-scale rapid-cycle projects that can be carried out quickly. It might even be possible to do these projects while the consultant is gearing up for the big study or even while the big study is getting under way. Don't be discouraged if your consultant is reluctant to tackle a rapid-cycle project: It injects an experimental mode in place of the consultant's well-laid-out comprehensive plan, and it subjects the consultant (and you, of course) to the test of measurable outcomes in a short period of time. Moreover, the fees connected with helping to carry out a few initial rapid-cycle projects are only a fraction of the fees that go with the big-fix study, which is another reason you may encounter consultant resistance. But hang in there. Why put millions of dollars on the table until you've had a chance to see what the consultant team can actually deliver—and how they work with your people—in a relatively low-risk project? Often once a few such projects are launched, each a mini experiment that tests some new approach or mode of operating, enough is learned that the costly up-front study is not needed—you can just keep advancing the way the PNC Bank did.

P.S. An Action Note to Consultants

If you are a senior officer in a large consulting firm and your performance review at the end of the year includes the income you generated by keeping many consultants fruitfully engaged, the rapid-cycle mode may not seem too appealing. But it is so rewarding for your clients that you may have to find some other ways to keep the big gang busy. Maybe they can be exploited at later stages in the work. Maybe they can be used in doing the technical research and development that will be needed to make the really big gains. In fact, maybe the big outsourced technical projects may still be necessary, but they should not be seen as "the consulting projects." This idea will be explored later.

One way or another, you should try shooting for rapid-cycle successes. The measurable results that your clients experience quickly are only one dimension of the outcome. As in the case of the Consolidated Edison package boilers and Dun & Bradstreet's Information Services business, the lessons learned in the first rapid-cycle projects provide important experience for both client and consultant on how to shape more ambitious strategic steps. The rapid-cycle approach permits clients to adopt the consultant's contributions a step at a time, absorbing what they are capable of absorbing and all the while producing tangible bottom-line improvements.

To make a consultant's contributions work well in an organization, many associated changes must take place in concert with the consultant's recommended steps. The initial rapid-cycle projects enable clients to learn how to manage all these other changes. A succession of rapid-cycle projects gives clients and consultants opportunities to move through the entire implementation cycle many times, with each implementation producing better results than the last. That is obviously much safer than the conventional game, where all your chips are on the table for a single roll of the dice.

Finally, in terms of job satisfaction for your people, the rapid-cycle projects are a boon. Most consultants I speak with enjoy their work, but are frustrated by the fact that after they've done the study and shared the recommendations with a client, they often don't have a chance to see their ideas translated into action and thence into bottom-line results. With rapid-cycle projects you and your people can have the pleasure of helping clients achieve results that are measurable and there for all to see.

Chapter 7

Build a Partnership to Achieve and to Learn

Clients and consultants can achieve outstanding results working in collaboration that they could never achieve working in parallel.

Two days after attending a meeting on improving order processing at MVE, Inc., of Bloomington, Minnesota, Karen Prasch, a customer service specialist, sent a three-page letter to the person who had run the meeting: J. David O'Halloran, at that time the company's president. Prasch was responsible for processing orders from all over the world for the company's cryogenic bulk tanks. Each order had many unique customer-dictated specifications, and this was further complicated by each country's special regulations for the importation of these vacuum tanks. The letter began by saying, "I left the meeting feeling angry and disappointed because the original goal of our group was not addressed." It continued by outlining many things that were going wrong with the handling of international orders. Prasch, who wanted very much to do a good job, was frustrated because she couldn't see what she could do to improve the situation beyond urging others to take action.

The list of problems outlined in her letter could have served as an open invitation to a lengthy, complex consulting study. The situation seemed to require a comprehensive diagnosis to determine the fundamentals underlying the order entry process problems. A set of recommendations would then have to be created. These would have to be reviewed with the client. Finally, some months later, the consultants would have to send in a team to help implement the recommendations, since no one in MVE had much experience with process redesign.

Instead, with the help of my associate Claude Guay, just a few weeks later Prasch was leading a work session with managers and employees from product management, engineering, finance, and traffic. After exploring the problems to be dealt with, they set an initial goal of correctly entering each order within twenty-four hours, instead of the several weeks it was then sometimes taking. They began creating a process map capturing the essence of the workflow for international bulk tank orders. The process mapping revealed that there were certain items, such as documentation packages, that could be attacked at once, while more complex issues would have to be addressed later.

In their effort to reduce order entry time to one day, they also reduced the time required for customer service representatives to enter orders. They improved the accuracy of freight quotes, and they reduced the number of missed shipping dates. Step by step, they attacked the main goal and a number of related ones. Gradually the turnaround time was reduced to about a day, while many other improvements were also occurring. The customer service group gradually developed the ability to process twice as many orders with the same number of people while translating customer orders into manufacturing specs with greater accuracy.

This was the beginning of an effort that grew into a continuing program of improvement in the company's order entry and related processes for a variety of products. As the work advanced, Prasch enlisted employees and managers from every related function to participate in the work of her team. And she initiated several new teams led by her or other team members.

Guay helped her gradually develop skill in organizing work teams, leading process mapping and process redesign workshops, and project management. She became an effective facilitator and discovered that she could have an enormous impact on introducing change and affecting bottom-line results. She felt justifiably proud and enjoyed a succession of successes. Her confidence expanded along with her skills.

All the work on this project was done within a partnership between a consultant with over twenty years of experience in performance improvement and a client who knew the details of her own operation but had virtually no team leadership, project management, or process mapping experience. The initial process mapping was done in collaboration by Prasch and Guay. The action steps were planned and executed in collaboration. Guay shared his insights and skills with Prasch and her associates. Sometimes he functioned as a member of a working team. Sometimes he simply helped various team leaders plan their work sessions. Sometimes Guay did some of the work that had to be done. The main goal was to maximize learning by MVE people and have MVE people do as much of the work as possible. A parallel effort, headed by Lois Tuma, another customer service specialist, was carried out in another product area. As they developed new skills on both of the projects, various team members went off and initiated other improvement team projects on their own. Meanwhile, Guay worked in the same flexible way with several of those teams.

On each of the projects there was a strong focus on results from the very beginning. The work began with several rapid-cycle projects matched to client urgency and to what the clients had said they were ready and able to carry out. The projects were successful. Eventually there was major progress on the entire order-to-delivery cycle. Beyond these tangible gains, the thirty-plus people who participated in these projects learned more from their successful experiences in producing results than they might have learned in a dozen training courses. As a consequence, the company developed a staff with capability in process mapping and redesign, team leadership, goal setting, and project planning that can be exploited in the years ahead. And Karen Prasch was promoted to a managerial job shortly after she demonstrated her capacity in this project.

Learning Through Collaboration

The MVE case illustrates how a consulting project can serve as a rich opportunity for developing clients' capabilities. The most effective way to exploit this opportunity is for the client and consultant to work closely together in a partnership mode. Both should share in performing any research that is needed as well as in analyzing the findings, deciding on the appropriate course of action, and implementing it to produce results. This is what Claude Guay did in working with MVE. The approach must be expanded on larger-scale projects, but the basic concept is the same.

One reason for the rapid-cycle design, in fact, is to provide repeated opportunities for the client-consultant partnership to move through the entire project cycle. That means beginning a project, carrying it through to success, and learning from it. Each time around the client people develop new skills and new confidence in executing change that expand their capacity to implement and benefit from the consultant's inputs.

This partnership approach overcomes a major deficiency of conventional consulting, where the consultant does the work and then presents a finished deliverable, one that often requires a huge dose of change for the client. But while the consultants are busy creating a challenging change project for the client, they probably aren't doing a single thing—during all those many months at work—to help the client expand its ability to implement change. And, as mentioned earlier, if the client's staff have not been deeply involved in the consultants' work—if they continued with their regular jobs while the consultants were studying the situation, debating the issues, and working out their solutions, the final recommendations are apt to come as a sudden shock. The best and most useful learning comes from the process of speculation and discovery and experimentation, so the hand-off mode guarantees that the consulting team will learn much and the client staff little. And it guarantees that consultants will have to remain on board to run around helping to implement the changes they are trying to advance.

High-impact consulting is predicated on the belief that a change project offers a rich range of potential learning experiences for both the client and the consultant, and projects need to be designed to exploit those opportunities.

Managing Projects in the Partnership Mode

To get into a partnership frame of mind, clients and consultants have to abandon the traditional view that a consulting project is essentially a task carried out by a consultant on behalf of a client. Instead, the project has to be seen as a joint undertaking to produce a joint result. Moreover, both sides have to accept the fact that much of the work that is traditionally carried out by very large consulting teams could and should be done by client personnel. If client personnel do the work, they will not only produce better results for less expense, they will also benefit from the learning inherent in the experience.

The project described next, for Morgan Bank's Administrative Services Department, illustrates well how the partnership mode works and how projects can be designed to serve as management development vehicles for client staff.

When Bill Hayes assumed responsibility for the Administrative Services Department at Morgan Bank some years ago, he decided that there was no justification for the other bank departments to continue spending $90 million a year for administrative services they might not want or could obtain in a less costly manner elsewhere. Therefore, he made the department's forty-plus unit managers responsible for "selling" their services to the other bank departments and negotiating fees for them. Hayes told his people that their units' survival required major improvements in performance and customer support.

To communicate his view of the importance of producing measurable results for their customers, Hayes convened his managers in a workshop and asked each of them to identify one important, measurable, short-term service improvement they could accomplish in the next few months with some consulting assistance. How these goals were translated into results is illustrated by the experience of Dorothy Jacobson, head of the Micrographics Department.

Jacobson's unit was responsible for transferring the daily operating data of every department in the bank from computer tapes to microfilm. Her unit promised twenty-four-hour turnaround service but rarely met that goal. Jacobson was told she had to start meeting the target. With the consultant's help, Jacobson carved off a first-step, rapid-cycle goal: within five weeks, her unit would regularly meet the twenty-four-hour deadline for a single bank department, known as 30 West Broadway.

Jacobson started by drafting an assignment memo to her key assistant, John Palladino, outlining the 30 West Broadway goal and asking him to give her a draft action plan outlining the specific steps that he and his people would carry out to achieve the goal. When Palladino voiced his skepticism that the goal could be reached without additional people and resources, Jacobson restated her resolve. "I understand that this appears to be difficult," she said, "but we're going to take this one step at a time. Expectations have been raised. We're not working at the same level anymore."

Palladino's action plan was put in place and key personnel were prepped on their new responsibilities. During the very first week of the project, the computer tapes from 30 West Broadway were misplaced for a day. Jacobson used this mishap to fashion some new procedures for the unit. First, she named one supervisor on each shift to take on a new role, "work flow coordinator." Every job was tracked throughout the three operating shifts. In addition, she created a temporary structure, called the Supervisor Action Committee, to resolve conflicts between the shifts. Finally, she created a wall chart to track the results of all work coming from 30 West Broadway. This allowed everyone in the unit to know on a daily basis how quickly work was getting completed and what progress was being made toward accomplishing the turnaround goal.

The consultants spent some time each week with Jacobson, Palladino, and the other active participants. As with the MVE case, they provided some expert inputs, but more important, they helped the client managers think through for themselves what they had to do to achieve their goal. The consultants provided ideas about tools and procedures the client might want to try. As the weeks passed, the number of days for which the twenty-four-hour goal was met increased, and people's confidence in working together to meet deadlines grew. At the end of the five weeks, the challenge had been met: 30 West Broadway was being turned around on a twenty-four-hour basis every day.

The effort left an indelible mark on the unit and its people. They had responded to a demand that they once considered impossible. In doing so, they had set and met goals, redesigned the flow of work in their department, refined the way people worked together, modified the organizational structure, and increased the amount of responsibility the department's people carried. Most important, they now believed in their own ability to tackle a difficult assignment and produce results. And they were prepared to move to the next goal: satisfying their other customers.

Management Development Through Management Results

Morgan Bank's consultant not only helped Jacobson and her people accomplish a specific, measurable performance improvement, he helped them develop their capacity to sustain the improvement process and to implement other improvements in the future. This kind of learning and development, which plays a small or nonexistent role in conventional consulting, is not merely an incidental benefit of high-impact consulting—it is a central ingredient. Every consulting project offers a rich array of such opportunities for helping clients expand their skills and insights. Although the twenty-four-hour project was focused on a very specific goal, many opportunities for development were exploited. Here are the most important ones:

1. Diagnosing Readiness

During the kickoff workshop, Jacobson was introduced to the concept of selecting a goal that she could be pretty certain her people would accomplish. After some thought about what might actually be achieved in a rapid-cycle mode, she decided to limit her first goal to just 30 West Broadway.

When she left the workshop, she and the consultant had several conversations about how she could push for a goal that seemed impossible but that she gradually discovered could be achieved.

2. Carving Off Achievable Goals

For Dorothy Jacobson and her people, the overall goal of meeting the twenty-four-hour turnaround time on microfilm delivery for the entire bank was not something they could get their arms around. It was just an unimaginable burden. With what she learned from the workshop and from follow-up help from the consultant, however, she and her colleagues in the department translated the turnaround-time goal into a series of subgoals, each with a start date, an end date, and a measurable outcome.

Many management groups faced with large-scale challenges don't have experience in carving off a series of achievable subgoals. Learning this skill is important, because when management groups survey the totality of a large-scale challenge, it can seem overwhelming. The consultant spent time with Jacobson and her people thinking through appropriate ways to carve the overall project into achievable steps.

3. Framing Demands for Goal Accomplishment

Managers may be hampered in achieving their goals because they are not experienced or confident in communicating with their people that major improvement *must* be achieved.

To make her project succeed, Dorothy Jacobson had to convey to her associates not that it would be *nice* to achieve their goal but that they *must* achieve it. She had a number of conversations with the consultant about making this shift. It was necessary for her to recognize that, like most managers, she was somewhat uncomfortable in making clear-cut demands for higher performance, and that she had to learn how to overcome her anxiety in working with her people on performance improvement.

4. Improving Performance Through an Action-Oriented, Experimental Approach

Like the forty or so other managers in the bank's administrative services department, Jacobson was overwhelmed at first by the department head's demand for major performance improvement. In that she was no different from most managers, who are sincerely doing the best they know how to do. Thus, when confronted by a demand for major improvements, they naturally feel that the goals are impossible.

The consultants introduced Jacobson and her fellow managers to the concept of focusing on short-term, manageable steps that begin to move a unit toward its broader goals and also permit the managers to learn as they go. The consultants worked along with the managers, intermittently, to help them design and carry out their projects. This required a few hours a week of consulting for several months.

5. Involving People in Performance Improvement

No matter how good a change idea or improvement recommendation may be, managers need to learn how to engage their people in planning the changes and carrying them out. The consultants helped Jacobson and Palladino experiment with some innovative ways to communicate with their people and bring them into active participation on the project. Here the consultants could provide a "menu" of ways this could be done, suggesting different ways meetings could be held and different ways people could play a role in the project.

The consultant also helped Jacobson and Palladino take the initiative in scheduling meetings with and reporting to some of the senior officers who were managing the improvement effort. Previously they had shared the view common to most middle managers: "When the boss wants to talk with me, I'll get a call." They developed the confidence to contact senior management when that seemed to make sense.

6. Developing Work Planning and Project Management Skills

Many managers lack well-developed skills in managing change. Such skills are essential to implementing the work of a consulting project. Therefore, consultants who want their clients to succeed must help them develop their skills in project planning and management. These include determining how a project will be organized, how it will be managed, and how it will be carried out. It means learning how to work with groups of peers, subordinates, and consultants to create disciplined work plans that show in detail what is to be done, with timetables listing milestones to be reached along the way.

Is there a need for a steering group or groups? Are the tasks to be carried out by individuals? By small task groups? What is to be the pattern for project progress reviews? Who should participate in the reviews? How often should they be held? Who should be there? What should the format be?

Who should be informed about project progress along the way? What should be done if the project does not stay on course? These were the critical questions the Micrographics people had to answer.

The consultants helped Jacobson and each of her key associates master the skills of breaking a task apart into steps and then assigning responsibility and accountability for each step. John Palladino and the various supervisors developed individual work plans. By using a wall chart to track the daily progress of jobs through the unit, Jacobson learned how powerful such tools can be in organizing and coordinating the work of a large group of people. Finally, Jacobson and Palladino both learned how to become the masters of their time rather the victims of random pressures. By creating and sticking with their project work plan, they avoided the distractions that sidetrack most managers.

7. Dealing with Conflicts, Frustrations, and Disappointments

No manager who attempts to improve performance and accelerate the pace of progress can entirely avoid obstacles along the way. When you meet an obstacle, should you tough it out and push forward? When does it make more sense to pause, regroup, and possibly change direction? How can a manager deal with resistant associates in a way that is supportive but also maintains the integrity of the project?

Jacobson and Palladino faced considerable resistance. The people in the department felt they were already doing the best they could with the equipment and staff available to them. The twenty-four-hour goal seemed impossible to reach. The opportunity to talk about her reaction to this kind of resistance with the consultant and overcome her unease about confronting it was one of the most important experiences for Jacobson.

8. Working with a Consulting Resource

Management consultants spend their entire professional lives working with client managers, but many managers work with consultants only once or twice in a whole career. It shouldn't be surprising, then, that most managers are uncertain about how to properly manage a consulting relationship. Yet having the client playing a strong contributing role is critical to designing and carrying out a successful project.

At the beginning of the microfilm project, Jacobson, Palladino, and their associates seemed to be waiting for instructions from the consultants. The consultants were explicit about the partnership mode and, by word and deed, showed what that meant. The managers became increasingly comfortable about asserting their views, declaring what kind of help they wanted from the consultants, and playing an increasingly active, leading role on the project.

9. Modifying Organizational Structures as Needed

Managers often fantasize that having a better organizational structure or a better person on the job will solve their problems. Some managers make organizational and personnel changes frequently, always hoping that such changes will provide the rewards they hope for. In a results-driven improvement process, however, managers are encouraged to get moving toward results, and to view organizational and personnel shifts as possible supplemental actions to support all the other steps being taken.

In the Morgan Bank case, for example, after they had achieved tangible progress on a variety of innovations, Jacobson and her people decided that several organizational shifts would help speed progress. Thus they created the work flow coordinator position and Supervisor Action Committee, described earlier. The consultant spent some time discussing the pros and cons of various moves and sharing parallel experiences in other organizations so that Jacobson and Palladino could sharpen their judgment about the sequencing of various change efforts.

10. Teaching the Consultant's Expertise

A fundamental obligation of the consultant is to teach members of the client organization as much as possible about the subject matter the consultant has been engaged to address. This requires different levels of effort for different people: major effort with the specialists who will be responsible for maintaining the techniques or technologies within the organization, and lesser effort with the managers who will have to use the techniques or technologies or implement the consultants' recommendations.

One of the specific skills Jacobson and her key managers learned from the consultants in pursuing the twenty-four-hour turnaround goal was process redesign. They used these skills to differentiate between steps that were essential for getting the work accomplished and steps that could be eliminated. Process mapping was another specific skill Claude Guay brought to the MVE project. By collaborating with participants, he helped them learn to do it themselves. Here's another example:

> Gunn Partners, a consulting firm that specializes in working with corporate staff functions, makes it a top priority to train client staff to play a major role in any project. Bob Moore, vice president and comptroller of the Union Camp Corporation, had this to say about the firm: "Conventional consultants want to be treated as the experts coming in to straighten us out. With them it is basically an adult-child relationship. With Gunn it was adult-to-adult partnership." Frank Rabil, manager of business processes for the company, commented, "So far we've saved about $5 million a year, with another $20 million identified. The consulting fees were only a small fraction of that. In addition, the consultants helped me to learn how to do business process redesign, and I will be working with the other divisions around the corporation to implement redesign. So we have developed internal capability as a result of the collaboration." And Jack Harrin, assistant comptroller, said, "The twelve people on the original pilot team all grew so much in stature and confidence. They have new perspectives on how work can get done."

One thing is for sure: if client learning is a key goal of the project, then the techniques and approaches the client is to learn need to be introduced at an appropriate pace. In Morgan Bank's microfilm department, people were trained in a "just-in-time" mode. Rather than dumping a huge load of new concepts on them in a training course, the consultants helped them learn new processes and procedures when that knowledge was needed to meet the challenge at hand. This strategy presents a dilemma for the large consulting organization that wants to shift to high-impact consulting. Large consulting teams, by their very nature, generate tons of material, often indigestible, that in the conventional consulting mode are delivered all at once at the conclusion of a project.

High-impact consulting is all about achieving results quickly while also learning how to achieve even more results, through a partnership relationship. The Morgan Bank and MVE examples show how a partnership approach can extend through every phase of a consulting project and focus on many learning dimensions.

While the microfilm project moved forward, over a hundred other Morgan Bank administrative services managers were carrying out parallel results-driven improvement efforts similar to Dorothy Jacobson's. Not only were most of their goals realized, saving many millions of dollars a year for the bank, but hundreds of people learned a whole array of new skills and techniques that equipped them to carry on. This learning that is going on all over the organization at the same time is what's needed to enable organizations to carry out very big strategic change. The consultants who dismiss rapid-cycle projects as merely picking the low-hanging fruit fail to see that these projects develop the organization's capability to go after the higher-hanging fruit. By contrast, conventional consulting reports that recommend big strategic changes beyond the client's ability get bogged down by the implementation gap and rarely pick any fruit at all.

Any client who fails to receive the learning and development benefits that should accrue from a consulting project is being cheated by the consulting process. Any consultants who fail to make this kind of learning integral to their work confine themselves to a sterile practice, constantly frustrated by client limitations, and barren of the joyful experiences that come from seeing one's clients learning and growing as well as achieving results.

Developing Learning Organizations That Really Learn

This results-based approach to managerial and organizational development is quite different from that advocated in a spate of recent writings on the subject of "the learning organization." A number of authors have usefully called attention to the fact that, in this time of ever-accelerating change, the only way organizations will keep pace is by providing opportunity for constant learning by their members. It is not enough for organizations to perform well today. Tomorrow's requirements are sure to be very different, so the leadership of organizations must devote major attention to making certain that their people learn what they will need to know in order to succeed in the future.[1]

These authors are making an important argument—that constant learning by its people must be a critical goal of every organization. These writings on the learning organization, however, slight the importance of results-focused experiential learning. The authors tend to succumb to the same belief about change that conventional consultants hold—the idea that the right concepts, if properly communicated, will somehow exert so much power that organizations will find them inexorable. This view is illustrated in the following quotation from David Garvin: "Organizational learning can usually be traced through three overlapping stages. The first step is cognitive. Members of the organization are exposed to new ideas, expand their knowledge, and begin to think differently. The second step is behavioral. Employees begin to internalize new insights and alter their behavior. And the third step is performance improvement, with changes in behavior leading to measurable improvements in results: superior quality, better delivery, increased market share, or other tangible gains."[2]

This thinking is based on the belief that cognitive change (insight and knowledge) leads to behavioral change, which in turn leads to results. There is an apparent lack of appreciation of the fact that setting and achieving sharply defined, challenging goals—and learning from the experience, as Dorothy Jacobson did—and then doing it again, can be the most powerful vehicle for expanding the capacity to set and achieve even more challenging goals. Peter Senge comes closest to an appreciation of experiential learning in his advocacy of "learning laboratories" and other simulations. He says that the effects of the learning laboratory can be seen most clearly when the managers implementing their learning "focus first and foremost on business results." And he adds, "If they can find new approaches to enhance results, they will commit time and energy to them" and have more staying power than those turned on merely by the learning process.[3] My colleagues and I have found that life is the most exciting learning laboratory, and on-the-job experience provides the most lasting learning.

To the extent that most of these writings on the learning organization refer to goals at all, they are mainly activity-based goals, such as, "improving actions," "correcting errors," "changing actions to reflect new insights," and so forth. The definitions do not reflect appreciation of the power of a challenging goal to trigger and energize the learning process. Garvin, in fact, seems to view interest in measurable results as possible evidence of short-sighted management: "Even half-life curves have an important weakness. They focus solely on results. Some types of knowledge take years to digest, with few visible changes in performance for long periods."[4] I don't deny that organizations must invest in critical long-term pursuits. Little learning occurs, however, in organizations that do not have frequent experience in setting tough goals and then mobilizing their wits and energies to achieve them.

And that is what high-impact consulting aims to provide for them (see Exhibit 7.1).

Consultants Also Need to Learn on the Job

While most managers and consultants would probably agree that consulting projects offer important opportunities for client learning, few appreciate the fact that there is much that consultants can learn on the job as well.

Consultants entering a new client situation (including internal consultants entering a new plant or department) are much like anthropologists exploring a culture that is new to them. Even though some of the artifacts, customs, and costumes may appear familiar, no anthropologist would claim to understand a new culture on the basis of such evidence without careful study. And thus it should be with consultants. Oh yes, you have been in other large commercial banks. You may know that in a paper mill a blanket is not used for sleeping. You understand the odd patterns on your client's balance sheet. You grasp the exquisite delicacy of semiconductor manufacturing. You've sat on the floor chatting with a gaggle of youthful dot-com company

Exhibit 7.1. Learning Opportunities for Consultants and Clients in Rapid-Cycle Projects.

Area of Learning	Description
1. Diagnosing readiness	Learning what people are ready, willing, and able to do now. Tapping into hidden reserves of energy, creativity, and motivation to get the improvement effort started.
2. Carving off achievable goals within a larger strategic framework	Tackling a piece of a much larger, seemingly overwhelming goal or challenge. Maintaining the focus on *results* in the short-term project.
3. Framing demands for goal accomplishment	Conveying a sense of urgency. Conveying expectations for improvement in ways that show confidence in people. Overcoming one's own resistance to asking more of others.
4. Improving performance through action-oriented experimentation	Using rapid-cycle projects to make incremental improvements in performance. Finding out what innovations actually produce a result.
5. Involving people in performance improvement	Learning how to use the power of the team to arrive at creative solutions and build commitment to new ways of working.
6. Developing work planning and project management skills	Learning how to use the basic tools of change management: work plans, project tracking tools, progress reviews, steering committees, and the like.
7. Dealing with conflicts, frustrations, and disappointments	Dealing with resistance, overcoming pitfalls, regrouping when initial solutions don't produce the intended results.
8. Working with a consulting resource	Learning how to use the consultant as a resource while maintaining project leadership and control.
9. Modifying organization structures	Ensuring structural change supports, rather than interferes with, goal achievement.
10. Teaching the consultant's expertise	Learning how to transfer the consultant's know-how in ways that expand but don't exceed the clients' absorption capacity.

founders. You may have extensive expertise of all sorts, but in a new client relationship, you know very little about the unique and idiosyncratic dynamics of that particular client organization. Unless you put your assumptions on hold, you may fail to learn what you need to learn about how the organization actually works and what it will take to improve its performance.

Consultants need to ask questions about the workings of the client organization as well as about the readiness issues the assignment raises. Exhibit 7.2 suggests some of the factors a consultant should investigate at the earliest possible moment in a new client situation.

The real-world questions in Exhibit 7.2 address the kinds of issues consultants need to understand before they decide how to work with a client and so they can make certain their specialized knowledge is fully exploited. Developing insight into these issues should be one of the objectives of the readiness assessment.

There is also much that consultants need to learn about once the project begins to move forward, as outlined in Exhibit 7.3.

The more consultants learn about how their relationship with the client is developing and how the client really operates, the more powerful their contributions will be. To develop these insights requires working with an organization for a while, attempting to make progress together, encountering and overcoming barriers, and learning from the experience.

Exhibit 7.2. Getting Oriented to a New Client—Some Key Issues.

1. How do things really work in this company? What has enabled its people to get as far as they've gotten? What's holding them back? What are the unique strengths and capabilities that current problems and difficulties might be obscuring?
2. Who are the people most open to new ideas and experimentation? Where can the most progress be achieved most quickly?
3. What are the relationships among key individuals and groups? What are the unique ways they have of working and interacting?
4. What might work here? What would be unlikely to work? Have I been in organizations like this before? What did I learn about the forces for and against change in those organizations?

Exhibit 7.3. Continuing to Get Oriented as the Project Progresses.

---

1. When a commitment is made, does everyone in the organization honor it?
2. How open to experimentation is the organization? Are there any taboo areas where no one will tread?
3. How do the people in the organization respond to consulting help? Do they see consultants as intruders or as helpers? What kinds of behavior by the consulting team elicits the best reactions from the client's people? Are we doing anything that turns them off or makes them resentful?
4. With respect to the specialized knowledge we have been asked to contribute, where does the client stand now? How well are its staff using what they have? How much more do they really need? How much can they absorb at once?
5. Have we learned anything about the organization that suggests that we should review our original project design with the client and possibly modify it?
6. Are we identifying the organization's "tender spots," the issues certain key players are sensitive or defensive about? Are they experimenting with different ways of handling these delicate issues?

If consultants work hard to learn about these issues during each individual project, they will also develop their overall grasp of how to facilitate large-scale change in an organization. The rapid-cycle approach, with repeated start-to-finish advances in a partnership mode, offers consultants numerous opportunities to develop insights into these vital issues. And with added insight comes greater ability to plan additional steps with more certainty.

Another dimension of this consultant learning is the development of effective working relationships with key client personnel. Over time a consultant can develop relationships that facilitate goal setting and action planning. Unfortunately, on-the-job learning and relationship building are irrelevant to those consultants who believe that their job is to deliver so many pounds of high-quality know-how. The following experience is not unique:

A very large, well-known consulting firm had a contingent of consultants working in a financial services company that was carrying out a major transformation affecting nearly every aspect of its operations. My firm was also working with the company, and I became aware that every once in a while one of the large firm's lead consultants disappeared, never to be seen again. When I inquired, I was informed that they had been reassigned or rotated onto other accounts. After a few months on the job, each lead consultant would simply disappear, to be replaced by another equally bright, equally well-dressed and well-coifed consultant. It was clear that their firm regarded them as interchangeable parts, valued for their knowledge and skills but not for anything they might learn about the client organization or any relationships they might develop with the client's people.

The concept of a client-consultant partnership was obviously meaningless to this firm. One of the easiest shifts a conventional consulting firm can make toward high-impact consulting is to face up to the need to learn about each client organization, to learn from each group of clients, and to value relationships with the clients' people.

Project Assessment: Mutual Learning

Project review and assessment sessions should be conducted periodically during the course of a project. They are somewhat structured mechanisms for making certain that the client and consultant assemble periodically to evaluate progress and to assess what they are learning. They can also spend some time deciding how to benefit from that assessment—that is, how the project can be strengthened and how learning can be enhanced. Exhibit 7.4 contains some suggested questions that should be on the review meeting agenda.

To make these reviews most useful, people need to be encouraged to believe that no aspect of the project is immune from examination and modification. The leaders of these sessions should endeavor to make them as frank and open as possible. Clients should not have to strive to be polite in such sessions; their honest reactions to the project are valuable data. Consultants need to try to understand and deal with client doubts and concerns rather than try to answer them or explain them away.

Exhibit 7.4. Project Progress Assessment.

- Is the project proceeding according to plan?
- Is anything turning up that should cause us to consider changing the assumptions around which the project was designed?
- How do we feel about how we are working together? What is working best? What is working less well? Should we test some different ways of working together?
- Looking forward, do we still hold to the timetable and goals we set at the beginning of the project? Are we still confident of achieving the results we said we would achieve?
- Are there people who are not in this meeting who need to be brought up to date on the project? Are there any who need to be consulted on how to proceed? Any whose help we may need but are not sure we can obtain?

Then, at the end of each project, a more extensive session should be held for the client and consultant to assess how well they accomplished what they intended to accomplish, both on the immediate project and in terms of making progress toward larger-scale, longer-term goals.

A few of the participants could be asked to prepare papers and presentations. In the partnership mode, it is often client people who make such presentations. Karen Prasch, for example, MVE's customer service specialist, made a number of presentations to senior management on the order processing project she was managing with the help of a consultant. Exhibit 7.5 contains some of the questions that might be addressed in such a session.

At the end of a project, clients are much more sophisticated about the specialized information and technology their consultants have introduced. They are more sophisticated about how to work with the consultants to manage change and improvements. The consultants have also learned much about how to contribute most effectively. The idea is that every participant's abilities keep developing.

Exhibit 7.5. Project Assessment Checklist.

- How much of what was intended did the project accomplish?
- What were some of the main lessons for the client about what it will take to continue to improve results and accelerate progress?
- How well did the client and consultant collaborate? Were their roles well spelled out, and did people carry out their roles as expected?
- If this project were to be carried out over again, how would we do it differently?
- What light was shed on the client's strategic goals and directions?
- What are the most potentially useful projects for the next step? Can strategic as well as operational advances be achieved in subsequent projects?

Clients should comment on what consultants could have done that would have been more helpful; consultants should do the same.

P.S. An Action Note to Client Managers

The fact that client-consultant collaboration adds so much value to a consulting project does not mean that you, as a client manager, will necessarily be eager to embrace the approach. You might feel as many client managers do, "I would love to work that way, but the place may fall apart if we do. My people are stretched out as it is." Or, "My people are 150 percent tied up with the new acquisition." Or, "We're right in the middle of year-end budgeting." And you might even add, "Hell, if my people had time to do this project themselves we wouldn't have had to hire a consultant."

You have to face up to the fact that, with any project of some significance to your organization, you will always pay a big price for hiding in the safety of the conventional consulting mode, with the experts doing their thing while you keep doing your job. In Chapter Four I described why both clients and consultants may feel more comfortable in the conventional mode even if it produces inferior results. One of the main reasons was to avoid the risk of having to make specific results commitments and then having to deliver on those commitments.

You and your people should explore how you can best work with your consultants on the project. If your consultants are not experienced in this type of discussion, this will be good for them as well as for you. You need to set the limits on the time investments that you and your people are willing to make. Actually, the time required for you and your people to participate responsibly can always be kept to a reasonable level. Your active collaboration on the project is so valuable that you do yourself a disservice by trying to avoid it. And if your consultants pander to your desire to dump the problem in their laps so you can quickly turn to your "regular job," they are doing you a disservice.

P.S. An Action Note to Consultants

Most consultants I've known, even those who enjoy working directly with clients, feel most comfortable going off on their own when the serious work of the project must be done. Yes, they want to interact with the client when the project is planned and when the recommendations are being reviewed. But during the working phase, while client people may be assigned to teams that are doing some of the research work, the consultants like to be able to move forward on schedule, doing what needs to be done.

If you want to really help your clients to learn and to grow, however, you will have to work more closely with them so that they can learn from the experience. That may not be easy. Many of you are simply not comfortable with adopting the role of change agent, collaborator, and coach. Yes, of course there are some conventional consultants who do client coaching, but not many are truly comfortable in the role of change facilitator.

This attitude about relationships with the client was graphically illustrated to me in a visit to the Harvard Business School some years ago. I learned that about eight hundred of the sixteen hundred graduate students in residence belonged to the school's management consulting club. At that time, a course was being offered on how to facilitate change in organizations. Of the eight hundred consulting club members only about ten felt

High-Impact Consulting

interested enough to sign up for the course. I dare say the same pattern would be repeated in most graduate business schools. The other 790 students understood that they would be welcomed into a consulting firm if they learned as much as they could about every management subject other than change management.

Thomas Kivlehan (mentioned earlier), who was then vice president of reengineering at Simon & Schuster, captured the value of the client-consultant partnership in describing the help his company received from a firm that practices in a high-leverage mode. "The capacity to manage change is one of the most valuable resources in any company today. When you work with consultants like Gunn Partners, you will be getting practical experience in how to make change happen, and you will become more skilled and feel more empowered to do so. It is an investment in your people. There is no training in the world that can substitute for that."

What an endorsement! This is quite different from serving up consultant wisdom or consulting products. It means providing continuous support as the client experiments with new modes. Since this is an unfamiliar role for most consultants, a good start for consulting firms would be to provide some training for your consultants who want to play such a role.

If you share a strong sense of responsibility for client successes or failures, and if you view each consulting project as a valuable personal learning experience for your clients and yourself, try out the strong partnership role. That is the key for making it happen.

Chapter 8

Leverage Resources
More Results with Fewer Consultants

The fifth reversal of the five fatal flaws is really a product of the other four. Because you can achieve so much more with the high-impact strategies already described, the need for hordes of consultants roaming the property is radically diminished. In fact, large numbers of consultants not only impose huge costs but can be a detriment to organizational learning.

In the spirit of the drive to "reinvent the government" that was advanced in the mid-1990s, the Occupational Safety and Health Administration in the Department of Labor engaged a conventional consulting firm with a human resources focus to help it make progress. The consultant's mission was to help identify core management processes and launch teams empowered to improve them. The consulting firm, with assistance from OSHA staff members, identified five "core processes" and formed teams to improve each of the five. The teams were given free rein to reinvent the way OSHA did things. The consulting firm provided training in quality improvement methods, problem solving, and group dynamics to representative groups from around the country. Consultant sessions with groups of staff focused on how to build teams, how to define problems, how to collect baseline data, how to create a "quality story," and other typical preparations-first activities that involved the very heavy use of consultants across the agency.

Six months into the project, Assistant Secretary Joe Dear, head of OSHA at that time, convened the teams to review the ideas and recommendations they had developed. The groups had few results to report, however, and they were discouraged about their progress. As Rob Medlock, area director of the Cleveland office and one of the team leaders, recalled:

"We were feeling pretty bad as a team because we had no tangible successes. The training we had gone through had laid down a very specific process. First you go through each of these steps, and at the end you reach a result. Then you evaluate the result. Then you start again. We were not allowed to circumvent the process, because each step led to the next. In theory, it was great. In practice, it was demotivating, because we had to spend so much time going through the steps before we could actually *do* anything. Remember, we had to keep our jobs going the whole time. The phones didn't stop ringing. We only had limited time, and most of it was spent on keeping things going, not on making changes."

Coincidentally, as part of a broader redesign effort under way in the Department of Labor, consultant Charlie Baum was assigned to work with OSHA at just about that time. Baum was experienced with high-impact change techniques, and he and Joe Dear agreed to try a new tack. They decided to aim at a tangible success on one critical core process: reducing the time required to eliminate workplace hazards called in to OSHA by workers. Instead of trying to reduce response time in all seventy area offices at once, one regional administrator, Mike Connors, volunteered to take the lead in two of his offices, Cleveland and Peoria. It was also agreed, despite some skepticism, to concentrate on only one of the two types of complaint processes. As Medlock recounted, "Charlie wanted to focus just on the non-formal complaint process. I was doubtful that would be useful. Our office already received more than one thousand such complaints each year, and we believed we were already experts in handling them."

Nevertheless, the team leaders agreed to test the non-formal complaint process first. Baum spent a day in each office, with teams led by the office director. Within an hour or so, the teams and Baum were able to map the workplace complaint process flow and identify several problems interfering with progress. Then, asked by Baum to define a results goal they would try to achieve (instead of identifying processes that they would work on improving), the two teams decided to try to reduce the average time it took an office to process a complaint by 25 percent within eight weeks. The teams then created action plans for achieving that goal.

With only telephone conferences with the consultant after the first day's workshop, the two offices began to experiment with alternative ways to process worker complaints. For example, instead of sending a formal letter filled with legalese to employers, they asked each complainant to provide a contact person and phone number at the company where the complaint occurred. Through same-day phone calls, OSHA staffers quickly notified employers of alleged problems. They then entered into open, relatively friendly discussions with employers about how the problems could be abated. Faxes were used to allow quicker back-and-forth communication with employers. Complainants retained all of their rights by being given the opportunity to verify abatement and to dispute the employer's response if they wished to do so.

By the end of the eight weeks, the Cleveland office had reduced the average time from receipt of an employee complaint to abatement of the condition from thirty-nine to nine working days. In Peoria the reduction was from twenty-three to five work days. Instead of the targeted 25 percent reduction, both offices achieved better than a 75 percent reduction. What is more, the OSHA employees who participated in the breakthrough process remember it as a time of learning, excitement, and growth. As Peggy Zweber, the Peoria office director and team leader, recalled, "It was the best thing that ever happened to this office! We worked as a team and accomplished so much. The most important thing was that each person's contribution was valued and treated with equal attention. There were six of us in the group, but I wish that everyone had been able to participate."

The project not only produced dramatic results but also laid the groundwork for rapid expansion of the improvement effort. After the first two successes, the process was rolled out across the country. Each regional office identified a senior "reinvention sponsor" who came to Washington for two days of training by Baum and key members of the Cleveland and Peoria teams. Nelson Reyneri, who headed up the reinvention effort, described the rollout: "Historically, we would have just sent out a memo, a compliance directive. We typically communicated just about everything that way. But we wanted the changes to be successful and to be lasting so we had the 'reinvention sponsors' come together personally. The great results in Cleveland and Peoria opened people's eyes to the possibility that they, too, could improve. The results have been excellent. The time to resolve non-formal complaints has been reduced by 70 percent across the country in the past year."

The amount of consulting support required to achieve the results in the Cleveland and Peoria offices was only about three or four days of consulting per office. The amount required to support the national rollout was only an additional four or five days.

The OSHA project focused on measurable client results. It began with a rapid-cycle success. The pace and scope, although a significant stretch for the participants, was designed to match what they felt they could accomplish. It was carried out as a learning partnership between client and consultant. When all those factors are fully in play, a relatively small amount of consulting effort can produce tremendous results. The performance of seventy offices nationwide was affected by less than a month's work by a single consultant. That's why high-impact consulting is also highly leveraged consulting.

In the OSHA case as well as the cases described in earlier chapters, the more the clients "made it happen," the more they learned the techniques the consultants were trying to introduce. They learned about project management. They gathered data themselves, instead of having to trust the consultant's findings and reports. They leavened the project with insights about their organization's operations that the consultants could not possibly have known. And they developed the ability to sustain progress on the ongoing projects while they launched new projects.

For all these reasons, even if high-impact consulting cost 50 or 100 percent more than conventional consulting, it would nevertheless be worth choosing it. But the wonderful thing is that high-impact consulting produces its results for only a fraction of the costs of labor-intensive conventional consulting.

Contrast the attitude toward engaging the organization's own people as evidenced in the OSHA case with the following more conventional approach:

A successful financial services company that marketed to corporate rather than individual customers decided that its future success would require it to work more closely with its customers' managers. To define more accurately what their customers' requirements might be, the managers in charge of the transformation decided that in-depth interviews should be conducted with senior people in a number of their customer companies. The consulting team helping to plan the new approach to customers supported this decision and devised an interview protocol.

When the question of who should do the interviews was raised, the consultants quickly suggested that they do them. "Customers might not speak as freely to your people, so you might not get a true picture." And, as if that were not reason enough, they also explained that the company's own people, though skilled as salespeople, might not be sufficiently skilled to follow the interview protocol. The consultants felt that doing the interviews themselves would definitely be the way to go. Perhaps at a later time, they said, it might be possible to have some of the client company's own people do some interviews. It sounded so logical that the client's senior people agreed at once with the suggestion. Predictably enough, the consultants learned a great deal about the customers—but so little of that learning could be conveyed to the client that relationships between client personnel and customer managers went on much as before.

This incident exemplifies the way conventional, labor-intensive consultants view their roles. The consultants believed that if they did the interviews they would be done well. And they were correct. They did not, however, consider the tremendous value to the company if its people could begin to learn how to talk with clients in more mature and sophisticated ways. The consultants failed to see that by doing the interviews they would rob the company's own people of the opportunity to develop new skills while also hearing firsthand what their customers were thinking. The slight loss of "accuracy" in the interviewing process was of little consequence compared to these potential benefits. Unfortunately the habitual pursuit of the labor-intensive "we are the experts who know how to do it, so we should do it" mode kicked in automatically. Not only did this client lose the benefit of its people doing the work, it paid far more for the project than it needed to, since the consultants were used in the most labor-intensive fashion.

The work in a number of departments of the State of Connecticut described in Chapter Four illustrates the difference between labor-intensive conventional consulting and highly leveraged consulting. The project began yielding reductions in workers' compensation costs almost from the first weeks. The seven-year collaboration between external consultants and various facility managers and internal consultants was able to buck the nearly universal trend of rising workers' compensation costs. Eventually the continuing savings grew to well over $10 million a year and continued to grow. Beyond those tangible results, there is now throughout the state a well-trained, experienced cadre of leaders and facilitators in place who are carrying the work forward.

At no time were more than three outside consultants engaged on the project, and they each worked half-time or less on it. The overall consulting fees for the entire seven years were less than $400,000. The project has yielded a continuing annual cash dividend amounting to twenty or thirty times the state's investment in consulting—and at the same time put the state in a position to carry on that type of work without further investments in outside help. That is highly leveraged consulting.

Highly Leveraged Consulting at Dun & Bradstreet

In Chapter Six I outlined the launch of the quality effort at Dun & Bradstreet Information Services, which was led by Mike Berkin, the division's quality manager, with the help of consultants Douglas Smith and Charles Baum. It began with the selection of eight rapid-cycle projects, and as Mike Berkin describes it, proceeded as follows:

Doug and Charlie were light-years different from the consultants I had worked with. They came on the scene, listened to us, and made us feel that they were on our side and were going to really try to help us. We did not want to invest further in training or anything else until we began to see results. We had seen over and over where people were trained and then did not accomplish anything.

Charlie did the hands-on consulting, and Doug worked more on the strategic level. We started with the eight projects. We picked leaders with the help of Charlie and Doug to make sure these initial projects were designed for certain success.

When we kicked off additional projects, I ran some of the launch workshops for the appointed project leaders, and Reuben Nyvelt, the training manager, ran a few. Charlie provided some coaching for us and sat in on some of these launch workshops.

All the projects in the first wave were successful. All the additional projects were successful. When we launched the third wave, we began to do it in clusters. Reuben, Charlie, a few other people, and I went to Canada as a team, and we launched a whole set of breakthroughs. In the morning we met with the leaders of all the projects, and then in the afternoon we had six simultaneous meetings, each facilitated by one of us. So by the end of the day, we had six breakthrough teams launched.

Charlie then created a workshop to train our facilitators. He ran some of those facilitator workshops with Reuben, provided him some support, and thereafter Reuben did the training of our facilitators. By the end of 1991 we had about twenty-five facilitators. And by that time Charlie was no longer involved with the work directly. Six months later, we had another seventy or eighty, for a total of over a hundred internal facilitators. Of the hundred facilitators, some have done as many as twenty or thirty projects, others only four or five.

Charlie has come around occasionally for an informal review of our progress, and we chat on the phone every once in a while; but after the first few months of 1991, basically all of the work was taken over internally.

We have done about three thousand breakthrough projects, so we don't have to go through all the preliminaries anymore. When there is a problem or a goal or a thing we want to tackle, we bring the people together into a team, and everyone knows that the goal has to be clear, measurable, and short-term.

By the end of 1993, all of the work to date was having an impact of about $30 million a year. By the end of 1994, there was $52 million worth of continuing and annualized impact from all the projects started since the beginning. These were in three categories: increased revenue generation, actual cost savings, and cost avoidance, by being able to produce more with the same expenses and resources.

In 1995 we began measuring only the impact of the current year's projects. In 1995 the incremental impact of the 1995 projects was $15 million a year, and that is a net figure—we subtracted all the expenses. That is on top of all the ongoing savings from previous years. And there may have been some additional projects, because not all got recorded.

When all of this started in 1991, we had four people in the quality shop. Today we are down to two.

Highly leveraged consulting? For an estimated $200,000 to $400,000 in outside consulting fees plus perhaps another few million dollars in internal consulting expenses, this division benefited to the tune of $60 or $70 million a year. Although they don't always hit this level, every high-impact consulting project aims for this same sort of leveraged return on consulting resources.

Some High-Leverage Project Designs

People who become interested in adopting high-impact methods often ask, what's the best way to try it?

First, you should test the shift to high-impact consulting gradually. Client and consultant should select some initial results-focused steps that appear achievable to both. They should be steps they both agree they'd like to try. Get started with them.

Second, it is useful in the early stages to have some structured ways to apply the approach. The next few paragraphs describe some of those structured methods.

"Model Week" Projects

As described earlier, we discovered that people are willing to shoot for amazingly challenging goals if they do not have to commit to meeting them indefinitely. That's what made it possible for United Aluminum's people to commit to and achieve 100 percent on-time delivery for a week when they had for years struggled to get much beyond 80 percent. And that's what made it possible for the furnace superintendent and his team at Vitrine Products to agree to try to improve furnace efficiency by 7 percentage points for a week although he had been certain that even 2 points was going to be a stretch.

Short-term, highly focused projects with a challenging goal often arouse a zestful game spirit. T-shirts or hats with slogans, martial music over the plant speaker system, senior managers visiting on the third shift—all add to the spirit of the endeavor. Once the participants have had the experience of reaching their apparently impossible goal, even for a week or for a few weeks, they have learned enough to sustain performance at the peak level or close to it. "Model week" projects are particularly appropriate with easily measurable improvements as the goal, such as speedier response to orders or customer requests, elimination of quality problems, and productivity improvement.

Breakthrough Projects

The "breakthrough strategy" is a discipline my firm developed for helping clients organize and sustain performance improvement. It is described in my book *The Breakthrough Strategy: Using Short-Term Successes to Build the High Performance Organization* and in many other articles and publications.

A breakthrough project is a rapid-cycle, results-focused project designed for client learning as well as achievement. Many of the rapid-cycle projects described earlier in this book were breakthrough projects. The Dun & Bradstreet profit improvement project just described was a product of over three thousand such breakthrough projects. The OSHA successes and many of the high-impact experiences described in earlier chapters used breakthrough projects as the key mechanism for performance improvement.

There are three key ingredients to a breakthrough project:

1. *Measurable client results.* Reducing patient-caused injuries at Fairfield Hills Hospital, increasing the number of eucalyptus logs loaded on each railway car in South Africa, reducing "opacity" incidents in Consolidated Edison's package boilers, getting Motorola's new products to market in ninety days—these goals, all easily measurable targets, had to be achieved in "rapid-cycle" time, without sacrificing any other activities under way in the organization.

2. *Client learning and development.* Clients learn how to select and organize a results-focused project, to mobilize the involvement of the right people, to lay out a practical work plan, and to coordinate all the steps needed to achieve their goal. After each breakthrough project, clients should be much more qualified to carry out the next one.

3. *Testing of consultant-provided insights, tools, and techniques.* Consultants introduce their ideas, concepts, and tools during the breakthrough project so that clients have a chance to see how they work before making a big commitment.

Almost every large-scale change or improvement challenge can be attacked via incremental breakthrough projects.

The GE "Work-Out" Model

Jack Welch, former CEO of General Electric, recognized a paradox some years ago. After downsizing and reorganizing, the company had only 60 or 70 percent as many people as it had before. Yet, Welch discovered, his managers were trying to get their work done in the same old ways. He decided that GE needed a massive shift to more effective work methods. In 1988 he commissioned a group of academics and consultants to help devise a method for accomplishing this goal. The result was the GE Work-Out process. With modest levels of consulting help, each GE business identified its key improvement requirements. Then, after some careful planning, it assembled a large group for a day or two to plan how the improvements were to be achieved. The ground rules required that the division's general managers attend the final session of the conference, listen to the group's conclusions and recommendations, and make on-the-spot decisions.

Thus, with very modest levels of consulting input, thousands of GE people were able to contribute to modifying their work processes and accelerating the company's progress.[1]

The Work-Out approach is valuable not only with a single organization but as a vehicle for interorganization collaboration. For example, consultants helped the senior managers of GE Lighting organize a meeting with the senior management of its largest customers, like General Motors. The aim was to improve the way they did business together, for the benefit of both businesses. With very modest consulting support, some major advances were made in intercompany partnership relations in these sessions. The book *The GE Work-Out* presents a very good orientation to the process.[2]

The Work-Out methodology represents a design for highly leveraged consulting input. At General Reinsurance, the method was adapted to achieve widespread employee involvement in the company's quality and change processes. These sessions, called "quality action workshops," are supported by internal facilitators. Zurich Financial UK, which had been losing huge amounts of money, used Work-Out methodology to drive a major turnaround—a process described in detail in Chapter Twelve.

Pilot Projects

In many situations in which a conventional consultant would want to conduct a detailed study to assess whether some course of action was correct, a high-impact consultant might be more tempted to cut to the chase and say, "Let's try it and see how well it works." As described in Chapter Six, General Reinsurance selected six active customers and two prospects for pilot testing of its plan to implement customer service teams. At Vitrine Products, a pilot program was designed to test the performance improvement of one furnace before creating a process for increasing output from all the company's furnaces. In the automotive-parts plant example in Chapter Four, one of six production lines served as the pilot for a plantwide quality and delivery improvement project.

All these approaches can be exploited in a highly leveraged, high-impact, results-focused consulting mode.

Moving Toward Highly Leveraged Consulting

To see what the highly leveraged approach might contribute to your situation, whether you are a client or a consultant, here is some how-to advice to consider:

• *Select initial projects that have a high probability of success.* One key to encouraging managers to become willing participants in highly leveraged projects is to demonstrate to them that their people can actually achieve more than they've been achieving. Success will provide the fuel to energize further progress. In getting started, therefore, begin with projects that offer the maximum chance of success, projects where the client can be most certain of getting the most done with the least effort. The consultants will be equally reinforced by the experience of success.

Often managers don't tune in quickly to the idea of selecting sure-win projects. For example, I was exploring with a potential client which group would participate in a certain project, and she said, "Group X needs the most help. Why don't we start with them?" This is not an unusual managerial perspective. But the group that needs the most help is unlikely to be the one with the best hope of success. Success in the early steps of a project is critical, so the project needs to involve those most likely to succeed. After generating momentum there, both parties will have the experience and insights needed to make something happen with "group X."

• *Emphasize skill development of client personnel.* Except for research or highly technical projects (where the so-called consulting is really outsourced work) many of the tasks that consultants carry out can be done by the organization's own people with some modest training and some ongoing support from a consultant. Over and over again I have seen client people at all levels and with all sorts of backgrounds surprise their associates by demonstrating an ability to learn these new techniques and apply them effectively.

Throughout our lives, we are trained to depend on experts to give us answers. Conventional consulting methodologies reinforce this habit by putting consultants in the lofty role of diagnosticians and solution providers. This mystical faith in what the consultant's magic potions can accomplish often discourages managers from getting deeply involved in projects. This is compounded by the recurring issue of client "busyness." Clients may resist investing the time required for training and development. Indeed, the training may seem wasteful to some client managers. Since the consultants already know how to perform the work that must be done, managers may feel, "Why not let them do what they are good at, and let my busy people get on with their jobs?"

To you client managers who feel this way, I urge you to consider that if consultants had done the bulk of the work in the Morgan Bank, in the OSHA project, or in any of the other high-impact projects described in this book, they probably would not have accomplished as much as the people in the client organizations were able to accomplish. Worse, when the consultants completed their assignments, they would have walked away with much of the valuable insight that the client paid for. By contrast, all participants in highly leveraged projects learn a great deal. Then—for the rest of their careers—they will be able to apply these skills and act with a new sense of confidence that never would have developed were they merely the recipients of consulting studies and recommendations.

• *Train internal consultants or facilitators to support the work.* The selection of some people in the client organization to serve as internal change facilitators supports the highly leveraged mode in a number of ways. First, these people can help ensure the success of the change effort and they can multiply the client's return on its investment in consulting. Moreover, they will be there after the consultants leave, able to apply their new skills indefinitely.

My own firm, dedicated as my colleagues and I are to highly leveraged consulting, almost never begins an assignment without identifying internal consultants who will multiply our consulting effort and carry it forward after we leave. The same is true of other high-impact consultants. They and we provide training to these internal facilitators and work in a partnership mode with them to help them expand their capability.

• *Develop an experimental, action-oriented mode of working.* Consultants who want to help their clients deal with large-scale, far-reaching strategic change efforts need to launch those efforts with dozens of smaller-scale success experiences. These need to be seen as developmental experiments in change. The experience gained from carrying out a number of such experiments provides the collective insight, skill, and confidence needed to manage increasingly larger-scale strategic changes.

• *Help senior people lead the change.* It is important to focus sufficient consulting time and attention to helping the key senior people to provide the best possible leadership in the change effort. This goes beyond briefing them on the particular techniques the consultant is introducing. As outsiders with unique experience, consultants can help senior managers sharpen their demand-making and improve their project management and project sponsorship skills. It is these senior managers who are likely to have the most motivation for advancing the project and can have major influence in stimulating others to move.

• *Use interventions that engage large groups.* Working with large numbers of people in structured workshops focused on organizing action to accomplish the needed changes is another means of multiplying modest levels of consulting input into large-scale change. The Work-Out model described earlier in this chapter and the experience of Dun & Bradstreet's Information Services Division illustrates how these multiplication strategies work.

These strategic elements are summarized in Exhibit 8.1.

Spreading the Word

When Joe Dear, who led the OSHA effort described earlier in the chapter, returned to the state of Washington as administrative assistant to the governor, he brought an affinity for high-impact modes with him. Governor Gary

Exhibit 8.1. Moving to High-Impact Consulting.

1. Select initial projects that have a high probability of success.
2. Emphasize skill development of client personnel.
3. Train internal consultants or facilitators to support the work.
4. Develop an experimental, action-oriented mode of working.
5. Help senior people lead the change.
6. Use interventions that engage large groups.

Locke was as determined to make gains in the performance of state government as any corporate CEO I have encountered. A quarterly publication titled "Governing for Results" summarizes projects from every department. The high-impact multiplication is illustrated by one major project.

> The Legislative committee overseeing the Department of Labor & Industries had mandated a significant reduction in what they viewed as excessive claims payments for workers compensation. The lack of measurable progress for a number of months after that mandate was issued led the department to decide on some consulting help. My colleague Rudi Siddik and I worked on this project over a two-year period.
>
> Many of the participants were skeptical about the value of consulting help, even after we explained about the "hidden reserve." After all, it was they who were the experts in workers compensation claims, and they were already doing the best they could to improve results. To overcome this skepticism and get them started on a new pathway to change, it was necessary to demonstrate quickly that the people in Claims Administration were capable of accomplishing much more.
>
> In two-day workshops we helped all twenty-four first-line supervisors select the first round of rapid-cycle projects to speed the claims process. (How-to #6: "Use interventions that engage large groups.") These were designed to be sure-win projects that focused on what the supervisors wanted to try out, even though they were not necessarily the most

critical contributors to the overall results. (How-to #1: "Select initial projects that have a high probability of success.")

The success of this first round of breakthrough projects gave the supervisors and their managers additional confidence to move onto the real key performance challenge—actually reducing the number of active claims in their inventory. Judy Moran, head of Claims, formed a team with a number of other people in Claims and its key supporting functions. We helped this team develop a master plan to meet the legislature's goal. This plan included new rounds of breakthrough projects at the supervisory level, programwide breakthroughs aimed at improving the management of medical decision making and vocational rehabilitation planning, and related processes. We also helped various support groups launch their own breakthrough projects to help speed the processing of claims. (How-to #2: "Emphasize skill development of client personnel.") The numbers of claims began to drop within the first six months of work.

From the very beginning, we collaborated with the agency's Quality Resources group to help them run workshops and breakthrough teams. These internal consultants supported most of the breakthrough teams. (How-to #3: "Train internal consultants to support the work.") We helped to train the Quality Resource consultants in high-impact consulting techniques.

We encouraged Gary Moore, the director of Labor & Industries, to become more actively engaged in the process and consulted with him periodically in how that could be done. (How-to #5: "Help senior people lead the change.")

The entire process was organized as a huge experiment in which they were all engaged. As a consequence, the managers and supervisors developed competency in setting short-term measurable goals, in engaging their claims adjudicators and clerical support staff in experimenting with work flow improvements, and in developing detailed work plans that lead to the desired results of reducing unnecessary claims. (How-to #4: "Develop an experimental, action-oriented mode of working.")

At the end of two years, the disability rolls had been reduced 19 percent without depriving any claimants of their valid benefits. The gains? At least $15 or $20 million a year in compensation payments. The consulting fees? Between $1 and $2 million, in total.

Simple Concepts, Profound Differences

In Chapters Four through Eight I have outlined how clients and consultants can shift from long-cycle-time, labor-intensive, high-risk conventional consulting to high-impact consulting. These chapters have described how to reverse the five frequently fatal flaws of conventional consulting and transform them into high-return contributors. As clients and consultants make these shifts, they will radically alter the way they work together and multiply by many times the returns on clients' consulting investment.

Consultants who want to shift to a more highly leveraged approach have to abandon some of the comforting but counterproductive structures of the conventional mode. They will have to welcome and get comfortable with the participation of clients in the design and execution of their projects. And they will have to learn how to adjust the project pace to what seems right for the client.

Also, consultants, especially the less experienced ones, will have to develop strong interpersonal and change management coaching skills, skills they may not have focused on or been encouraged to develop. They will have to develop the skills to help their clients to think in new ways, to learn and grow. There must be a management development and organizational development component in what you do. For many consultants, this will require some new learning.

Finally, there are the economic issues: if yours is a large, traditional consulting firm and your economic health is rooted in large-scale, labor-intensive projects, you may anticipate adverse economic consequences from switching to high-impact consulting. That is not necessarily the case. The clouds have a silver lining: if the work your large teams of consultants are doing is truly valuable to your clients, then there is no reason not to provide such help profitably. What these large groups of professionals are doing, however, might more likely be some sort of outsourced expert labor and not what I call management consulting. In fact, consulting firms might wish to consider identifying those individuals who are really management consultants and differentiating them from the larger pool of professionals who are actually doing outsourced research or systems development work for the client.

Consultants may be required to do this as clients increasingly demand more demonstrable linkages between their investments in consulting and the benefits produced. It is my fervent desire that this book contribute to that market pressure.

To move effectively into a mode in which clients and consultants share responsibility for producing results, the parties will have to work out their project agreements (that is, their contracts) more carefully and deliberately. Consultants will have to pay more heed to the way senior client managers convey performance improvement requirements to their people. And, finally, clients and consultants will have to learn to overcome their anxiety-produced defense mechanisms and communicate much more effectively.

The next few chapters describe how these shifts in their working relationship can support high-impact consulting, with highly leveraged results. The shifts will contribute not only to making consulting much more effective but also to making it much more fun and personally gratifying.

Part Three

Creating High-Impact Partnerships

Chapter 9

Create a Contract for Collaboration Instead of a Proposal for a Job

W hat's wrong with this story? Write your views down before reading the text that follows it.

A state government agency wanted to reduce the frequent delays and errors that occurred in issuing professional licenses—covering dozens of categories from physicians to pharmacists to tattoo artists. Individual professional people and their associations all across the state were complaining about the long turnaround times, the difficulty in having questions answered, and the errors being made in the processing of their license applications. Several consultants were asked to bid on a contract to help correct the problems. While the details varied somewhat, each of the firms submitted a proposal that described how they would conduct some research into the causes of the delays and errors and recommend process improvements that would correct the problems. Several of them also described how they might help with the implementation of their recommendations.

This case illustrates the way consulting projects are often launched. When an organization believes that some consulting might help it, its managers give the consultants a description of their needs, answer the consultants' questions, and then wait for them to present a proposal outlining how they will meet those needs. These proposals, like those in this case, are typically composed by the consultants themselves and describe the work they will do. Then the client makes the decision.

But consider: any real solution to the licensing problems in this case will clearly have to be a close collaboration between consultant and client. The possibilities for success of that collaboration needs to be tested by exploratory discussions between the parties. The notion that consultants, working on their own, can conceive a plan that will actually result in solving the problem is ludicrous. After they have read the request for proposal and participated in an interview or two with the agency's senior people, the consultants have no inkling of what might really work in that setting. For clients to ask for proposals in this fashion, as if consulting is an intellectual commodity that can be purchased like an electrical installation or an asphalt-topped roadway is self-defeating.

In fact, this very act of passing a proposal request to a consultant ("What will you, the consultant, do to solve the problem?) sets the stage for the typical back-and-forth handoff mode that is loaded for failure. The next step, of course, will be for the consultants to pass back a proposal to the client. Now they are slipping into the well-worn conventional consulting groove. Once the project is launched this way, there is little chance it will ever evolve into a collaboration.

Clients request these proposals and consultants write them because they all view consulting as a set of tasks carried out by consultants on behalf of their clients instead of a collaboration between them, as advocated in this book. In addition, the policies and practices that govern organizational purchasing processes are applied to consulting with costly consequences. In the case of the state government licensing case, the client agency was undoubtedly following state government protocols. Unfortunately, those protocols often set the stage for failure.

The licensing proposal request viewed the consulting task as devising the best solution possible, a purely intellectual task rather than a collaborative project. The consultants were given no opportunity to test readiness as described in Chapter Five. Moreover, the consultants were given no opportunity to observe that the people who would have a role in making the final decisions, busy as they were with dozens of other issues, had not really discussed their respective views on this project among themselves. A few questions would have revealed that on some of the key issues, irreversible decisions had already been made. On other issues there was no consensus. Some readiness questions and "What if?" testing of possible conclusions would have revealed that there were resource and organizational relationship constraints that any solution would have to adhere to. So it was quite naive for the consultants to prepare a proposal and assume that a go-ahead from the client would mean likely support for the project's recommendations. The process completely failed to encourage a collaborative examination of the best way to carry out the project so as to ensure its success.

The willingness of consultants to accept responsibility for preparing proposals, as in this case, allows clients to disengage and assume little or no responsibility for shaping the project, thus putting themselves in a passive role from the start.

These are the kinds of weaknesses that characterize the typical consultant-designed proposal, which in most conventional consulting serves as the instrument for defining and launching a consulting project.

Collaborative Contracts, Not One-Way Proposals

Implementing a high-impact consulting project, by contrast, requires the client and consultant to thoughtfully explore what they want to achieve together and how to achieve it. As they reach agreements, they jointly document those agreements. The result of this process is the *project contract*. This is a carefully written statement, prepared by both parties, outlining their respective roles and commitments in their joint undertaking, from the beginning of the project to the end. If only the most immediate steps can be specified when the contract is created, provision is made for the parties to review their progress and create a more detailed plan for subsequent stages.

The fundamental consideration in creating a contract should be how the client and consulting team can best work together to accomplish results, not whether the consultants are the most technically proficient in any given area. If the client takes the conventional stance of a customer purchasing services from a vendor, as in the state licensing case, it will be more difficult to create a meaningful dialogue on issues like client readiness. Only in a true partnership mode can the parties design low-risk, rapid-cycle projects that are loaded for success.

Instead of rushing off to prepare a proposal, the prospective consultants to the state agency should have asked a few of the client's people for their ideas about the best solution. They then might have gathered, if only briefly, some of the key players to gauge their agreement on what they wanted from the consulting project and what sort of solutions might be workable. They might have made notes of what they heard in these discussions and circulated the notes back to the agency's senior managers as a draft "contract" for the project. If there were still some open issues, those would be the agenda for continuing discussion. If there were any conflicts within management, they would need to be identified and the project designed to deal with them.

This is the mutual contracting process in contrast to the "submit a proposal" process. Contracting in this mode reflects a partnership more than a buyer-vendor interaction. Although the client is certainly the "buyer" and the consultant the "vendor," they do not conduct their initial exploration as if they were negotiating a sale. The buy-sell mode can work if the consultant is selling a package of technical work or other outsourced services and not assuming responsibility for client outcomes. If, however, the aim is to create a working relationship among people who will be jointly accountable for significant client results, then a typical buy-sell back-and-forth negotiation will not accomplish that end.

In high-impact consulting, in fact, the contracting process is as important as the contract itself. It consists of a structured approach to managing all the issues detailed in the preceding chapters: identifying the most urgent client goals, assessing client readiness, defining specific goals for the first subprojects, and agreeing on the best way for the client and consultant to work together on the project.

Identify the Accountable Client

Perhaps it seems odd to make the point now, since I have made so many general references to "the client," but one critical step early in the contracting process is to specify who *the* accountable client really is. *The* client is the one person (or the small, explicitly defined group) who accepts personal accountability for seeing to it that the client organization makes use of and benefits from the consulting help.

Often a number of client managers are involved in negotiating a new project with a consultant, but no effort is made to specify the one person who will be accountable for the relationship once the consultant is hired. This need to identify *the* client is frequently overlooked. Consultants are hired and projects launched because a number of managers believe that "something needs to be done," and the consultants offer to do it. But at the end of the project when the recommendations are presented, there is no one person clearly designated to receive them and make sure they are dealt with.

Here are two vignettes that highlight the difference between working with a management team as a diffuse "client" group whose members all share an interest in the project's success, and pinpointing the single accountable client.

Mary McKreath is senior vice president of engineering for a telecommunications equipment company. Her company's CEO and its executive committee have agreed that their corporate strategic planning unit (the internal consultant) should study the rapid shifts occurring in the company's customer base. The issue is whether the company should reorganize its businesses to respond to those shifts.

Scenario 1

McKreath, as a member of the committee, attends the meetings when the study plan is discussed and participates actively. She reads and comments on the consulting group's proposal. Once the proposal is approved and the strategic planning unit gets to work, McKreath, along with all the other members of the executive committee, turns back to her very demanding job.

Scenario 2

As in Scenario 1, the executive committee agrees to the study. But the CEO also announces that he is asking Mary McKreath to take responsibility for the project on behalf of the executive committee. Her mission will be to work with the strategic planning unit to guide their work and make certain they do the best job possible. She'll act as liaison with the executive committee. And once the plan is accepted, the CEO adds, McKreath will be spearheading the implementation process.

Scenario 1 could easily lead to a situation in which everyone supports the consultant's findings but no one takes responsibility for ensuring an effective response. In Scenario 2, McKreath is clearly *the* client for the work to be done by the strategic planning unit. One can be certain she will be thinking about implementation possibilities well before the end of the project.

It is much easier, incidentally, for internal consultants than for external consultants to drift into projects where there is no clearly identified client because their fees usually do not have to be negotiated. So when they are in a meeting and a senior manager says, "We ought to look into—" or "Would it be possible for someone to find out how much demand there would be if—" an internal consultant, eager to contribute, may take that as an assignment and crank up a project without defining a client or creating a contract.

We have seen many corporate staff consulting projects that got started because there was a shared conviction by some senior managers that "something needs to be done about—" and that conviction was conveyed to internal consultants. In response, the internal group launched its efforts, overlooking the fact that no one was accountable for the project. Thus there was no one to play the partner role with the consultants nor to make sure that the consultants' work was translated into bottom-line results. I have seen such projects go on for years, racking up huge expenditures, with the internal consultants fruitlessly trying to "sell" senior people on doing something about their recommendations and the senior people all agreeing that "something really should be done."

No matter how many other people are involved in exploring and conducting the project, it is *the* accountable client who, from the first moment, is the consultant's counterpart within the organization. This point was touched on in the section on mapping in Chapter Five.

Create the Contract

Once the accountable client is defined, that person or group and the consultants need to work jointly on creating the contract. Here are some guidelines you might follow in creating a project contract (summarized in Exhibit 9.1).

• *Specific goals of this project.* The contract needs to specify answers to these questions: What is the aim of this project? What will be the measure of its success? This section will include the specific client results and the new methodology and systems to be introduced by the consultant.

• *Overall organization goals to which the project should contribute.* What overall organization strategies should this project promote? The contract should specify how the project fits and will contribute to the major strategic efforts going on in the organization. Thus it needs to address questions like these: What are the longer-range goals to which the project should contribute (for example, new marketing strategies, major cost reduction, speeding turnaround time, developing new products and services, meeting customer needs in new ways)? Are there by-product outcomes from this project that are important in creating momentum for ongoing progress?

Exhibit 9.1. Elements of a Typical High-Impact Consulting Contract.

1. Goals of the project
2. Overall organization goals that project should promote
3. Some possible rapid-cycle projects
4. Project roles and contributions
5. Project work plan and methodology
6. Possible future projects evolving from success of this one

Are there some specific client development and training goals? Are there any organizational structure issues? Are there culture change goals? How must the project be designed both to meet its immediate aims and to create a foundation for future progress?

• *Some possible rapid-cycle projects.* From the array of broad project goals, client and consultant should identify one or several possible rapid-cycle subprojects. These are the kinds of breakthrough projects that were described in Chapter Six. The goals of these projects have to be discussed and negotiated not only between the accountable client and consultant but also with the people in the client organization who will be responsible for achieving results. In identifying the first few possible subprojects, client readiness needs to play a key role. Initial projects need to be selected on the basis of what is learned about what the client might be ready, willing, and able to do.

It also bears repeating that each of these rapid-cycle projects differs from the "phases" of a conventional consulting project: there may be a long sequence of phases in such a project, but there is no promise of any real results until all the phases have been carried out and the entire project has been completed. Rapid-cycle, high-impact consulting projects, whether they aim at large or small goals, are designed to produce some tangible results quickly.

• *Roles and contributions.* The contract should describe the contributions of the various parties. What are the unique expert contributions the consultant will make? Will it be study and interpretation? Will it be ideas for major shifts in strategy? What will client people be expected to contribute? How will the consultant's expertise and know-how be blended with know-how in the client organization? How much time and energy is each party going to invest? In addition to the main players, what support will be required from other units inside or outside the organization, and how will that support be engaged?

• *Project work plan and methodology.* The parties need to create a tentative work plan outlining how the project might be carried out and how the clients and consultants will work together. The work plan should include the complete cast of characters (from the client mapping) and descriptions of the roles of each group and each person.

The plan should also include a work schedule, outlining the steps of the project, the people who will be involved in each step, and the way it will be carried out. The work plan should cover all of the steps up to the point when the initial results should have been achieved. Key milestones should be identified, along with the progress that should have been achieved by each milestone.

In laying out the work plan, the parties must ask the following questions: How will the project be directed? How will the various interested parties in the client organization be wired into the project? How often will progress reviews be conducted? how? by whom? If the senior people who are contracting for the project are not to be actively involved in it, how will they be kept informed and involved? If fresh insights are developed during the project and it appears that a change in direction should be considered, who will be responsible for raising the issue? How should such changes be accomplished?

• *Possible future projects evolving from success of this one.* Since high-impact consulting divides large-scale client change into short-term, manageable increments, it is important to keep the longer-term strategic issues always at the forefront. Thus, as part of developing the contract for a consulting collaboration, it is useful to sketch out some possible next-step projects once the current project succeeds. Specifying these possibilities is helpful in considering the design of the current project and making certain that it yields full benefits.

To accomplish its purposes, the contracting exploration must encourage real give-and-take between the parties. To facilitate open discussion, both consultant and client should do some homework before meeting. They should be prepared to walk through the elements covered in the above outline, discussing each one, testing possible ways to move, testing the connection between some possible rapid-cycle projects and longer-term goals. This kind of discussion tends to break down people's expectations for a stereotypical customer-vendor relationship.

Contracting for high-impact consulting is an iterative process. At the end of each exploratory meeting, someone should be responsible for summarizing the conclusions of the meeting in the form of a draft outline of project goals and activities. Sometimes this person will be the consultant.

Sometimes one or two members of both the consulting and client teams can be given the job of recording the consensus. The product of this work will be the beginnings of the project contract. The principal client leaders and the consulting team need to meet to review the draft, assess it against their expectations, and discuss how to strengthen it.

Sometimes clients complain that this exploratory process will take too much time. But usually this kind of exploration can be done in a few meetings. And even if it does take a bit longer than just having the consultant do a proposal, it won't be nearly as costly as doing the wrong project or getting the wrong results. This process also gives both client and consultant sufficient opportunity to raise and resolve readiness issues.

Versatility: A Key Ingredient of the Contracting Process

To design the project so that it aligns well with what is being discovered about the client's readiness issues, the consultant must be flexible and responsive. Many consultants are capable of this kind of flexibility, but it's not an easy task for many others who have favorite well-structured methodologies that they employ to deal with particular kinds of situations. With a solution or an approach already in mind, the consultant may become trapped, as illustrated by the following anecdote:

> A graying, slightly portly gentleman entered the "Smith & Company Formal Wear" emporium. He explained to Mr. Smith that he had been invited to a black tie dinner celebrating his employer's silver wedding anniversary. "Would you have a size 46 tuxedo for me to use next Saturday?" he asked. Smith had just finished outfitting the principals of a wedding that was to take place on the same day, and several of them were the same size as this customer. He realized instantly that the only thing available in size 46 was a powder-blue tux with wide satin lapels, which had last been worn to a high school prom by the football team captain.

I ask participants in my consultant training seminars to guess what Smith says at that moment. They laugh and offer possibilities like these: "Sir, you look like someone who would never want to dress in the same dull way as everyone else" or "Wow, would you look fantastic in blue! Let me see if I have something in blue." Since I tell this anecdote just after discussing the importance of testing client readiness, I challenge the seminar participants with this: "Isn't it important for Smith to test his customer's readiness, that is, his wishes and desires?" They respond: "No way! Smith is going to push the baby-blue number with the satin lapels."

The moral of the story is this: if you have only one suit to rent, that's the suit you are going to push. If you have a favorite consulting solution in mind, that's the solution you will tend to recommend. Consultants who become too locked into their standard ways of working have trouble fine-tuning their approaches to match client readiness. In fact, when such consultants speak about the importance of being well prepared for client meetings, they usually mean that they should be prepared to explain and defend their preferred approach. There is probably not one consultant in a hundred who would be willing to go to a restaurant that had no menu, where the proprietor simply tells you what is the best food to eat. But many consultants think nothing of offering their clients the single best solution without offering them any other choices.

Versatility is the alternative. Versatility is the process of offering clients a menu of different approaches. It encourages consultants to make available to their clients the same power that all of us want in our role as consumers of products and services: choice! To provide a menu with choices, however, means having a variety of choices ready to respond to a client's requests. With a range of options, the parties can review the possibilities, discuss them, and speculate about how each would play out. Gradually they can converge on a jointly created and mutually agreed-upon contract.

Such an exploration leads to a sense of joint ownership of the direction selected. A typical proposal, by contrast, dishes up the consultant's favorite approach. So it should seem clear that if consultants are to make use of what they learn about client readiness, it is necessary for them to develop "design versatility," which is the capacity to provide, in each situation, a menu of project possibilities that can be shaped to match unique client readiness.

Trapped by Right Answers

A difficult barrier to versatility exploration is the entrapment of consultants by their views of the "right answers." In any new situation, when a potential client describes what the organization needs, it is natural for the consultant to develop a sense of how the consulting project should be designed. And once this conviction takes shape, there is a tendency for the consultants to do less listening and more selling. This sales mode is even more exaggerated when the consultant has a somewhat different view of the situation than the client. Worse, the client may not seem even capable of grasping the issues "properly." This freeze-up reaches its height when consultants feel the potential client is trying to get them to do the "wrong" assignment.

Just as soon as consultants sense this gap in viewpoint emerging, their anxiety begins to rise. They become preoccupied with not being trapped into accepting the wrong assignment. At that moment, their listening mechanisms tend to shut down, and real dialogue becomes difficult. How often does this happen? Very often. Remember, clients and consultants always view the situation somewhat differently. Those differences can make the relationship productive, but it can also lead to a freeze-up. Consider this case, which I have used in seminars with many hundreds of consultants:

> Electron Digital is a distribution company that handles a variety of electronic control equipment for manufacturing and other automation uses. The president was recruited into the company a few years ago, and since that time performance has stagnated. The president calls on a consulting firm to see if they can provide some help.
>
> At the first meeting with a partner from the firm, the president comes to the point quickly. He feels the key is to accelerate sales volume. He admits that the company has a number of other problems that need to be dealt with, but he wants the consultant to focus on improving the performance of the sales force first. Since the salespeople seem to lack many basic skills, the president's first priority is for the consultant to design and conduct training for the sales force. Once this is under way, the president says, the consultant can also begin looking at the incentive

compensation plan and related issues. How does the consultant feel about taking on this assignment?

Now the moment of truth has arrived. The consultant's review of the briefing materials, the cursory research before the visit, and even the little that the president has said in this meeting all suggest that this company has many problems that cannot be cured by sales training. The company's prices seem to be high. Its distribution methods are inefficient. It has had some quality problems. One of the consultant's informants admitted that the company's technical support group is very weak.

So what should the consultant do? I have seen hundreds of consultants role-play this case, and most of them became preoccupied with not accepting the wrong assignment. They felt they would be doing the client a disservice to conduct a big training program that would not solve the company's problems. In role-playing this case, almost every consultant stops listening to the client early in the interview and concentrates on subtly (or not so subtly) maneuvering the client away from his desire for training. In almost every case this maneuvering irritates the CEO.

Once consultants get anxious about being saddled with the "wrong" assignment, they don't do much listening or readiness testing.

I ask seminar participants who are adamant that a training program would be the wrong solution in Electron Digital to describe exactly what the CEO meant when he used the word "training." It doesn't take them long to admit that the CEO didn't say much about it, and since they did not probe into the president's views, they really have very little idea what he meant. They were projecting their own images into the situation. When otherwise qualified consultants fail to establish rapport with a new client, it is often because they are uncomfortable with the client's description of the project and are trying to correct it.

Designing with Versatility

In negotiating new assignments consultants need to create a menu of possible project approaches. Then, by keeping their anxiety at bay and probing for the reasons that a client is asking for something in a certain way, they can begin to identify accurately what the client really wants. Then, at an appropriate time, they can present some of the choices on the consulting menu. As these are explored with the client, the consultant will gain deeper understanding of what might work. And with this understanding, the consultant can work with the client to fashion a "common ground" project design—that is, a project that is a good match with what the client wants to do and also makes sense to the consultant. The Electron Digital case illustrates how it works.

After discussing the concept of design versatility and the idea of presenting a menu of project possibilities, I ask the same seminar participants who have been arguing with the CEO whether they can possibly imagine even one possible "common ground" first step that they would undertake with Electron Digital. Such a step would have to meet two requirements:

- It would accept, at least for the moment, the CEO's belief that "sales force training" is what should be done.

- It would be a step that the consultants would consider a useful one to take—not merely surrendering to the client's perception.

At first this seems impossible to many in the group. Then one person makes a suggestion like this: "How about if we were to suggest interviewing the managers in one or two branches about what they think are the differences between their top-performing salespeople and their poorest salespeople? We could then come back and discuss the findings with the CEO and discuss some tentative next steps." Everyone agrees that step could provide some useful insight and permit further dialogue with the CEO without challenging his perception of the situation. Then I ask the group for another illustration, and then another, and then I ask everyone to think of four or five such steps. Not everyone can come up with that many, but most consultant groups can develop a list of twenty or thirty possibilities.

You might try to think of some ideas yourself, and then consult Exhibit 9.2, which lists a number of the versatility ideas various consultants have suggested. Some of them are just some next steps the consultants might take in exploring the project and some of them are actual results-yielding project ideas. It doesn't matter which it is. The idea is to have in mind a menu of next-step possibilities that avoids confrontation with the potential client and keeps the consultant in a collaborative dialogue.

At this point, I summarize the lessons of the case. First, no consultant should show up in a new situation and try to straighten out the client in the first few minutes. Second, consultants need not go into battle formation as soon as they find themselves in disagreement with a client.

The consultant should work with the client to try identifying a few modest next steps that make sense to both of them. They may do no more than sketch some next steps in their exploration (the first half of the list in Exhibit 9.2). Or they may actually be able to visualize some initial rapid-action projects (the second half). To make this approach work for themselves, many consultants will have to abandon the notion that their immediate goal is to design a major project involving a large team of consultants. Instead, their aim will be to offer a menu of next steps and then to narrow them down to a few sure winners.

After we have identified a menu of possible get-started steps and we review these "lessons" with seminar participants, I ask seminar participants to try the role-play interviews again with their Electron Digital "CEOs." In these follow-up role plays, the consultants no longer need to maneuver the client to abandon a stated position, and they become much better listeners. In virtually every case, offering a menu of a few possible first-step projects gets the interview moving out of a selling mode and into a collaboration mode. When the client asks the consultant, "How might you approach a task like this?" the consultant can respond, "I have a few thoughts about how this project might get started. Let me share them, and then you can give me your thoughts, and we can see whether there are others we can think of."

As consultants become more flexible in thinking about project design, they will find that it becomes easier to think of many design variations when confronted with a client's statement of need. The greater the number of variations that consultants think of, the more likely it is that one of them will respond to client readiness and be loaded for success.

Exhibit 9.2. A Versatility Menu for Electron Digital.

A. Some next steps in exploration:
- Interview some sales managers about what they think makes for successful selling in the company.
- Interview the best salespeople to find out what skills or actions they consider to be keys to their success.
- Interview some customers (of Electron Digital and of its competitors) to find out what the major influences are on their buying decisions. What role does the salesperson's performance play in their buying decisions?
- Spend some time in one or two branches, chatting with managers and salespeople about what they think are the keys to success and what would be required to increase sales volume.
- Conduct a formal companywide survey of current sales practices.
- Review sales results across regions to identify differences between better and poorer performers.
- Review the current or most recent programs used to train salespeople and assess their impact on sales results.
- Assess the sales practices of successful competitors, and compare them with Electron Digital's practices.

B. Some first-step rapid cycle projects:
- Select one or two pilot branches and conduct an experiment with the managers of those branches for a few weeks. Let them try out a few ideas about how they could work with salespeople to improve sales, and then see how these ideas work.
- Similarly, collaborate with the sales managers in one or two branches and work directly with salespeople on a sales performance effort.
- Work with a small pilot group of supervisors. Meet with them periodically over a month or two. Have them each create and then try out an experiment in improving sales in the branches. At each session, review progress and identify what is and what isn't working.
- Coach supervisors to work more effectively with a subset of their salespeople.
- Focus on one branch or region, and as an experiment, provide whatever support and training appears needed to increase its sales performance.

When first experimenting with versatility, consultants may have difficulty breaking free of their old patterns. It will take some practice to develop the spontaneity and flexibility needed to devise a variety of approaches to any given client situation. Client managers should also do some versatility preparation. What are some of the different ways you believe consultants might be able to attack the challenge you are trying to deal with? What are the advantages and limitations of each? If both client and consultant have a range of options in mind, then they can lay a foundation for a highly creative exploration.

To make this approach work and to be ready to offer a menu of choices to clients, consultants need to do some homework before their meetings. Telephone interviewing can be the enabler on this.

Telephone Interviewing

Since consultants are very busy when they are actually in a meeting with a client, they can't possibly have much opportunity to brainstorm versatility ideas. It is useful, therefore, if the consultant brings a few versatility ideas to the meeting. That means doing some creative thinking beforehand. To do this in advance, however, the consultant needs to find out enough about the situation. The key often is to conduct a pre-meeting telephone interview. This is most useful when a potential client describes the current situation and goals only in the most general terms in a telephone call setting up an appointment for the meeting.

At that very moment, the consultant should avoid ending the conversation with, "Fine, I'll see you Thursday morning." A consultant who does that won't have any basis for advance thinking and strategizing. Instead, the consultant should add, "If you have a moment, maybe you could say just a bit more about what our agenda will be so that I can do some thinking in advance and be certain to bring along any papers that might be useful." See Exhibit 9.3 for some other useful questions to help set the stage for a successful meeting.

That question often encourages the client to provide further insight. Sometimes a rather extensive conversation can evolve. This permits both

Exhibit 9.3. Eliciting Valuable Information Prior to Client Meeting.

- "Are there particular aspects of this issue that you especially want to explore at the meeting?"
- "Is there some particular information you want to get from me in relation to this issue?"
- "Is there anything you would like me to think about in advance in preparation for our meeting?"
- "Is there anything you would like to send for me to look at in advance so we can make the best use of the meeting time?"

parties to do some more detailed preparation, including the development of a menu of action possibilities. Thus the telephone discussion to agree on a time of meeting can serve to generate some useful data.

Then the consultant can brainstorm versatility ideas in advance with a colleague, if that is possible. If it is not, at least put down on a pad as many ideas as you can think of. You may or may not use any one of these, but they'll give you the confidence that if you listen carefully to the client you'll surely have in your hip pocket or handbag some next-step possibilities that will satisfy both of you.

P.S. An Action Note to Client Managers and Consultants

Clients should always feel cheated when consultants recommend only one approach to dealing with the client's situation. Usually that means that they are pushing "the standard product." Clients should insist on hearing a range of options from a consultant and having the pluses and minuses of each option explored and discussed. Why did the consultants recommend what they recommended? What were the alternatives considered, and why were they rejected by the consultant?

182

Conventional consulting projects get off to the wrong start at the very beginning by asking the consultant to "propose" a plan and having the client "dispose" of the proposal. Yes, this approach works acceptably when the so-called consulting project is really nothing more than outsourced labor. But if better client results and client development are critical goals, the approach won't work. No matter how competently it is done, the deck is stacked for failure, because both parties are into the hand-off mode instead of the collaborative mode. In sharp contrast, high-impact consulting begins as a collaboration. With some open back-and-forth dialogue, careful listening by both parties, and the consideration of a variety of possible get-started projects, both of you—client and consultant—will piece together a mutual contract for your joint project. In contracting this way, both sides move into a partnership mode from the first moment. The contract you develop is not merely a job description for the consultant that will be carried out and handed to the client. It is a joint pledge by both parties to collaborate in producing some measurable results.

P.S. An Action Note to Client Managers

By urging a collaborative exploration in the contracting process, I am not suggesting that clients shouldn't "shop around" in hiring a consultant. When a client is uncertain about which consultant to hire, an initial screening can be performed by requesting an informal introductory memorandum from potential consultants; this serves as a get-acquainted step. Once the client managers have narrowed the field to a few consultants, however, they should shift modes and pursue the process described in this chapter with all the remaining candidates. In that way, the shopping process will permit the right kind of dialogue to take place. It will give client and consultant a chance to engage in some healthy interaction and exploration. Where it appears that the consultants are being asked to spend more time than would be required by the traditional write-a-proposal method, the client should consider offering some modest compensation to the firms engaged in the exploration. To those outraged by this possibility, I say the amount you will spend compensating these groups is trivial compared to the difference in value between the right consulting project and the wrong one.

This same pattern can be followed in government contracting where several consultants may have to be screened before one is hired. But that does not require moving to the sterile "RFP" followed by an equally sterile proposal. The key is to break out of the arms-length interaction that often characterizes competitive bidding and that treats consulting projects as commodities to be purchased rather than as joint efforts to produce results.

Chapter 10

Senior Managers Must Insist That Their People Produce the Results

A senior manager who wants a consultant to help achieve certain results but does not convey to subordinate managers that they—not the consultant—are responsible for achieving those results is apt to be in for a big disappointment. Take this example:

A partner in a well-known consulting firm was asked by the vice president of manufacturing at a hardware company to visit a recently acquired plant. The consultant was told that the plant was a poor performer that needed help in many areas, including productivity, inventory control, employee relations, and quality. When the consultant asked what had been communicated to the plant manager about his impending visit, the vice president replied that he had sent the plant manager a memorandum advising him that the consultants would be coming. It asked that the plant management cooperate, and it assured the plant people that the consultant's fees would be paid as a corporate expense.

When the consultant, with several associates in tow, arrived on the scene, the plant manager and his principal associates readily admitted that theirs was a poor-performing plant. "And why wouldn't it be?" they asked, explaining over the course of several hours how corporate management was actually standing in the way of any improvement. The plant was allocated no funds to replace inadequate equipment. The most difficult products to manufacture were assigned to the plant. They had been forced to cut people whose services were needed. And corporate staff was constantly pulling their people off the job for safety training, quality training, leadership training, and other corporate programs that were not directly related to getting the job done.

When the consultants described their mission, the plant people groaned and insisted that trying to improve the plant without capital and other corporate support would be futile. The consultants said they would convey those feelings to senior management, but in the meantime they would get started on the assignment. They began. But whenever they invited the plant manager or other plant people to collaborate with them in the process, it was always the wrong time, or something else had to be done first, or there was "no sense doing it until corporate management loosens up the purse strings."

Months went by, and the consultants presented a variety of recommendations for improvement to the plant management and the vice president of manufacturing, but very little progress was achieved.

Consultants frequently get trapped into working with clients who don't have a strong drive to make a consulting project succeed. The key to avoiding this trap is be certain that the senior manager communicates clear performance expectations to the lower-level "implementing clients" who will be working with the consultant. This chapter will describe how high-impact consulting encourages senior managers to do this. The traditional consulting process, with its focus on the consultants' studies and consultants' systems design, does not pay much attention to implementation issues early in projects and thus may fail to deal with the need for senior managers to communicate strong expectations to the people who need to be motivated.

Hiring a Consultant Cannot Substitute for Making Demands

What consultant has not been thwarted by a chain of events exactly like those described at the beginning of the chapter? A top-level manager, determined to achieve significant performance improvement, engages a consultant to help. This senior executive describes the challenge and outlines the goals. Once the deal is struck, the consultant, assignment in hand, heads out to work with the lower-level "implementing clients." Out in the field, however, it turns out that the people on the spot have little or no motivation to accomplish the results the consultant has been hired to help them accomplish. And they have lots of reasons to explain why they are not the cause of the problem and why they have little power to ameliorate it. This forces the consultant to choose among three bad options: complaining to the boss about the lack of motivation of the subordinates, ignoring implementation issues, or becoming a missionary and trying to persuade people to implement the recommendations.

In the case described here, the vice president of manufacturing instructed the plant manager to welcome the consultants and cooperate with them, and that's exactly what the plant manager did. He and his associates were very open and hospitable. What the vice president had failed to do was convey to the plant's management that they were required to improve the performance of the plant by certain specific amounts with the help of the consultant. Like many senior managers who hire consultants, the vice president was hoping that the project, if done well, would produce the results. That unrealistic hope allowed him to sidestep the emotional strain of demanding that the plant managers meet higher standards.

The defect lies in a pattern of intraorganizational communication that is all too common when a consultant is involved. Exhibit 10.1 portrays how the strongly motivated senior client conveys the improvement requirement to the consultant but fails to convey it to the implementing clients. Consequently, highly motivated consultants are placed in the position of trying to get the job done with less-than-enthusiastic or even resentful working-level clients.

Consider the following two assignments, which almost any management consultant would be delighted to receive:

Inventory Control

The president of a multidivisional corporation told the director of its technical services department, an internal consulting group, that control over rising inventory and a significant increase in inventory turns were two of the corporation's most important goals. The director was charged

Exhibit 10.1. Misdirected Demands.

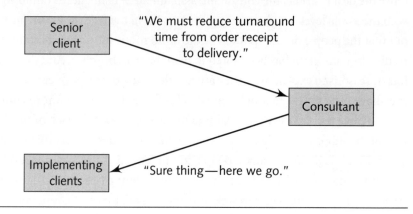

with taking steps to achieve some significant gains during the following year and to bring overall inventory growth under control.

Administrative Productivity

A consulting firm was invited by the CEO of a health maintenance organization to help reengineer its operations to increase productivity and improve service to subscribers. The consultants were given carte blanche to proceed, and department heads throughout the operation were instructed to give their complete support to the effort.

In both of these cases, an executive with the necessary power and position gave a challenging assignment to a consultant. Both assignments addressed important client goals and were broad in scope and concept, and in each case the key executive indicated a real commitment to cooperate with and support the consultant. But what happened when the consultants went forth to accomplish the mission?

Inventory Control

When the consultants began to move into the corporation's divisions and manufacturing plants to work on inventory control, they encountered a mixed reaction. Several divisions pointed to inventory control programs that were already under way. Others said that reduced inventories would mean reduced service. Since this took place during an economic downturn, some divisions implied that keeping their business afloat took precedence over controlling their inventory. There was relatively little interest in working on the goals the consulting group had been charged with achieving.

Administrative Productivity

The consulting team introduced a new work flow design and dozens of sound scheduling and control programs in several of the largest departments. There was, however, little noticeable effect on productivity, quality, or service.

Because the success of consulting projects depends so heavily on the assigned implementing clients' actually implementing some change, it is important that they are motivated to do so. And that means that the senior managers need to convey expectations in ways that stimulate this motivation.

Expectations Profoundly Affect Performance

Over twenty years ago I wrote, "Few managers possess the capacity—or feel compelled—to establish high performance-improvement expectations in ways that elicit results. Indeed, the capacity for such demand making could well be the most universally underdeveloped management skill."[1] All of my observations since then have confirmed this conviction. Every year, a profusion of organizational improvement tools and techniques are adopted by thousands of organizations as hoped-for magic cures. Yet the single most critical difference between high-performing, fast-moving organizations and their less successful counterparts remains the same. It is the capacity (and resolve) of the senior executive to convey to associates that much better results will be required, and to convey that message convincingly.

The differences between excellent demand making and weak demand making are very clear to management observers. Everyone with an interest in organizational performance was impressed by the impact Jack Welch's demand making had on General Electric. When he told his business heads that they would have to be number one or number two in their sector or they would be replaced or have their business sold, there was little doubt in the minds of these executives that they had to respond. Most did respond, and rather successfully. When GE vice chairman Larry Bossidy became CEO of AlliedSignal in the early nineties, he too issued some tough demands to company business heads, and within a year they had produced major advances in profitability, cash flow, and costs.

When senior executives like Welch and Bossidy convey the message that performance must improve, the recipients of the message become highly motivated. One benefit of such an environment is that the value of a consultant's contributions is multiplied significantly. In fact, one of the most dramatic examples I have observed of effective demand making and its impact on the benefits of consulting occurred early in my career in a regulated public utility—an industry not noted for such performance breakthroughs.

When this project took place, Bell Canada's productivity was about average in comparison to all of the regional telephone companies in North America. For a number of years, the business had been growing rapidly, including the number of telephone customers, the number of telephones, and overall telephone use. And right along with these numbers, the size of the workforce was rising equally rapidly.

But then, at a particular moment and rather suddenly, there was a dramatic shift. The total workload continued to rise—even more rapidly than before—but the number of employees actually began to decrease for several years. Within a few years, the company's productivity had improved over 30 percent, ranking Bell Canada among the very best telephone companies in North America. The value of these improvements was more than one-third of the company's net income at that time, a tidy sum.

What produced this gain? Neither new technology nor labor-saving machinery was a significant factor. There was no change in the organization's structure. Productivity-enhancing electronic switching was yet to come. The key to this turnaround was the determination of the new executive vice president for operations, Robert C. Scrivener, who felt that the company could, and therefore should, make substantial productivity gains.

When Scrivener first broached his views to his associates, they thought that Scrivener, as a new executive, was merely out to glean some favorable publicity for himself. They were sure that the idea would blow over fairly soon. They joked about the "impossible" goals he had established.

They asked Scrivener where they could let service deteriorate in order to achieve the cost reductions he had insisted must be made. He shocked them when he told them there would be no degradation of service. Cost improvement would come as a result of doing things better and faster and doing them right the first time, not the second or third time. He had to endure the skepticism, criticism, and even ridicule of his associates. Yet he stuck to his demands and produced dramatic gains.

One of my associates and I were the consultants who supported this effort. As we went to various company units to provide help, at none of them did we receive a brush-off from the implementing clients like the consultants at the hardware manufacturing plant described earlier. Once it had been made clear that they had no choice but to meet Scrivener's expectations, managers throughout Bell Canada welcomed any help in getting it done.

This was my first large-scale application of high-impact consulting. While many organizations have the potential to achieve gains as great as or greater than Bell Canada's, few will ever realize it—because few managers are willing to endure the interpersonal pressures that are required to communicate high performance-improvement expectations compellingly. And the phrase "making demands compellingly" includes much more than telling people they have to do better. It includes getting a work plan from them outlining how they will make the improvements. It includes reviewing progress with them. It includes mentoring them. It includes not letting them off the hook when they seem to be in trouble. When senior managers make such demands for results convincingly, the implementing clients will be much more receptive to the help a consultant can offer (as the people at Bell Canada were). When the demands are clear, the consultant does not have to play the missionary role, conveying the senior client's desires. Instead the consultant is able to concentrate on being a helpful resource to highly motivated implementing clients, as illustrated by Exhibit 10.2.

Exhibit 10.2. Ideally Directed Demands.

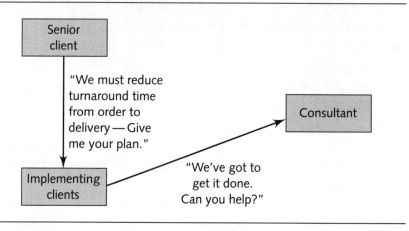

Consulting Projects Can Become Avoidance Mechanisms

The reason that both client managers and consultants need to pay more attention to the demand-making issue in consulting projects is that the problems consultants are called on to solve often are rooted in weak demand making. If this issue is not confronted, the consulting project itself can perpetuate the very problem that gave rise to the need in the first place.

It all begins with understanding that conveying high expectations to people in ways that actually elicit high-performance results is one of the most difficult of all managerial tasks. Demanding better performance of subordinates can be very risky for managers. A manager who sets high targets that associates feel are impossible to achieve is immediately exposed to possible public failure. The fellowship that most managers enjoy with their people can easily be threatened by making tough demands. Also, when managers set high targets they are subject to challenges they do not have to deal with when they select more modest goals: "Hey, boss, what makes you think such goals are achievable?" "How did you pick those numbers?" "Our toughest competitor doesn't have such high targets, and they have more modern facilities." "If you really believe we can achieve the goals you suggested, how about telling us how it can be done?"

High-Impact Consulting

Moreover, by setting very clear and very challenging goals, senior managers put themselves on the line to be judged themselves. Their success will be a matter of public scrutiny. Moreover, once the targets are clearly announced, the senior managers have placed themselves in a position where they will have to deal decisively with people who fail to achieve the targets. Moreover, for managers to demand performance significantly beyond the organization's norms is a conspicuous step, often subjecting them to jokes about their sanity.

Given all these threats to their comfort and security, it is no wonder that only truly exceptional managers dare to demand performance that is well beyond the acceptable standards—and do so in ways that elicit effective responses. Most avoid the confrontations that these tough demands require. One of the most common escape routes from tough demand making by managers who nevertheless want to see improvement is the let's-get-a-consultant-to-look-into-it route. By hiring a consultant and launching endless studies, activities, and preparations senior managers can feel they have taken decisive action without having to change their own behavior.

An example of how that works: Many sales managers would be very uncomfortable informing a group of salespeople that they will be required to deliver 20 percent greater sales in the next quarter than they did in the last. One good way to avoid (or at least delay) the need to make this sort of demand is to focus on the preparations needed before the people can tackle the goal: "We can't expect them to deliver better results, can we, until we provide them with better training? Of course we can't." "We certainly need to improve the compensation system so that when they sell more they'll be properly rewarded. No doubt about that." "They have said repeatedly they need better intelligence on the competition, so we better make sure we have that available." And on and on. It is so much easier psychologically for managers to undertake all these preparations, gearing up, and alignment activities than to get on with the job of making improvements happen.

Consultants are the frequent unwitting co-conspirators in this avoidance game. When hired to do so most are delighted to give client managers plenty of studies, programs, training, and other preparatory activities that allow the managers to delay (or completely avoid) making sharp demands.

Ironically, after launching such a study, instead of feeling guilty for having delayed real progress, senior managers typically congratulate themselves for having taken decisive action. After all, they rationalize, knowledgeable and experienced consultants are digging into the facts, and they will undoubtedly come up with the right answers.

P.S. An Action Note to Consultants: Helping Managers Sharpen Demand Making

Most consultants seduced into the role of substituting for tough demand making probably do not see that they are being used as the instruments of delay and avoidance. As they see it, they are providing vital studies and creating essential tools that will be the foundation for progress. But in fact they may be providing, however unintentionally, the mechanisms of managerial avoidance. In fact, I believe that one of the attractions of conventional long-cycle-time, labor-intensive consulting is that it permits managers to delay, sometimes indefinitely, the task of confronting their people with the need to get moving, at once, toward better performance.

It would be impossible to estimate the billions of dollars that are wasted each year on consulting projects whose success requires a high level of commitment and effort from the members of an organization but which don't go anyplace because the senior officers failed to make the necessary demands in a way that would evoke such commitment and effort.

High-impact consulting requires consultants and managers to discuss what demands can reasonably be made and sustained, and to design every project so that there is a good match between the senior client's demands and the project's requirements. This process will not only raise the odds of success considerably, it will ensure that success on early projects will increase senior management's ability to make demands for subsequent projects.

An important contribution clients should expect from their consultants is help in expanding their own ability to convey demands. Then, as the initial results-focused projects yield their tangible results, the client managers' confidence in their ability to sharpen and strengthen demand making skill should increase continuously.

There are a number of ways consultants can help clients sharpen their demands during the launching of a new project, even if those clients are not fully ready to examine their demand-making strengths and shortcomings (see Exhibit 10.3). The challenge is to make the steps as easy and workable as possible, so both client and consultant can select and modify the approaches that meet the unique needs of each situation. Exhibit 10.3 gives a list of ways consultants can help clients in this area.

- *Work together on formulating and clarifying project requirements.* Interview the senior client about the project. Ask probing questions to help define what to convey to the implementing clients in terms of information, explanations, and demands in order to be clear about what is expected. Draft what you hear into a working paper to share with the client.

Then, before the project goals are finally defined, bring together the senior client and the implementing clients to discuss what must be accomplished in the project. Keep notes and summarize the meeting's conclusions in writing.

During the process, conduct some informal explorations with various project participants to get their impressions of the possibilities for achieving the project goals. Share these insights with the senior client, and discuss their implications for selecting and conveying demands.

Finally, work with the client to spell out in the clearest terms possible what the project's goals are to be and begin to consider how these are to be conveyed to the implementing clients.

Exhibit 10.3. Helping Clients Sharpen Project Demands.

---

1. Work together on formulating and clarifying project requirements.
2. Work together to determine how to communicate demands clearly.
3. Help the implementing clients as they begin to respond to the senior client's demands.
4. Develop a process for following up on the senior client's demands.

• *Work together to determine how to communicate demands clearly.* Once the goals of the project are defined, help the senior client clarify what the implementing clients are to accomplish, and help draft an assignment memorandum from the senior client to the implementing clients that communicates these demands. Then review and edit the memo with the senior client.

Help the senior client frame the demands in terms of a range of possible goals; this allows the implementing clients to select, from within that range, the specific first project they feel best about attacking.

Help the senior client clarify the exact responsibilities of various implementing clients.

Decide with the senior client whether it would be better to bring all the key people together and convey expectations to the entire group or to brief a few people first. Also, discuss and agree on when and how to pass on the written version of the assignment.

• *Help the implementing clients as they begin to respond to the senior client's demands.* Arrange a meeting with the responsible people to discuss the implications of the senior client's demands.

Help the implementing clients create a plan to fulfill the project's requirements. Begin to lay out the necessary action steps, and decide how to track and report on progress to the senior client. Define the roles of both client and consultant personnel as this plan is created.

Conduct a workshop to help the implementing clients brainstorm possible solutions and to provide consultant input on related skills (process redesign, for example).

• *Develop a process for following up on the senior client's demands.* Help the senior client decide on the frequency and form of progress reports to be required from the implementing clients.

Help the team to prepare for progress review meetings, to run them, and to analyze what needs to be changed in the way the project is being run.

As with the other checklists presented in this book, neither clients nor consultants should feel burdened or limited by the foregoing list. It is simply a way to stimulate your thinking. The greatest value will accrue as managers and their consultants discuss these issues together and modify the ideas to suit their unique situations.

Consultants need to be aware of the fact that this may be a very sensitive area for senior managers. Some managers are open to feedback on their demand-making capabilities, but many others would feel threatened or attacked if a consultant were to imply that they have shortcomings in this area. Thus, though consultants need to focus on the issue of managerial demands, they also need to be somewhat subtle in helping managers deal with it. Exhibit 10.4, at the end of this chapter, provides a questionnaire for senior managers to use in assessing their demand-making characteristics. It could be used as the basis for opening a dialogue between clients and consultants on the subject.

P.S. An Action Note to Client Managers: Demanding Results Compellingly

As a senior manager, if you ask a consultant to work with your people to achieve an objective but fail to make your expectations clear to the implementing clients in your organization, you force your consultant to become a missionary, as shown in Exhibit 10.1. By contrast, if you commit yourself to achieving measurable results and ask your people to commit themselves too, you effectively block off the consulting study escape route. This does not mean that you will not ask the consultants to do in-depth studies. Nor does it diminish the value and importance of the unique technical inputs consultants can make. What it means is that those inputs will be made in a sharply results-oriented context.

This means that on every consulting project, the senior executive must demand from the implementing clients the kind of tangible, measurable results described in Chapter Four:

- "With the consultant's aid, lay out a plan for increasing inventory turns by 20 percent within three months, and then carry out the plan and achieve those results."

- "Reduce heat losses from furnace #16 by 15 percent by June 30, using whatever help is needed from the consultant."

In high-impact consulting, the focus on achieving some measure of tangible results right from the beginning requires senior managers to convey to those who must get the job done the expectation that they will produce specific bottom-line results fairly quickly. The message to the implementing clients from their boss is neither to make the consultants feel welcome nor to cooperate with them; it is to produce some measurable results with their help.

Early in the contracting process, especially in a new relationship, a consultant needs to assess the ability and willingness of the senior client to clarify the essential demands. This is a key dimension of readiness testing. Sometimes consultants will discover that the implementing clients are willing to commit themselves to goals beyond what their senior manager would require of them. If so, go with those. If not, then it is risky to design a project with goals that go much beyond what their superiors are ready to expect and demand. Thus one cardinal consulting rule should be to tailor consulting projects around the demands the client is ready to make and pursue.

For managers who would like to examine their demand-making patterns, Exhibit 10.4 at the end of the chapter provides a self-assessment questionnaire. After you have filled it out, you might want to talk over the results frankly with your consultant as part of shaping any project you might be working on.

In any event, the aim is to make sure that by one means or another the senior client, not the consultant, communicates a demand for results to the implementing clients in your organization. It should not be left to the consultant to play the role of communicator ("I know your boss really wants to see this project succeed") or missionary ("This project could save your division several hundred thousand dollars a year"). The ideal relationship between the consultant, the senior clients, and the implementing clients is the one portrayed in Exhibit 10.2.

This relationship was demonstrated quite clearly in the Vitrine Products case, described in Chapter Five. Joe McCray, the manufacturing vice president, asked his consultant to help the furnace superintendent increase furnace efficiency by a significant amount. It was only when the consultant encouraged McCray to convey clearly to the furnace superintendent what he expected in the way of performance improvements that the furnace superintendent became ready to accept help.

Exhibit 10.4. Demanding Better Results and Getting Them: A Self-Assessment Exercise for Senior Managers.

Think of one or two recent situations when you asked your people to accomplish something and you were disappointed by the results. Maybe they had a "good explanation" for why it didn't get done; maybe they thought they had responded but really hadn't. Keep these experiences in mind as you fill out the following questionnaire. Use your own definitions of "sometimes" and "too often."

Selecting and Defining Goals

Expectations need to be clearly defined and focused. Accountability must be assigned. There should be a very few top-priority goals. Do you ever do the following?

	Never	Sometimes	Too Often
1. Establish too many goals?			
2. Define expectations in vague or unmeasurable terms?			
3. Set target dates too far in the future?			
4. Fail to clearly assign accountability for results?			
5. Fail to check to make sure the recipient's view of the goal matches your view of the goal?			

Negotiating Expectations

Getting people to fully commit to performance targets requires toughness, resiliency, faith, and perseverance. Do you find yourself adopting any of these patterns?

(Continued)

Exhibit 10.4. Continued.

	Never	Sometimes	Too Often
1. When my people insist "it can't be done," I ease the goals or give them more time.			
2. I accept goal trade-offs ("Sure, boss, I can accomplish goal A, but you'll have to forget about goal B").			
3. I accept vague agreement ("Sure boss, I'll give it a try").			
4. I signal that the goal should be achieved "if possible" (versus saying "it must be achieved").			
5. I hear myself offering inducements to get people to do what they should be doing anyhow.			

Making Sure Goals Are Actually Achieved

It is necessary to have a work plan, with a timetable, and to review progress regularly. Do any of these statements ring true?

	Never	Sometimes	Too Often
1. I don't insist on written work plans that state how people will achieve their goals.			
2. I do not review progress regularly. Mainly I do it when we get near the deadline or when I feel something's going wrong.			
3. My people don't really believe that there are significant consequences for success or failure.			
4. I do not forcefully confront people when projects go astray.			

Mastering Your Doubts About Asking for Higher Performance

When people don't see how to deliver greater results, they may resist. You need to be sympathetic but also firm in your insistence that it be done. Do you find yourself acting out any of these statements?

	Never	Sometimes	Too Often
1. I feel very uncomfortable asking people who seem stretched to do even more.			
2. Unless I can actually see how a result can be accomplished, I hesitate to ask people to achieve it.			
3. I worry that people will quit and go to a competitor.			
4. I feel guilty about making my people work under pressure, and so I do some of the work for them.			

Build Communication Bridges and Overcome Anxiety

A s Sigmund Freud described many years ago, certain situations in life create fear and discomfort for no "logical" reason. Starting from earliest childhood, each person develops unique susceptibility to this discomfort, which is known as anxiety.

The symptoms of anxiety are easiest to observe in extreme cases. We all know people who are afraid to fly or who freeze up while taking examinations or who sweat profusely when standing before an audience. Those are the extremes, but anxieties afflict us all. The events that spark anxiety in each of us, and our unique methods for coping with or avoiding anxiety, have a profound effect on our work lives, even though we may not be conscious of how it happens.

In this chapter I discuss the way anxiety patterns, anxiety avoidance, and the techniques clients and consultants employ to minimize anxiety all influence the consulting relationship. Anxiety avoidance can trap clients and consultants into perpetuating some of the least successful patterns of conventional consulting.

At this point let me simply note the fact that when clients try to minimize their anxiety, it often is counterproductive to the project. For example, they may not be fully open about problems or defects that might make them appear deficient. They may not take on project tasks and roles unless they are certain of success. In short, the more anxiety, the more avoidance behavior to minimize it, and the greater the negative impact on the project.

Anxiety in the Client

Many aspects of client-consultant relationships provoke anxiety. When managers engage consultants, they turn over important responsibilities to people who are often virtually unknown. Such dependence on people not under the manager's direct control, especially if they are strangers, is a natural anxiety arouser. This anxiety can be exacerbated by the fact that the very act of engaging a consultant—even an internal consultant—can be perceived by fellow managers as a sign of weakness.

The actual arrival of a consulting team can be a very unnerving experience for managers. Coteries of bright young people descend on the organization with a license to wander and probe. They are certain to discover what is not working well. They are programmed to uncover shortcomings in the way managers have been doing their jobs. They will unearth matters that haven't been attended to but should have been. They will shine the spotlight on problems that have been kept in the shadows. All these possibilities are anxiety arousers.

Further, when the time comes for the consultants to make their recommendations, they may suggest changes that could disrupt comfortable working habits. They may tip the balance in strategic disputes in favor of one side or another. They may make recommendations that will require more time and energy to implement than is available. Client managers will have to follow their recommendations or defend their choice not to. Implementing the consultants' recommendations may require skills and knowledge not abundant among client staff. Individual members of the organization may fear that the consultants will recommend steps that diminish their role or downplay their skills and background.

The consultants may present material with recondite charts and graphs that client people don't fully understand. The consultants' conversations may be sprinkled with unfamiliar technical terms that suggest deep knowledge of the subject under discussion. They will refer to the marvelous things other companies are doing that far surpass what the client organization is doing. They focus on weaknesses and may even convey a hint of disdain when they ask, "You mean your people haven't yet—?"

Also, when consulting reports point to weaknesses in the organization or suggest realignment of tasks, individual managers can feel that the consultants are singling them out. Consultants may, for example, preface their criticism with slightly condescending remarks like, "Considering the effort that management has been making to overcome their failure to enter this market soon enough, they should not be criticized unduly for. . . ." And when there is criticism, it is easy for client managers to feel that the consultants are taking direct aim at them. They may brood about the possibility that the consultants are conveying criticisms about them to their superiors or to the board of directors.

Thus there are many ways by which consultants, without even trying, can arouse all sorts of anxiety in their clients.

Anxiety in the Consultant

It isn't just clients who are affected by anxiety. Because consultants work on the client's premises, away from their own cozy offices; because they are dealing with issues of great significance to the client; because they must deal with conflicting views among different client people and between themselves and their clients; and because their success often depends on the cooperation of people over whom they have no control, management consultants are more subject to anxiety than many other professionals.

In addition, for each consultant there are unique situations that can trigger discomfort. For some it is making public presentations. For others it is confronting what they think of as "difficult" clients. For still others it is being uncertain of the direction to take in ambiguous situations, or meeting with clients who are very powerful or very affluent, or dealing with clients who refuse to give them sufficient time or help, or coping with clients who get angry or criticize the consulting work, and so forth. For many consultants, the simple act of coming together with a client—any client—can trigger some degree of uneasiness. This anxiety is multiplied in consultants who feel compelled to perpetuate the illusion of omniscience and feel that they must always be prepared to present a brief lecture at any moment, no matter what subject is raised.

Some consultants are made uneasy by the human foibles they discover in client organizations: managers not performing as they should, systems not working properly, groups not collaborating, client people not giving straight answers to the consultant. The consultant thinks, "How will I ever be able to make something constructive happen here?"

For example, in the Electron Digital consultant teaching case (described in Chapter Nine), the CEO asks the consultant for a training program that appears to be the wrong solution. That situation arouses anxiety in almost every consultant who role-plays opposite the CEO. When trapped in such a situation, the consultant's anxiety can trigger subtle expressions of resentment or anger about a client's perceived inadequacies. Those messages, however subtle, simply make the client more uneasy, giving rise to behavior that becomes the part of a mutually reinforcing process that undermines progress.

Clients who feel hostile toward consultants have a variety of techniques for putting consultants in their place. Jokes about consultants, mostly very bad and very old, are repeated—jokes about fees, jokes about bringing the same solution to different clients, jokes about borrowing the client's watch to tell the client the right time. Even though such remarks may stem from clients' own anxieties, they can easily trigger anxiety and defensiveness in consultants.

Storm Warnings: Anxiety at Work

Often behavior on the part of consultants—and client managers—that appears bizarre to others is nothing more than the reaction to intense feelings of anxiety. Here are a few illustrations to help consultants (and their clients) better understand why they behave as they do.

- *Leaping to answers.* When clients raise a question, consultants want to answer—and a factual answer is often the right response. Equally often, however, a question is simply the client's way of beginning a discussion; the client is not really interested in hearing the consultant's view. The appropriate response in those cases may be a moment of silence, or to ask for the client's view, or to offer a menu of possible answers. But anxiety drives many consultants to provide definitive answers almost automatically, as if the failure to provide one will demonstrate ignorance of the subject.

- *Compulsive talking.* There are consultants who tend toward compulsive talking. Some, in fact, become very impatient when the client wants to do the talking. These consultants allow the client to talk for a while just to be polite, but they jump in as soon as they can with what they consider to be the real stuff, their own explanations and illuminations.

Clients also may express anxiety by talking continuously. Some years ago in beginning a new assignment I met and interviewed the CEO of a large metropolitan hospital. He said he wanted me to have a good understanding of the situation and began to provide the details. When after two hours he had to leave for another meeting, we made an appointment to continue. After four such meetings, I realized he would never end the interview. It was as if he had an unconscious conviction that nothing bad could happen to him as long as he held the floor and kept talking.

- *Having a cast-iron front.* Many consultants feel it is important to appear self-assured and knowledgeable. For example, they are reluctant to discuss clearly the limits of their own competence. They will almost never say, "I am not sure" or "I'll want to look that up." Clients can also be the same way. They want to appear to know their business thoroughly, and they feel uncomfortable admitting a lack of knowledge or decisiveness. This defensive stance is so common that it is startling to witness exceptions to it. I still recall one client, who was then chief financial officer of a major commercial airline, describing to me his three key goals at our first meeting twenty years ago. In contrast to the way 99 percent of senior managers behave, he ended the story with a broad smile and this comment: "There's only one trouble, Bob. I don't yet know how the hell to accomplish them."

- *Using jargon and other forms of one-upmanship.* Consultants who feel a bit uneasy often seek reassurance by using jargon and technical language that the client is apt not to understand. Clients do the same thing by referring to their own operations in ways that an outsider couldn't possibly understand. Both clients and consultants can use subtle and not-so-subtle put-downs to gain some sort of upper hand in the psychological duel that characterizes much client-consultant interaction.

Thus in hundreds of ways, minor and major, all sorts of anxiety-stimulated barriers get in the way of real communication and mutual understanding between clients and consultants. Ironically, one of the appeals of conventional consulting is that its patterns tend to shield the parties from many of these sources of anxiety, but only at the price of having projects carried out with large gaps in mutual understanding. It's worth the time to examine those dynamics further, because clients pay much too big a price for this psychological protection.

Buffering Anxiety at a High Cost

If one were to design a method of consulting with the major objective of minimizing anxiety by both client and consultant, the method would undoubtedly be very similar to the conventional consulting model. The conventional model's five frequently fatal flaws do permit the parties to minimize anxiety—but at a very high cost.

Flaw #1. *Defining projects in terms of consultant expertise or products.* Conventional projects are usually defined by the consultant's expert inputs and technical products, so discourse tends to focus on technical or abstract discussion of the consultant's systems and procedures and how the consultant will do the study. Neither client nor consultant has to make any commitments about actual bottom-line achievements. The consultants are happy to delegate the task of achieving results to the client once the "real work" of the project is over.

Clients can also avoid making any clear commitments to take action. Once the consultants begin their work, client managers can turn their attention to other matters until the consultant delivers the recommendations. Then, if they choose not to take action, they can always call the project a success anyhow because they "got some valuable new insights about the business." Or they can blame the failure to achieve the project's goals on the consultant's shortcomings.

Both clients and consultants may feel safer discussing the consultant's research findings and new systems and recommendations than agreeing on a measurable goal and making a public commitment that they will achieve it. So the focus on consultant technology and products rather than client results clearly protects both parties from anxiety.

Flaw #2. *Determining project scope based on the subject to be studied, not on client readiness.* In conventional consulting, project scope is based not on what the client can reasonably expect to accomplish but on the kind of technical analysis that the consultant believes should be done. Consultants define projects in terms of the way they view those subjects. So the dialogue tends to focus on factual issues: "How many days of inventory do you carry?" "What sort of delivery times do you promise to customers?" In this mode, neither client nor consultant venture into important but potentially anxiety-arousing territory: "Do your associates share your enthusiasm for this project?" "What have you been doing about this problem until now?" "Do you think you'll be able to get the cooperation of your CEO and the other functions to make these changes?"

As soon as the parties move into an exploration of client readiness, all sorts of sensitive social, psychological, and political issues surface. No wonder this subject is avoided more often than confronted.

Flaw #3. *Aiming for one big solution.* As discussed earlier, when consultants are new to a situation, it feels very risky to speculate about possible directions and to launch any concrete action. They want to dig and analyze and then dig some more until they "have all the data." By gathering all the data, they are convinced, they will avoid wrong moves or recommendations that later turn out to be ill-founded. Many client managers feel the same way. That's why the large, formulaic study mode is so reassuring to both client and consultant.

Usually the consultant firm already has on hand a readily available template that lays out the steps. This serves to avoid the anxiety that might be aroused in either their clients or themselves by having to explore creative new possibilities for the project.

More structure of the assignment means more control for the consultant, since the template guides and constrains the client's behavior as well as the consultant's. So structured routines and templates that can be modified slightly for each new assignment are an important source of psychological security for consultants. For large firms, these standardized models serve the additional purpose of permitting people to move from job to job and still follow the prescribed procedures.

Finally, another costly benefit of the large-scale project is that it takes a long time. That means that both client and consultant will not have to face up to decisions, action, and implementation for a long time. No matter how urgent the project, this postponement can be a relief to both parties.

Flaw #4. *Dividing responsibilities sharply.* The closer consultants get to their clients, the more exposed both may feel. When they work in close collaboration, their own weaknesses and human frailties may be revealed. Consultants are not nearly as comfortable "thinking out loud" in the presence of clients as they are doing their homework in private and then making well-rehearsed presentations to management.

No wonder people feel safe with the conventional mode of handing responsibility back and forth. There is much less need for open communication in this mode than in a partnership mode. The hand-offs permit consultants to keep their own work separate from the client's activities. The consultants can exercise control over their work, the staffing of assignments, and their work schedule. They do not have to let client people work closely with them, tune in to their thinking, and try to influence the course of events.

The hand-off mode is safe for clients as well. They can sit back in a somewhat detached manner, make whatever contributions they care to make, and then evaluate the consultants' efforts.

Flaw #5. *Making labor-intensive use of consultants.* Finally, conventional consulting makes labor-intensive use of consultants. It is expected that the consultant's team will perform the work and then turn over a finished product to the client. Since the client's people are busy and the consultant is happy to staff up for the job, both are content with the arrangement. In fact, for many clients, the thought that an army of consultants is attacking the problem at very great expense provides reassurance that the job will be done well.

Working Past Anxiety

There is no doubt that these conventional consulting work patterns provide the structure, distance, academic focus, and avoidance of commitment to results that permit both clients and consultants to minimize their anxiety. But all this safety is earned at a high price: ineffectiveness. High-impact consulting, on the other hand, requires both consultants and clients to come out into the open and take some risks. But the risks are minimal, and the potential benefits are enormous. For those who want to try it, the next sections outline some techniques for breaking through the communication and anxiety barriers described here. I also suggest some ways clients and consultants can gain insight into their own counterproductive anxiety-avoidance behavior. There is no doubt that greater awareness of some of these dynamics will help both parties determine how they can work together more effectively. They will be able to experiment with communicating more openly with each other, and they will feel freer to experiment with results-driven approaches.

Building Communication Bridges

High-impact consulting requires a high level of interaction between client and consultant. To create high-performance client-consultant partnerships that accelerate the pace of change, it is essential that the partners have the best possible understanding of each other. Each of the five major shifts from labor-intensive to high-leverage consulting requires, encourages, and reinforces good communication between clients and consultants.

Here are some of the challenges posed by high-impact consulting in terms of client-consultant communication:

- The need to define the project, right up front, in terms of specific client goals and results to be achieved requires some very thoughtful collaboration right at the beginning. To maximize the likelihood of success, clients and consultants need to explore openly and freely what they might actually accomplish. They need to develop a good mutual understanding of what the goals should be and how much they should shoot for.

- The need to base the scope of each project on client readiness means that the consultant can not move forward without some pretty accurate understanding of the client situation. The client and consultant must be able to determine together what the client is likely to be able to implement successfully. This requires some careful discussion of what might be possible, what would not work, where is the best place to start, who are the people most likely to produce success, and what are the likely impediments. Rapid-cycle projects that can be accomplished readily need to be created and designed.

- The aim of leveraging the consultant's effort by having client people play a significant role requires some creative design work. Consultants have to be very sensitive about how to best encourage client people to take initiatives. Both parties need to be able to freely explore where the consultant's inputs are needed and where they are not. The goal is to avoid too much consulting, but not to go to the other extreme of too little consulting. Both parties have to learn to communicate with each other very effectively to make this happen.

Expanding the Consultant's Range of Interaction

It is clear that high-impact consulting requires new levels of communication between clients and consultants, but how are these new levels to be reached? Few consultants have received much training in establishing a dialogue with clients, and most do not have any sense of how to improve communication.

Two processes go a long way toward achieving this goal. The first is for both client managers and consultants to take an accurate look at how their own anxiety patterns may be affecting their collaboration. The way to do this is to complete the appropriate column of the questionnaire in Exhibit 11.2, "Anxiety Self-diagnosis," at the end of the chapter. There is one set of questions for consultants and one for clients. The second is for consultants to spend some dedicated time to examining the nature of their interactions with clients, and consider the possibilities for improvement.

The questionnaire in Exhibit 11.2, based on one first published in the *Journal of Management Consulting,* offers both clients and consultants a unique opportunity to examine how anxiety may be undermining the effectiveness of their collaborations. The greatest benefits will accrue if clients and consultants either fill it out together or share their answers after they have filled it out.[1] My colleagues and I have worked with hundreds of consultants and clients who have filled out this questionnaire. Every one of them has discovered that some of the descriptions match their behavior. You will too. Don't let the uneasiness of anticipation keep you from doing it. Virtually every one of the people who has gone through the questionnaire is happy to have done so, and pleased with the insights that were gleaned from the exercise.

As to the modes of interaction with clients, consultants assume that working with clients is just a matter of talking to them—and the consultants have been practicing *that* all their lives. Most consultants can, in fact, appear to do pretty well at carrying on a dialogue with clients and prospective clients. However, after considerable observation on the matter, I have discovered that most of what consultants say to or ask their clients tends to fall into three fairly narrow categories:

1. They ask for information.

   "Does the average sales per salesperson vary much from region to region?"

   "Does your integrated system permit you to produce your monthly statements more quickly?"

   "How do warehousemen record the removal of an item from inventory?"

   "Has the profile of your major customers shifted much in the past few years?"

2. They react to the information and ask for more information.

"So it takes over twelve months on average to bring out a new product? Do you have a chart that shows the process and about how long each step usually takes?"

"You have fourteen different information systems at headquarters and in the various subsidiaries. How compatible are these systems with each other?"

"Eliminating sales calls to your smaller customers has not improved profitability. Where do the extra costs come from?"

3. They tell and sell.

"We think that an analysis of the shifts taking place in the business structure and goals of your key customers would provide the basis for deciding on a new strategy for your key product groups."

"There is no doubt that the product-oriented organization structure you now have is going to become obsolete as technology diminishes the price spread between plain vanilla and gold-plated products."

"If we were to lay out the entire process from the time an order is called in until the product is shipped and you get paid, we could begin to see what steps can be eliminated and how the process can be speeded up, and then—"

Ninety percent or more of what conventional consultants say to clients falls into one of these three "standard interaction modes." The three modes are all necessary, but they represent only a small part of the communication repertoire that consultants require. These three modes keep the conversation in the territory of "just the facts," as Sergeant Joe Friday would say. This tends to be nonthreatening territory, but it also makes it impossible to break through the communication walls between clients and consultants.

To develop the kind of communication needed to enable clients and consultants to become collaborative partners, the three standard modes of consulting interactions need to be augmented.

High-Impact Consulting

Bridge-Building Modes of Communication

There are a number of modes of client-consultant communication that help to establish connections between the parties. These "bridge-building" modes of communication go beyond the facts and create new levels of understanding. Unlike the three standard modes, they help to build understanding between client and consultant. There are five such interventions. They are powerful modes, but relatively few consultants use any of them with any frequency.

• *Eliciting clients' views and perspective on the issues.* To work in a partnership mode, the consultant needs to understand not only the information clients can provide but also the views and perspectives of the client people on that information. The consultant needs to ask the client to share personal views of the situation: "What are some of the solutions or approaches you have thought about?" "What are your thoughts about how each of them might contribute to what you are trying to achieve here?" "How do you think the division got into such a situation?"

• *Helping clients think out loud.* In a partnership, both parties participate in the thinking process. So if the issue is one that the client does not have much confidence about addressing, the consultant needs to encourage the client to think out loud: "When you consider the various courses of action that are possible, describe the ones that appeal most to you. Don't be constrained at this moment by how workable they seem to be." "How might each of them play out?" "Describe how each of these approaches might contribute to or interfere with some of the other major programs you have under way here."

• *Summarizing the client's views and testing the consultant's understanding of them.* To the high-leverage consultant, it is vital to understand the client's perspective. Consultants should take steps during the course of meetings to make sure there is real understanding. One way to do this is to repeat, in their own words, what they have heard the client say. This tests how well the consultant has been hearing what the client was conveying. It also gives the client a chance to hear what message was received by the consultant—and to amend the picture. So in a dialogue with a client, the consultant might say things like, "What I heard you say is. . . ." or "So you feel that. . . ." In addition, consultants should periodically test their understanding of what the client has said: "Let me see if I can summarize the key points you've been making. . . ." "Am I correct in understanding that you believe the drop in sales can be explained by. . . ."

• *Reacting to how the client feels about an issue as well as to its business implications.* The people engaged in a consulting collaboration are human beings, with feelings, likes and dislikes, fear and anger, joy and gratification. These feelings influence both consultant and client behavior. If strong bonds of communication are to be built, the parties will have to recognize and discuss some of these feelings. So, in addition to reacting to the facts and the numbers, the consultant can ask clients how they feel about an issue under discussion and they can recognize client feelings that have been expressed: "You sound pretty angry that. . . ." "I detect some pride in what you were able to accomplish in that new product release." "You sound very disappointed that. . . ." Consultants should encourage their clients to express their views about the consultants and the project.

• *Allowing the client to pause and reflect on the topic.* Sometimes it is useful to keep quiet for ten or fifteen seconds and let the client think. Many consultants have trouble with this one. They seem to feel that the valuable part of their discussions with clients is when they are expounding on the subject at hand. Some consultants get so preoccupied with getting their ideas across to their client that they almost hurry the client to finish talking so they can get to what they want to tell the client. Competing with the client in this way simply arouses anxiety, whereas allowing some silence permits the conversation to be more thoughtful.

These bridge-building modes are summarized in Exhibit 11.1.

To develop your own perspective on the issues discussed in this chapter, try carefully observing the next few meetings you witness between consultants and clients or potential clients. You'll be able to verify for yourself my assertion that 90 percent or more of the consultant's comments conform to the three "standard categories" of asking for information, reacting

Exhibit 11.1. Bridge-Building Modes of Communication.

1. Eliciting clients' views and perspective on the issues
2. Helping clients think out loud
3. Summarizing the client's views and testing the consultant's understanding of them
4. Reacting to how the client feels about an issue as well as to its business implications
5. Allowing the client to pause and reflect on the topic

to it, and telling and selling. You'll see very little of the five bridge-building modes of communication.

As mentioned earlier, because most consultants have engaged in conversation all their lives, they assume that they are already well practiced in this "consulting tool" of conversing with the client. In fact, for most consultants who have not been practicing in a high-leverage mode, their conversational patterns may elicit only a fraction of the information needed to design a successful project. They may not be good at creating a basis for a fruitful partnership with the client. To make the shift, consultants might try selecting just one of the five bridge-building modes to focus on. Then practice it deliberately in the next conversation with a client. When you have mastered one, try the next. Gradually you can develop new patterns that work best for you.

Overcoming Communication Barriers

Two other techniques can help consultants improve their communication with clients.

- *Help clients develop greater insight into their own work patterns.* One valuable contribution consultants can make is to provide feedback to clients about issues that, while not in the official project contract, are nevertheless significant potential contributors to the client organization's effectiveness.

Consultants can almost always, for example, see in the style and work modes of the key managers they are working with behaviors that appear to be self-defeating. What should they do? If they blurt out their views, they risk alienating the client. If they hold back, they fail to provide uniquely valuable data.

The key is to develop some ways to share such insights on a low-risk basis. The easiest way to take the risk out of it is to ask clients whether they would be interested in hearing the feedback: "After hearing your people talk about it, I have some observations about how they view the division's new goals. I'd be pleased to share them with you when you have a few minutes." Client managers will rarely come right out and say, "No, I don't give a damn about how they feel." But if they are truly interested in the feedback, they will make it their business to ask you for it. If they don't really want to hear it, they will let the matter drop. Be guided by this behavior. If they do drop it, you may wish to try again later. Sometimes it takes a few tries.

• *Maintain an open dialogue about consultant contributions.* Gunn Partners, a firm dedicated to high-leverage consulting, makes it a point to review weekly or even more frequently with the client the status of the consulting relationship and assess its value. In this way, work is never carried out merely because it was previously agreed to in the contract or because the consultant thinks it is a good idea. The client must continuously manage the relationship to make sure both parties are doing their best and the investment in consulting is being rewarded.

Many consultants feel threatened by discussions about the value of their work and therefore avoid them. In such cases, unfortunately, clients who might have concerns about a project hesitate to voice them until they are ready to explode, because they quickly recognize that their consultants are really not interested in feedback. If consultants want to stay in touch with how their clients feel about a project, they have to make it easy for clients to let them know.

The Gunn firm is more diligent than most about client feedback on the consulting contribution. For those who want to do more of this, the progress assessment work sessions discussed in Chapter Seven offer excellent opportunities for frank dialogue on how the collaboration is working and how it could work better.

Again, the more the client and consultant can share about how they perceive what is happening and how they feel about it, the more likely that the issues that need to be addressed will be addressed.

P.S. Action Note for Both Client Managers and Consultants: Establishing Human Contact

To produce the most valuable results from their collaboration, clients and consultants need to gradually shift from the structured roles and formalized mechanics of conventional consulting and begin communicating with each other in a much more human fashion.

Both parties need to address the fact that a formal meeting in which the consultant presents so much material that the client cannot absorb it or presents it in a way that frustrates client understanding and inhibits client participation is not a communication process. It is anti-communication.

Consultants will have to experiment with portraying themselves in a manner aimed less at maintaining an image and more at forging a partnership. They will have to admit the limits of their knowledge. They will have to accept the human and therefore somewhat flawed condition of every organization they deal with, including their own. And they will have to search more diligently for (and show more respect for) the knowledge, wisdom, and experience that resides in their clients' organizations. As clients become more comfortable with their consultants, they should be able to open up about what is and isn't working. This will help their consultants focus on the right issues.

Indeed, the ability to overcome the handicaps of anxiety avoidance and to learn to communicate increasingly well is another developmental dimension of the client-consultant adventure. It will not only be more productive and rewarding, it will be much more pleasant.

Exhibit 11.2. Anxiety Self-Diagnosis for Clients and Consultants.

Client Managers: Respond to issues in this column	Never or Hardly Ever	Often or Too Often	Consultants: Respond to issues in this column

To what extent do you pattern your behavior in interactions so as to minimize anxiety?

	Never or Hardly Ever	Often or Too Often	
1. I keep the conversation to areas I am comfortable with and avoid discussion of areas in which my expertise may be shaky.	☐	☐	1. I keep the conversation to areas I am comfortable with and avoid discussion of areas in which my expertise may be shaky.
2. I prefer to work with consultants who are not critical and are easy to work with.	☐	☐	2. I tend to pay more attention to client people who are friendly than to those who are hostile or resistant.
3. I tend to give consultants my views quite strongly on subjects I feel strongly about—even if I don't have strong evidence to back me up.	☐	☐	3. I tend to respond to client questions too quickly with direct answers, rather than with speculation, questions, probes, or silence.
4. I find myself talking more than I'd like, when I should be drawing out the consultant's views.	☐	☐	4. I probably talk too much and may be too impatient to listen carefully to the client.
5. I hesitate to reveal "dirty linen" to consultants. I don't want them to be able to use it against us.	☐	☐	5. I'm not free enough to discuss the limits to my range of expertise, knowledge, or ability.

Client Managers: Respond to issues in this column	Never or Hardly Ever	Often or Too Often	Consultants: Respond to issues in this column
6. I sometimes make consulting jokes or allude to high fees if the consultants are getting too big for their britches.	☐	☐	6. I may subtly highlight client shortcomings as a one-up technique.
7. I get very irritated if consultants focus too much on our problems and don't seem to recognize what we have accomplished here.	☐	☐	7. I'm too preoccupied with whether the client fully appreciates my abilities and contributions.
8. I prefer to deal with the consultants in structured meetings and work sessions, to avoid losing control.	☐	☐	8. I prefer to deal with client managers, especially the higher-ups, in structured meetings and work sessions, to avoid losing control.

How many of these anxiety "storm signals" do you recognize in yourself?

	Never or Hardly Ever	Often or Too Often	
1. I may give the consultant too big and too global a question to permit an incremental attack on the problems.	☐	☐	1. I like to give my clients big-picture ideas, whether they can absorb them or not.
2. I'm too busy to take enough time to think about project strategies and work plans.	☐	☐	2. I'm too busy to take enough time to think about project strategies and work plans.

(Continued)

Exhibit 11.2. Continued.

Client Managers: Respond to issues in this column	Never or Hardly Ever	Often or Too Often	Consultants: Respond to issues in this column
3. I may worry too much about dominance or submissiveness when consultants are around.	☐	☐	3. I may worry too much about dominance or submissiveness in client situations.
4. I tend to feel too defensive when the consultant is critical or makes suggestions.	☐	☐	4. I tend to feel too defensive when the client is critical or makes suggestions.
5. I tend to get impatient with the pace at which consultants are able to move ahead.	☐	☐	5. I tend to get impatient with the pace at which clients are able to move ahead.
6. I may ascribe disappointing results to the consultant—and overlook my own shortcomings.	☐	☐	6. I may ascribe disappointing results to the client—and overlook my own shortcomings.

Chapter 12

Test the Shift to High-Impact Consulting
It's All Upside and Risk-Free .

Patrick O'Sullivan knew he had to transform both the financial performance and the corporate culture of the Eagle Star General Insurance Group (as it was known then) when he took the helm in 1997. He was the sixth CEO in as many years. The company had lost more than US$2 billion in mortgage underwriting products in the past ten years and was still on a downtrend. As he put it, "Almost no one had any idea how bad the situation was. Moreover, some senior managers, whom I called the permafrost, were quietly resistant, sensing a threat to their positions and to a system they didn't want to change."

Several large, conventional consulting firms were at work in the company. One of the firms, the consulting arm of a global accounting firm, was conducting the preliminaries for a total reengineering effort in one of the largest divisions. This effort was going to call for radical change—in a company that had little demonstrated capacity to execute change. Another firm was conducting a comprehensive strategy review to identify the best directions for the company and to pinpoint where cost reductions had to take place. But, on-target as their insights were, they were going to be valueless because Eagle Star simply didn't have the capacity to act on them. These two firms each had eight to ten consultants on the scene for many months, drawing huge fees from a company suffering exceptionally poor performance. Other conventional consultants were also busy, all creating huge implementation gaps by making suggestions that the company couldn't carry out.

O'Sullivan thought that the "Work-Out" process he had participated in as a General Electric executive might help break the logjam. He believed the approach could generate some urgently needed cost reductions and revenue enhancements. At the same time, it could help develop the organization's fundamental capacity to implement changes.

As adopted by Eagle Star, Work-Out involved assembling fifty to seventy-five managers to create action plans for each important improvement target. To launch the effort, sessions aimed at three target areas: reducing overpayments on claims, general cost reduction, and the simplification (and speeding up) of certain core customer processes.

Each assembly broke into small working groups for two or three days and developed a set of recommendations for making progress rapidly on their particular issue. In the final session of the workshop, they shared their recommendations with senior managers. The ground rules specified that the senior managers would, with few exceptions, make yes-or-no decisions immediately. This was not as difficult as it might sound because these groups were required to develop steps that would produce rapid results with no additional capital or expense. A yes decision was not the end of the process but actually the beginning. It triggered the appointment of a team immediately after the sessions to organize and carry out rapid-cycle projects to implement the steps they had recommended.

For example, claims representatives in twelve large sales branches launched a series of short-term projects targeted at reducing the cost of auto claims by over US$1 million in the first year. In an effort to improve productivity and answer more incoming calls while also improving sales, sales staff cut the average length of a sales call by over 25 percent in two months.

These first rapid-cycle projects had the additional aim of helping senior management learn how to provide overall sponsorship for such rapid payoff, results-focused change. The entire effort was supported by my colleague Matthew McCreight and two other associates. Their efforts were multiplied by a small team of company staff people that was formed into an internal change consulting group. They were trained in facilitation and results-focused consulting modes, and as the process progressed, they were increasingly active in leading it.

At first the projects met with resistance and skepticism, particularly on the part of the top several hundred managers—who were accustomed to the revolving door on the CEO's office and figured O'Sullivan would soon go the way of his predecessors. To overcome this resistance O'Sullivan actively sponsored many of the first year's projects on his own or with members of his own team. He held monthly meetings to review progress on all these efforts. Soon, progress toward the achievement of these critical business goals was reviewed as part of monthly CEO meetings with the corporate managers and the business heads. O'Sullivan also traveled extensively around the company to make the case for change. For the first time in the history of the company, the whole staff learned of the dire financial straits the organization faced. And he shared his vision and strategy for turning the company around. His active participation in many Work-Out sessions and projects provided a valuable link between himself and the rest of the organization. In the first year, over thirty Work-Out sessions launched well over a hundred rapid-cycle improvement projects in key areas that produced measurable savings in excess of US$10 million. The momentum was building.

These incubator projects provided the insights and data needed to develop new management processes and systems. For example, rigorous implementation tracking was developed and introduced into the project work. The aim was to begin to build the kind of accountability and review process needed to see these important projects through. In addition, special training for senior managers was developed so they could play the sponsoring and supporting roles needed to lead the process. And intensive just-in-time training was developed so that dozens of people at all levels of the organization could begin to play new roles as facilitators of the change process under the aegis of the internal consulting group.

Building on the learning and new confidence from the early work, the process expanded in the second and third years, eventually addressing all of the company's important business and change needs. For example, a new information system had been planned at a cost of well over US$15 million. Careful review indicated that it was not needed. Experiments in partnering with customers, suppliers, and insurance brokers were tested. Ways of making major organizational changes in record time—such as reorganizing claims handling across five branches—were developed and sharpened.

The change process had to absorb the extra work that was required when the company was taken over by Zurich Financial Services. Here again, though, instead of sitting and waiting, the two companies staffed and ran rapid-cycle, results-focused experiments that played a crucial role in bringing them together rapidly. Time and again, people would emerge from these projects saying "we started this effort as two companies, but we emerge from these projects feeling we're all working for the same organization."

Hundreds of Work-Out-like project launching sessions have been held since the beginning of the transformation initiative. O'Sullivan reports having achieved annual savings of "over 35 million pounds, (about $50 million US) in verifiable operational savings" from the work. In addition, he is "convinced that millions more have been generated."

During this time, the company's management conferences were transformed from passive "days off" to hard-driving working sessions in which any improvement idea might be turned at once into an experimental, results-targeted change project. The strategic planning and goal setting process also changed as the improvement program progressed. At first there was a heavy emphasis on setting and accomplishing the stretch goals that the company needed to achieve to ensure viability. Later, as people developed their confidence and their capabilities, the focus shifted to developing the strategies for more comprehensive changes.

In summary, Eagle Star provides an example of a company that used high-impact consulting to organize a comprehensive turnaround. Three consultants helped to produce huge improvements and generate a totally transformed culture. In contrast with the long cycle times of traditional consulting, bottom-line results were generated almost from the first day.

Today, other parts of the worldwide Zurich organization and many organizations in the United Kingdom are now looking to this organization—a failure three years ago—as a model for successful change.

That's high-impact consulting.

Physician, Heal Thyself!

The management consulting profession is dedicated to helping organizations replace less effective processes with more effective ones, to accelerate their pace of progress, to become more customer-responsive, to eliminate non-value-added activities, to replace human labor with sophisticated technology, and to fearlessly face the changing realities of the marketplace.

That is indeed a worthwhile set of objectives. And if there ever was an enterprise that desperately needs help in every one of these areas, it is the management consulting profession itself, including all its branches and specialties and both consulting firms and corporate staff consulting groups.

The entire superstructure of the profession is built on an unsupportable foundation: namely, the belief that providing better solutions, better tools, and better ideas about what needs to be done represents the ultimate contribution to organizations. As specified earlier:

- Instead of defining project goals in the customer's terms (such as "reduce costs" or "speed deliveries"), most consultants continue to define them in their own narcissistic terms (such as "install a system" or "recommend a strategy"). Thus they can call their projects "successful" because they deliver the consultant-defined product they promise to deliver, without regard to how much it actually benefits the client.

- Instead of matching project scope to what clients might be able to carry out, most consultants virtually ignore client readiness.

- Instead of carving off rapid-cycle subprojects so they can deliver early payoffs and test the effectiveness of their approach with minimum client investment, most consultants employ a once-around-the track, big-investment, total-systems approach.

- Instead of working in close partnership with clients, with both parties contributing to and learning from the process, most consultants organize projects so that they do the work. Client learning and development take a distinct second place to job efficiency.

- Instead of aiming to empower clients to carry out the project work, thus yielding greater results with fewer consultants, most consultants expand their task definition endlessly. Like Hollywood films of the thirties, many firms feature a few stars and "a supporting cast of thousands." The staffing on many assignments can only be described as grotesque.

All this remains the prevalent pattern in management consulting, despite overwhelming evidence that brilliant ideas about what *ought* to be done come much more easily than the capacity to actually make them happen. And that gulf between them, the implementation gap, sabotages the intentions of many clients and consultants. Billions and billions of dollars and millions of staff days are spent developing great visions about what clients should do and installing tools and systems to allow them to do it, with results that are often not worth the investment in time and money.

Consulting firms and internal consulting groups are constantly introducing new practice modes to exploit the latest popular trends. Many corporations, for example, are increasingly concerned with developing their ability to carry out complex change. No problem! Consulting firms with little or no experience helping organizations manage change suddenly sprout change management practices. Some of these firms have shifted hundreds of people into this specialty; and at least one firm claims to have several thousand people in its change management practice.[1] The fascinating aspect of all of this change is that consulting firms may develop new services, new products, and new approaches, yet they inevitably preserve the labor-intensive conventional paradigm.

In a *Business Week* cover story on management consulting several years ago, John A. Byrne made this piquant observation on consulting firms' habit of reinventing their offerings and their people: "It's still a little early to know whether the new more engaged and expansive style of consulting will pay

228

off any better than the older, more superficial model did. But even if it turns out to be another disappointment, rest assured that the consultants will cook up something else."[2]

In that same article, Byrne also states that clients are increasingly demanding greater accountability from consultants and more substantial evidence that their consulting investments will lead to measurable results. Perhaps this is so, but from what I have seen, the conventional consulting train is running down the conventional track with so much momentum that it will take much more market pressure than has been exerted thus far to slow it down or change its direction.

The Proof Is in the Results

If you are a senior manager and you use either internal management consultants or outside consulting firms, you should really confront this fact: there isn't a shred of doubt that the simple shift away from the five frequently fatal flaws of conventional consulting and toward the results focus of high-impact consulting can significantly reduce the risks and increase the returns from your consulting investments.

My colleagues and I have been demonstrating this fact and writing about it for over thirty years. As described earlier, the high-impact paradigm first took shape in the project that helped Robert C. Scrivener increase Bell Canada's productivity some 30 percent or more. The consulting input there was contributed over several years by two consultants, sometimes augmented by a third, each working about half-time. Since then, we and other high-impact firms have completed numerous projects that produced similar highly leveraged results.

In each of the high-impact cases described in this book, only two or three consultants, generally working part time, were able to help engage very large numbers of client people in carrying out far-reaching changes. And those cases cited could easily have been replaced by dozens of others.

But it isn't just my own firm. Any number of consulting firms, individual consultants, and staff consulting groups throughout the world who practice in a similar highly leveraged mode have experienced similar success. The Lexington, Massachusetts, firm of Rath & Strong also works in a high-impact mode. Their projects are frequently defined in client-results terms, because, as described in a company newsletter, "producing measurable success in fairly short order [creates] enthusiasm, which [leads] to additional projects with additional goals." Most of the consulting work is done by client people, with the consultants acting as catalysts and coaches.

The General Systems Company of Pittsfield, Massachusetts, is headed by brothers Val and Donald Feigenbaum, both of whom disdain the label "consultant." Their practice nevertheless exemplifies the high-impact mode. Their staff members work alongside the client's to help produce major advances. The Feigenbaums focus on "quick results." As Don Feigenbaum describes it, "Results become self-generating. When people see it's going to help, it jacks them up to go to the next level."[3]

Rodney Blanckenberg introduced the high-impact approach into South Africa many years ago, and more recently it has been promulgated there by Gerard van Hoek and Johan Jordaan. Amatai and Eva Niv practice in a high-impact mode in Israel. In Germany, Hirzel Leder & Partner practice in ways that reflect the high-impact mode. There are numerous others, each of whom can document innumerable successes, where success is measured in terms of tangible client returns that are many times the client's investment, with client learning and development as important by-products of the effort.

The contrast was highlighted for me by Tom Barron, then leader of Dun & Bradstreet's Worldwide Shared Transaction Services. He had the assignment of leading the redesign of the corporation's payroll, general accounting, employee benefits, procurement, and related back office operations, which were being performed both at headquarters and in fifteen divisions around the world. The consulting firm Gunn Partners was instrumental in helping design and launch the process.

By the third year of the transition, the annual savings achieved was $40 million. The cumulative cost of the effort to that point was slightly under $60 million (of which consulting fees were a very small part). That is high-impact consulting!

By contrast, two years before Dun & Bradstreet launched its effort, Barron reported, a corporation which he asked me not to name (call it X), with slightly fewer employees than Dun & Bradstreet, brought in one of the "Big Six" consulting firms to help accomplish an almost identical task. At the end of five years that corporation had not accomplished as much as Dun & Bradstreet had in three years. According to Barron, they had by that time invested well over $200 million in the effort.

At Dun & Bradstreet, a few Gunn Partners consultants supported a number of interfunctional task teams of client people who did the bulk of the work and developed their skills in the process. At Corporation X, Barron reported, the Big Six firm sent teams of fifteen to thirty consultants to each location, up to a total of two hundred during the project's early stages, to do the work.

Although this companywide project was not at all related to the Dun & Bradstreet Information Services Division case cited earlier, both of them clearly illustrate the difference between conventional consulting and high-impact consulting. (Gunn Partners calls it "lean consulting.") Over and over, highly leveraged consulting produces greater immediate results and much more significant, lasting value.

Gearing Up for Large-Scale Changes

As noted earlier, many consultants who hear about high-impact consulting with its rapid-cycle subprojects are disdainful, alleging that it deals with small issues but not with the big strategic ones. As illustrated by the Zurich UK (Eagle Star) case and many others cited in this book, however, this oversimplification misses the essential point. Yes, rapid-cycle subprojects focus on helping client managers achieve some focused successes quickly. But a critical aim of this approach is to develop managerial capacity to carry out further change. The successes produced by the rapid-cycle projects develop managerial confidence and managerial skill. If all managers did was to pick some low-hanging fruit, they would have learned nothing. The initial rapid-cycle subprojects focus on challenging goals that represent a real stretch for participants. They must also be designed to be achievable. At the end of the first rapid-cycle subproject, there must be success, a real sense of accomplishment, some solid learning, and an anticipation about putting the learning to work on more challenging goals. In this way, high-impact consulting helps organizations build a foundation for continuous improvement and for large-scale strategic change.

By contrast, conventional consulting with its large-scale studies, major reengineering schemes, or corporate strategy paradigm forces both clients and consultants to slog through the ponderous sequence of steps:

- First the consultants must do their research and investigations, as thoroughly as they can. The client must wait until this is all done. Months slip by.
- Then the consultants digest their data and develop reports, conclusions, and recommendations. More months.
- Then they lead the client through a process aimed at digesting all of this consultant-developed input and developing the right vision and the right master plan—more months with no action under way.
- When the master plan is accepted by senior management, it must be elaborated so that all of the details are laid out on paper. Still no action.
- Finally, after so many months, a switch is thrown, and the transformation begins.
- Then there is supposed to be a turbulent period, after which, the theory goes, the organization will be up and running in its new mode.

I call this the "big-leap" model of organizational transformation. As implied throughout this book, however, this model is fatally flawed. The failure rate of these large-scale change processes has been scandalous and the costs ludicrous. A key reason for this high failure rate is that in such large-scale transformations, everyone in the organization must suddenly learn to work differently and to change the way they coordinate with everyone they deal with, all while thousands of related work-method changes are being implemented. The implementation gap in such projects becomes a veritable Grand Canyon.

The big-leap model, therefore, places very high demands on organization members to develop the capacity to make all these changes at once, and yet it makes no provision for this learning to take place. During the many months of the study and planning phases, client people learn little or nothing about how to carry out the changes that will eventually be necessary. The consultant learns nothing about how best to help the organization implement the changes successfully. Thus, no matter how much studying, strategizing, master planning, and benchmarking is done, neither party gets a shred of experience during all these preliminaries.

In the high-impact mode, large-scale change capability is a direct product of the collaboration between client and consultant.

Change as a Learning Process

Organizational learning results from success experiences. A series of rapid-cycle subprojects provide repeated opportunities for clients to hone their individual skills in managing change and coordinating numerous related changes. As its change management capability expands, the client organization can mount increasingly large-scale efforts with low risk and constant payoffs. Its people can understand strategic issues with more insight and can judge what they might and what they might not be able to do. Instead of a long, sequenced approach, long-term planning studies take place simultaneously with a constant stream of rapid-cycle projects that constantly produce results and expand management capability.

Thus management can get moving on major changes rapidly, without long delays, and can learn from their experience as they go. Hamel and Prahalad are two scholars who share the view that in the strategic realm, implementation experience is as important as conceptualization. They point out that in new product marketing, for example, a firm can pursue the conventional approach and pour resources into market research, segmentation, competitor benchmarking, industry analysis, and so forth in an effort to be sure to "get it right" the first time. Alternatively, it can make a series of quick, low-cost, low-risk forays into the market with real products, and learn from their customers' responses. As they put it, "Staking out uncharted territory is a process of successive approximations. What counts is not being right the first time but . . . how fast can a company gather insights into the particular configuration of features, price, and performance that will unlock the market, and how quickly can it recalibrate its product offering. Little is learned in the laboratory or in product-development committee meetings. True learning begins only when a product—imperfect as it may be—is launched."[4]

Motorola's rapid testing of radios for fast-food restaurants, described in Chapter Six, demonstrates the validity of this assertion. Hamel and Prahalad also argue that "strategic intent" is not by itself enough to motivate and sustain change. They insist that the vision must be translated into a series of "clear corporate challenges that focus everyone's attention on the next key advantage or capability to be built."[5] A truly high-impact mode of attack.

My associates and I apply to large-scale change projects the same philosophy that Hamel and Prahalad apply to a new product launch. Both client organization and consultant will learn less from months of thorough analysis and a report thick with brilliant recommendations than they will from setting a few clear goals and acting to reach them successfully, and then learning from the experience.

In high-impact, highly leveraged consulting, there is no limit on speed or scope except the limits imposed by client managers. Subprojects that produce millions of dollars of return on the client's investment within a year or two of start-up can evolve into large-scale strategic change processes, in every kind of business and public and nonprofit agency.

Motorola's Organizational Effectiveness Process is a good example. It was launched in 1984 in order to overcome what CEO Bob Galvin felt was unwarranted self-satisfaction and to get the company moving much more rapidly so it could compete with the best companies in the world. The process created considerable momentum and served as a foundation for the corporation's other improvement thrusts in the late 1980s and early 1990s. I provided the external consulting support, along with a few associates. We worked part time. We focused on supporting and collaborating closely with Joe Miraglia and his human resources staff. This partnership helped Motorola design, launch, and sustain the process. Similarly, far-reaching strategic and performance changes were supported across the entire corporation by very small numbers of consultants in the General Electric "Work-Out" program. As reported earlier in this book, similar projects have been carried out at General Reinsurance, SmithKline Beecham, and numerous other large, global organizations.

The Dun & Bradstreet Information Services Case: Lasting Change from High-Impact Help

The experience of Dun & Bradstreet's Information Services Division cited earlier provides another excellent example of how a large number of rapid-cycle projects, used as learning vehicles, can evolve into large-scale strategic change. In Chapters Six and Eight I described the quality-focused effort led by Mike Berkin, who reported that by the end of four years there were $60 to $70 million a year in documented results, with the amount increasing every year. This occurred after an investment of a few hundred thousand dollars in consulting fees and an estimated several million dollars in internal consulting support. But were these savings merely the sum of numerous tactical improvement efforts, or did the effort, driven by rapid-cycle projects, contribute to the fundamental health of the business? I asked Berkin, "You have had thousands of these breakthrough projects, and they have produced huge improvements. What has been the overall impact on the company and on its competitive capability?" He responded as follows:

> There has been a major cultural shift. Managers shifted away from our old culture, where they would tell people not only what had to be done but how they were to do it. Now we tell people what has to be done, and they go about it on their own. In fact, they are taking much more initiative with what needs to be done.
>
> In 1991, the span of control ranged from four to nine people, with an average of about five. Today (1995), there are many managers who have fourteen, fifteen, or sixteen people reporting to them. Because of the shift

in people's sense of personal initiative, we have more than doubled the spans of control.

Now when information or complaints or requests come from customers through the "Voice of the Customer" data, it all comes into one place and we send it out to the entire organization. Everybody acts on their own initiative. Nobody has to go out to them and urge them to act on a problem that needs to be corrected.

The whole performance appraisal system has become more disciplined. We use numbers more than impressions of performance. Groups are aligned with each other around common goals. Everyone has become much more focused on results. And that has got us all working on developing better instruments to measure what we are doing and where we have to concentrate. Today, when customer service information comes in, everyone grabs for it to see what they have to do.

During the four years, while our revenues were only up about 5 percent, our operating income was up 38 percent.

The Unique Role of Internal Consultants

Because (as should be clear to all managers and consultants) large-scale organizational change and the learning associated with it must take place continuously over extended periods of time, internal consultants are in a unique position to exploit high-impact consulting for the benefit of their organization. They have a distinct advantage over consulting firms on this score. In consulting firms, the realities of keeping large groups of professionals gainfully occupied mean that most projects, especially those of larger firms, are scheduled to occur in large spurts. But because they have to schedule work that way, firms that deploy large teams of consultants are almost doomed to delivering huge packages of largely indigestible analyses and recommendations at the end of each spurt, in order to justify their fees.

Internals don't have that problem. They remain on the scene, working with their clients over time. They can maintain a dual focus, working on a never-ending succession of rapid-cycle, results-focused subprojects while simultaneously helping their clients design longer-term strategies. The Motorola case illustrates this point. There is no way that the change acceleration process that Bob Galvin was driving in the 1980s would ever have happened without the ongoing catalytic role of Motorola's own internal human resources consultants. While the effort was augmented by external consultants, a major focus of the external consultants' efforts was to help develop and support the internal staff. Joe Miraglia enjoyed close working relationships with senior management in developing and monitoring the overall change effort. And in every sector there were staff consultants who helped generate action—sometimes in collaboration with the outside consultants, sometimes not.

This unique ability of internal consultants to facilitate major change and performance improvement on a continuing basis is an important advantage. It makes it possible for them to play a critical role when they are collaborating with external consultants. They can serve as multipliers who absorb and then disseminate the external consultants' know-how. In Connecticut's worker injury reduction effort, internal consultants played a significant role from the start, and a major aim of the external consultants was to support and develop the internal consultants' capabilities. As the project moved forward, the results obtained by the internal consultants expanded rapidly, as did the ratio of internal to external consulting effort.

In 2000 I made three trips to Hamersley Iron, a subsidiary of Rio Tinto Mining located in western Australia. This company owns a complex of seven mines, spread over a hundred-mile span, with a two-hundred-mile railroad to carry ore to the port. The major focus of the consulting work was a project to expand the throughput of the entire system (which had reached capacity) without additional capital investment. A kind of model week project was designed with the goal of running sixty-five ore trains during a "batch" period, just under two weeks. This was three more trains than the company included in a regular batch. One of the first rapid-cycle projects cut the time to reassemble ore trains (which were disassembled for unloading) from ninety minutes to thirty. Additional rapid-cycle projects were organized at nine key locations. When the trial period came, Hamersley ran sixty-six trains during the batch—one more than their target. This represented a gain of several millions of tons of ore per annum. How was that accomplished in twenty-four or twenty-five days of consulting input? The key was a strong onsite team of internal change consultants. By collaborating with and supporting them, I helped to achieve prodigious results that could not have been possible otherwise.

In the Dun & Bradstreet Information Services case, Mike Berkin valued and made good use of external consulting help, but it is clear that he and his internal group were the critical catalysts in attaining the far-reaching results that were achieved. With a Mike Berkin in place, a few hundred thousand dollars of external consulting can produce tens of millions of dollars of continuing improvement. Without a Mike Berkin, it is doubtful whether even $10 or $20 million spent on external consultants will produce a fraction of that gain.

Employees who serve in an internal consulting or facilitating role not only make unique and valuable contributions to their organization's change efforts, they also learn invaluable lessons about how to make change happen. For this reason, many organizations assign people whose jobs don't normally involve internal consulting to serve as facilitators in change efforts. At General Reinsurance, for example, more than seventy-five people throughout the corporation were trained as facilitators to support the company's quality and change management process. These facilitators served part time as the need arose. Other companies have released such internal facilitators from their regular jobs for periods to enable them to support major changes full time.

P.S. A Final Action Note to Client Managers

As the Zurich UK, Dun & Bradstreet, Washington State Labor & Industries Department, and other experiences dramatically demonstrate, you don't have to shift into idle for a few years while you gear up for large-scale change that is always off in the future. The best way to prepare for large-scale change is to get moving at once, to carry out some actual changes rapidly and successfully and to learn as you go. Consultants—both internal and external—can learn to work in a results-focused, highly leveraged mode if you insist that they do so. It will be a psychological wrench for you and for them, but it isn't all that complicated. You have to be sold on the importance of your active involvement in consulting projects. And you each have to be open to learning how to work with consultants in this new way.

Begin by insisting that your consultants focus on achieving results. This means making sure they are committed on every project to helping you achieve measurable bottom-line benefits. You might try insisting that they redesign the project proposal until they can make a results commitment. If they say they cannot do this, you need to ask yourself whether you really want to invest in their services.

To make the shift successfully, it will be important for you and your consultants to develop the ability to divide large jobs into shorter incremental steps. Remember, however, that these steps are not phases of a single project but complete rapid-cycle projects that go from start to finish quickly and achieve measurable results. Your consultants should demonstrate with tens of thousands of dollars of your money that they can produce some significant returns before they ask you to invest hundreds of thousands or millions of dollars.

A number of consulting firms have adopted some of the high-impact techniques described here, and there are many more who would devote energy to learning them if their clients insisted on it. Based on my own firsthand knowledge, I am confident that there are many individual consultants within large firms who would, if they had the chance, prefer to practice in this mode.

Of course you should insist that your own staff consultants shift toward high-impact consulting. They do not have to keep large groups of people busy, expand their own profitability, and maintain high stock prices. They have only to serve the needs of your organization, and so they should be much more amenable to the shift.

Be reassured that you will not find yourself becoming overly enmeshed in doing the project work with your own hands if you move into high-impact consulting. It is almost always possible to find ways to play an appropriate role without adding unreasonably to your workload or your people's. In fact, having to take on more responsibility for your projects with consultants can encourage your people to make constructive shifts in their use of time. So don't let busyness get in your way. There is so much to lose (beyond the consultant's large fees) when you simply turn a project over to the consultant and hope for the best. Unless it is purely a matter of outsourcing specialized work, you and your people should play a major role. The jobs will go better. Your people will learn more. And you'll keep the consultants on course. If your consultants cannot or will not learn how to do it, there are many who can and will.

P.S. A Final Action Note to Consultants

If you have any interest in the ideas expressed in this book, you can try them without making revolutionary changes all at once. You can begin with a few low-risk, low-cost breakthrough projects. The risks are so small and the potential benefits so enormous that you almost owe it to yourself and your clients to try it.

A former associate of mine helped a number of consultants at McKinsey & Company experiment with high-impact consulting, and he collaborated with them on a number of projects. As a clear demonstration of my assertion that most competent conventional consultants who are motivated to do so can make the shift to high-impact consulting, a number of McKinsey consultants have since successfully exploited the approach on their own. In a 1994 article, two of the firm's principals, Jonathan Harris and Warren L. Strickland, described their approach to high-impact consulting as putting small groups of people to work on sharply defined goals to be achieved in six to eight weeks. They described how the approach was used to help an insurance company reduce costs: "The first-wave breakthrough used 65 teams involving 520 team members and 20 facilitators including 5 consultants. By the third wave, the company was launching over 100 teams per wave, using exclusively internal facilitators. In the first year, over 300 break-through teams achieved expense reductions and revenue enhancements totaling $60 million."[6]

Five consultants got the effort going, then internal facilitators gradually took over and supported the entire effort with some modest continuing help. In the first year alone, they had $60 million in savings to show for the effort. That is high-impact, highly leveraged consulting. What a far cry from the Big Six firm that dispatched herds of fifteen to thirty consultants per location in Corporation X, as described earlier in this chapter. Harris and Strickland also describe how McKinsey helped an oil company reduce operating costs by $250 million through highly leveraged assistance.

As with all the other cases I've described, no matter how spectacular the measurable benefits from these projects, there are always, in addition, developmental and learning dividends for the client organization. Harris and Strickland assert that the learning and excitement generated by the initial performance improvements created "an improved environment for other changes" and set the stage for "institutionalizing and locking in continuous performance improvements." They reinforce the notion that when an organization develops increasing competence and confidence in carrying out dozens or hundreds of tangible performance improvements, it creates an environment that permits strategic thinking and action to take place more effectively.

Undoubtedly, your consulting firm has people who can learn to work in this same fashion. As a first step, determine which of the strategies I have been recommending would be easiest for you to adapt and fit most smoothly into the way you have been doing your consulting. Then decide where and how to begin.

Consultants who want to try some of these shifts (assuming their firm supports them) can scout around to find some clients who also might like to try them. You should be frank with clients. Tell them you would like to try a slightly different approach that you think promises better results. Explain the approach and ask if it makes sense to them. Let them read this book.

Maybe a good place to begin is a project where some bottom-line results are urgently needed. You are more likely to find client readiness in a situation where management is saying something like, "Our cash flow has suddenly taken a nasty turn downward, and we aren't really sure what to do about it." There is likely to be less readiness when the client is saying something like, "I've been wondering about our organizational structure. We might begin examining over the next year or so whether a more matrixed organization would suit our needs more appropriately." Once you have a client and a project area, you can select one of the rapid-cycle project designs mentioned throughout the book that facilitate the shift to a high-impact mode:

• *Performance breakthrough projects.* These are short-term projects targeted at specific performance improvement goals and also designed to test out the consultant's technical or methodological inputs and to provide development experience for client managers and employees. Hundreds of these were carried out in the Dun & Bradstreet Information Services project, for example.

• *Strategic breakthrough projects.* These are short-term breakthrough projects that aim to test, quickly and in a low-risk fashion, some major strategic idea rather than to aim at a performance improvement. Motorola's rapid development of a mock-up radio for fast-food restaurants and its informal testing in a few local restaurants is an example of such a strategic breakthrough project.

• *Model week projects.* These are projects that ask people to test, for some limited period of time, how well they can do on some key performance variable. United Aluminum's 100 percent on-time shipment project was one example. Vitrine's 7 percent furnace efficiency improvement goal was another.

• *Results-focused process redesign projects.* These are projects that carve off one part of a large business process, assemble representatives who are involved in the various steps in this subprocess, and have them map and then redesign the process to achieve some specific improvement goal. The electric utility that was helped to improve its maintenance operations is an example of a client that used this sort of results-focused process redesign. The MVE order entry project is another example. OSHA's complaint-handling projects also illustrate incremental results-focused process redesign.

You can carry out such an effort within the framework of a large-scale reengineering project or where a client must improve results that depend on a chain of events involving multiple groups (such as speed of customer payment, inventory, and customer service).

- *"Boundary-busting" projects.* These are rapid-cycle projects conducted by a supplier and a customer or among different units of a single organization who have to coordinate more effectively. The joint planning sessions between GE Lighting's management and General Motors and other customers is an example of how this can be done.

- *The Work-Out approach.* If you want to get many client people involved in improvement quickly, the Work-Out process, pioneered by General Electric, is a good way to go.

Again, all you need is one or two clients who are willing to try it. You can do it as a frank experiment, in partnership with the client, with the mutual understanding that the intent of the project is to learn how to work together to achieve results and learn how to achieve more results. Exhibit 12.1 lists the six design options.

An Exciting Future

Once a client and consultant have begun the shift toward highly leveraged, high-impact consulting and enjoyed the shared pleasures of collaborating to achieve some real results, neither will ever want to revert to the more

Exhibit 12.1. Rapid-Cycle Project Designs.

1. Performance breakthrough projects
2. Strategic breakthrough projects
3. Model week projects
4. Results-focused process redesign projects
5. "Boundary-busting" projects
6. The Work-Out approach

conventional style. And both will have gained new insights about what to do next.

If you are a client, you will have taken an important step toward liberating yourself from the notion that the experts will solve your problem for you. You will have learned to play an active leadership role in every change project in your organization—even if consultants are involved in a major way.

If you are a consultant, you will have taken a first step in what can be a lifelong journey of discovery. You will learn how to be more and more effective in helping organizations accelerate change and improve their performance.

The relationships that develop between clients and consultants can be sustained over time. Each round of projects develops the skills, confidence, and insight of both client and consultant and expands their capacity to shoot for constantly more ambitious undertakings. Although high-impact consulting aims for the highest possible return from the smallest possible investment, consultants do not have to "work themselves out of a job." The high-impact model requires much less consulting input per project, but it encourages long-lasting client-consultant relationships.

No matter how long you have been locked into the conventional mode, and no matter how uneasy you may be about making the shift to a more multiplicative mode, you can move into it modestly. There is very little up-front investment required. You won't be required to take an oath of loyalty and fealty to high-impact consulting. Nor do you have to renounce the use of large-scale technology when it seems like the best answer to you. All you need—whether you are a client or a consultant—is some belief that what you've read about in this book might work for you. And then try it. Ultimately the marketplace will decide.

NOTES

Preface

1. R. H. Schaffer, *Maximizing the Impact of Industrial Engineering* (New York: American Management Association, 1966).

Chapter 1

1. R. Schaffer, "Rapid-Cycle Successes Versus the Titanics: Ensuring That Consulting Produces Benefits," in M. Beer and N. Nohria, eds., *Breaking the Code of Change*, Boston: Harvard Business School Press, 2000, p. 364.

2. Schaffer, "Rapid-Cycle Successes Versus the Titanics," p. 365.

Chapter 2

1. Pittiglio, Rabin, Todd, and McGrath, *Productivity Survey* (Mountain View, Calif.: American Electronics Association, 1991).

2. "The Cracks in Quality," *Economist*, Apr. 18, 1992, pp. 67–68.

3. G. Hall, J. Rosenthal, and J. Wade, "How to Make Reengineering Really Work," *Harvard Business Review*, Nov.-Dec. 1993, pp. 119–131.

4. J. Champy, *Reengineering Management* (New York: HarperBusiness, 1995).

5. "Management's Field of Dreams, Headstones in Management's Graveyard: 50+ Fads and Panaceas in 50+ Years," *Consultants News*, June 1994, p. 4.

6. S. Hansell, "An Ambitious Internet Grocer Is Out of Both Cash and Ideas," *New York Times*, July 10, 2001, p. 1.

7. N. Nohria and J. D. Berkley, "Whatever Happened to the Take-Charge Manager?" *Harvard Business Review*, Jan.-Feb. 1994, pp. 128–137.

8. T. Neill and C. Mindrum, "Human Performance That Increases Business Performance: The Growth of Change Management and Its Role in Creating New Forms of Business Value," in M. Beer and N. Nohria, eds., *Breaking the Code of Change,* Boston: Harvard Business School Press, 2000, p. 354.

9. D. A. Blackmon, "Familiar Refrain: Consultant's Advice on Diversity Was Anything But Diverse—For Big Fees, Towers Perrin Gave Many of Its Clients Nearly Identical Reports—Nissan, Westinghouse Balked," *Wall Street Journal,* Mar. 11, 1997, p. A1.

10. Neill and Mindrum, "Human Performance That Increases Business Performance," pp. 354–355.

Chapter 3

1. A. N. Turner, *Influencing Clients to Produce Needed Change* (Harvard Business School Teaching Note). (Boston: HBS Case Services, 1984).

2. For a more detailed discussion of these zest factors see R. H. Schaffer, *The Breakthrough Strategy: Using Short-Term Successes to Build the High Performance Organization* (New York: HarperBusiness, 1988), pp. 52–60.

3. A. N. Turner, *Expert or Facilitator?* (Harvard Business School Teaching Note). (Boston: HBS Case Services, 1983).

4. C. S. Sloane, "A Practitioner's Perspective on University Education for Management Consulting," *MAS Communications,* Mar. 1982, 6, 23–29.

Chapter 4

1. M. Hammer and J. Champy, *Reengineering the Corporation* (New York: HarperBusiness, 1993).

2. E. M. Mandrish and R. H. Schaffer, "Putting the Engine into Reengineering," *National Productivity Review,* Spring 1996, 7–15.

3. C. Argyris, *Behind the Front Page* (San Francisco: Jossey-Bass, 1974), p. 275.

4. J. Champy, *Reengineering Management* (New York: HarperBusiness, 1995).

Chapter 6

1. M. Beer, R. A. Eisenstat, and B. Spector, "Why Change Programs Don't Produce Change," *Harvard Business Review,* Nov.-Dec. 1990, pp. 6–12.

2. D. K. Smith, *Taking Charge of Change* (Reading, Mass.: Addison-Wesley, 1996), pp. 155–156.

3. E. M. Mandrish and R. H. Schaffer, "Putting the Engine into Reengineering," *National Productivity Review,* Spring 1996, pp. 7–15.

Chapter 7

1. C. Argyris, "Double Loop Learning in Organizations," *Harvard Business Review,* Sept.-Oct. 1977, pp. 115–125; C. M. Fiol and M. A. Lyles, "Organizational Learning," *Academy of Management Review,* 1985, *10*(4), 803–813; D. A. Garvin, "Building a Learning Organization," *Harvard Business Review,* July-Aug. 1993, pp. 78–92; G. P. Huber, "Organizational Learning: The Contributing Processes and the Literatures," *Organization Science,* 1991, *2*(1), 88–115; B. Levitt and J. G. March, "Organizational Learning," *American Sociological Review,* 1988, *14,* 319–340; P. Senge, *The Fifth Discipline: The Art and Practice of the Learning Organization* (New York: Doubleday/Currency, 1990).

2. Garvin, "Building a Learning Organization," p. 90.

3. P. Senge, "Leading Learning Organizations," in F. Hesselbein, M. Goldsmith, and R. Beckhard, eds., *The Leader of the Future* (San Francisco: Jossey-Bass, 1996), p. 48.

4. Garvin, "Building a Learning Organization," p. 90.

Chapter 8

1. R. Ashkenas, D. Ulrich, T. Jick, and S. Kerr, *The Boundaryless Organization: Breaking the Chains of Organizational Structure,* 2nd ed. (San Francisco: Jossey-Bass, 2001); R. Ashkenas, "Beyond the Fads: How Leaders Drive Change with Results," in C. E. Schneier (ed.), *Managing Strategic and Cultural Change in Organizations* (New York: Human Resource Planning Society, 1995), pp. 33–54.

2. D. Ulrich, S. Kerr, and R. Ashkenas, *The GE Work-Out: Implementing GE's Revolutionary Method for Busting Bureaucracy and Attacking Organizational Problems—Fast!* (New York: McGraw-Hill, forthcoming).

Chapter 10

1. R. H. Schaffer, "Demand Better Results—And Get Them," *Harvard Business Review,* Nov.-Dec. 1974, pp. 91–98.

Chapter 11

1. R. H. Schaffer and R. N. Ashkenas, "Anxiety: The Consultant's Unwelcome Companion," *Journal of Management Consulting,* 1983, *1*(2), 30.

Chapter 12

1. S. Whelehan, "Capturing a Moving Target: Change Management," *Consultants News,* Feb. 1995, pp. 1–3; S. Whelehan, "Leading Players in Change Management," *Consultants News,* Mar. 1995, pp. 4–5.

2. J. A. Byrne, "The Craze for Consultants," *Business Week,* July 25, 1994, p. 66.

3. J. A. Byrne, "Never Mind the Buzzwords. Roll Up Your Sleeves," *Business Week,* Jan. 22, 1996, pp. 84–85.

4. G. Hamel and C. K. Prahalad, *Competing for the Future* (Boston: Harvard Business School Press, 1994), p. 87.

5. Hamel and Prahalad, *Competing for the Future,* p. 136.

6. J. Harris and W. L. Strickland, "Achieving Real-Time Performance Improvement Using Breakthrough Teams," in *Property and Casualty Insurance Annual Report* (New York: McKinsey & Company, 1994), pp. 37–49.

INDEX

A

Ability, client. *See* Willingness and ability
Acceleration strategy, 87–88
Accountability: ambiguous, 20; of client, 169–171; in conventional consulting, 23–24, 55; demands for, 229; in high-impact consulting, 4–5, 55–60; for results, 40, 55–60; shared, 4–5, 55–60, 72, 74. *See also* Partnership; Responsibility
Accountable client, the: identifying, 169–171; management team *versus,* 169–170
Acquisition integration, results-focused approach to, 63–64, 69
Acquisition planning, readiness assessment and, 85–86
Action plan, 12
Activity-based goals, 135
Administrative productivity case study, 188, 189
AlliedSignal, 190
American Electronics Association, 18
American Greetings, management development project of, 70
American Standard, 63, 69
Andersen Consulting, 19
Anger, 206
Answers, leaping to, 207
Anxiety, 162, 203–222; assessment of, 220–222; in client, 203–205; in consultants, 205–206; overcoming, with communication bridge building, 211–219; "right answers" entrapment and, 176–177; symptoms of, 203, 206–208; working past, 211
Anxiety avoidance, 20, 203–204, 219; behavioral signs of, 206–208, 220–222; conventional consulting flaws and, 208–211
Anxiety self-diagnosis questionnaire, 220–222; use of, 213
Argyris, C., 71–72
Arthur D. Little, 18
Ashton, P., 58, 59
Assessment, project, 139–141, 196, 218–219
Assessment of readiness. *See* Readiness assessment
Assumptions, false, 7–11; about efficacy of making recommendations, 7–11, 15–16
Automakers: success *versus* failure among, 8
Automotive parts plant case study, 53–54, 156
Avionic Instruments, 99–100, 102
Avoidance. *See* Anxiety avoidance; Risk avoidance

B

Backlog reduction: rapid-cycle subprojects for, 106–107; results-focused approach to, 64, 69
Barker, A., 104–105

249

Infrastructure improvements, rapid-cycle subprojects and, 105, 109–110
Insight sharing, 217–218
Institute of Management Consultants, 19
Insurance company case studies, 30–31, 115–116
Internal change facilitators/consultants, 157–158, 160, 170, 236–238
Interorganization collaboration, Work-Out approach to, 155
Interviews: initial, telephone, 181–182; with senior client and implementing clients, 195
Inventory control case study, 187–189
Inventory management system, 114–115
Inventory reduction project, conventional *versus* high-impact approach to, 118
Israel, high-impact consulting in, 230

J

Jacobson, D., 125–126, 127–128, 129, 130, 131, 133, 134
Japanese automakers, 8
Jargon, 208
Jokes, about consultants, 206
Jordaan, J., 230
Journal of Management Consulting, 213
Just-in-time training, 132–133

K

Kearney, A. T., 18
Kickoff workshop, 127
Kivlehan, T., 74, 143

L

Labor-intensive use of consultants, 29–30, 145–146, 149–150; anxiety avoidance and, 210–211; learning and, 145, 149–150, 228; leveraged use of consultants *versus,* 45–46, 145–162, 228
Large group workshops, 158, 159
Large-scale, big-picture solutions: anxiety avoidance and, 209–210; as flaw of conventional consulting, 10–11, 26–27, 52–53, 209–210; labor-intensive use of

consultants for, 29–30, 145–146, 149–150; rapid-cycle subprojects *versus,* 42–43, 46, 99–101, 117–118. *See also* Incremental solutions; Solution; Subprojects
Large-scale change: carving off subprojects for, 105–117, 128–129, 136, 227, 231–233; gearing up for, 231–233; improvement *versus,* 110–111; of information systems, 114, 115–117; laying a foundation for, 103–105; leveraged consultant resources for, 145–162; low-risk test before, 112–113; rapid-cycle subprojects for, 100–102, 103–118, 223–244; rapid-cycle test in adjacent area before, 113–115; starting small with, 106–107; target selection for, 107–108. *See also* Change, organizational
Large-scale, comprehensive studies: anxiety avoidance and, 208–210; consultants' addiction to, 71; as flaw of conventional consulting, 10–11, 46, 52–53, 104, 232; partnership mode *versus,* 121–122; pilot projects *versus,* 155–156; rapid-cycle subprojects *versus,* 42–43, 46, 99–100, 104, 118–119, 231–233; senior managers' failure to make demands and, 193–194. *See also* Preparations-first approach
Large-scale interventions, 158, 159
Lassen, C., 58
Lean consulting, 231
Learning, client: in breakthrough projects, 154, 241; conventional consulting and, 132–133, 134, 138–139, 149–150, 228, 231; experiential *versus* cognitive, 133–135; just-in-time, 132–133; levels of, 131–132; leveraged use of consultants and, 145, 148–149, 156–158, 159, 228; in partnership approach, 44–45, 122, 123–135, 136, 139–141; from project review and assessment, 139–141; with rapid-cycle subprojects, 44, 120, 122, 123–135, 136, 231–244; with results-focused approach, 44, 120, 122,

Preparations-first approach: anxiety
avoidance and, 208–210; to consulting,
51–55; fear of failing and, 111,
193–194; to management development, 64–65, 70; senior managers' demand making and, 193–194;
subprojects approach *versus,* 111,
118–119, 231–233. *See also* Conventional consulting; Large-scale, comprehensive studies
Presentations, client-led, 140, 141
Process consulting, 47; outcomes and,
54–55
Process mapping: client learning of, as
skill, 122, 123, 133; results-focused approach to, 60–61, 68
Process redesign: client learning of, as
skill, 122, 132; leveraged use of consultants for, 145–148; rapid-cycle subprojects for, 108–110; results-focused
approach to, 60–61, 242–243
Progress assessment, 139–141, 196,
218–219
Project attention span, assessment of, 83
Project contract. *See* Contracts and contract process
Project definition: as client results, 39–41,
46, 51–74, 212, 227; communication
and, 212; as consultant deliverables,
22–24, 39, 46, 51–55, 68–70, 71–72,
208–209, 212, 227; in conventional
consulting, 22–24, 46, 51–55, 68–70,
208–209, 227; in high-impact consulting, 36, 39–41, 46, 51–74, 212, 227
Project design: common ground, 178;
communication and, 212; in conventional consulting, 26–27, 42, 43, 46,
100, 117–118, 227; in high-impact
consulting, 42–43, 46, 99–120, 227,
242–243; high-leverage, 152–156, 212;
phases in, 117–118, 172, 232; rapid-
cycle, 101–103; versatility in, 174–181,
182; ways to approach, 105–117,
242–243. *See also* Subprojects
Project design statement, 44

Project management skills: development
of, in partnership mode, 122, 123,
129–130, 136
Project review and assessment, 196,
218–219; checklist for, 141; mutual
learning in, 139–141
Project scope: assessment of client's view
of, 83; big-picture or grandiose, 10–11,
26–27, 42, 43, 46, 227; client managers'
action note for, 97–98; communication
about, 212; consultants' action note for,
98; in conventional consulting, 24–25,
46, 75–77, 209; in high-impact consulting, 36, 41, 42–43, 46, 75–98; labor-intensive use of consultants and, 29; matching,
to client readiness, 75–98, 174–176, 179,
209, 227; readiness assessment for determining, 78–98. *See also* Subprojects
Proposals and proposal process, 22; collaborative contracts *versus,* 165–184;
consultant versatility and, 175; in conventional consulting, 165–167, 168,
175, 183, 184; project definition in, 40;
weaknesses of, 165–167, 175, 183
Psychological issues: anxiety and, 204–222;
fear of failure and, 111, 192–193;
highly leveraged consulting and,
161, 162; partnership approach and,
141–142; readiness assessment and, 81,
84, 209; results-focused approach and,
67, 71–73; in senior managers' demand
making, 191, 192–194, 197. *See also*
Anxiety; Anxiety avoidance; Fear; Obstacles; Resistance; Risk avoidance
Psychological issues, assessment of, 79
Psychological myopia, 21
Put-downs, 208

Q

"Quotom Supply" case study, 15–17, 20

R

Rabil, F., 132
Rapid-cycle subprojects. *See* Subprojects
Rath & Strong, 230